5-24

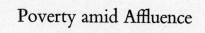

Poverty amid Affluence

Poverty amid Affluence

edited by Leo Fishman

NEW HAVEN AND LONDON, YALE UNIVERSITY PRESS, 1966

Contributors

BENJAMIN CHINITZ
Professor of Economics and Director, Appalachian Project, Center for Regional Economic Studies, University of Pittsburgh

DONALD A. CRANE
Research Associate, Center for Regional Economic Studies, University of Pittsburgh

OTTO ECKSTEIN
Professor of Economics, Harvard University; former member, Council of Economic Advisers, Executive Office of the President

JOSEPH L. FISHER
President, Resources for the Future, Inc.

HAROLD A. GIBBARD
Professor of Sociology, West Virginia University

OSCAR HANDLIN
Winthrop Professor of History and Director, Center for the Study of the History of Liberty in America, Harvard University

HARRY G. JOHNSON
Professor of Economics, University of Chicago

ROBERT J. LAMPMAN
Professor of Economics, University of Wisconsin

ALEXANDER H. LEIGHTON
Professor of Social Psychiatry, Cornell University Medical College

DOROTHEA C. LEIGHTON
Associate Professor of Mental Health, University of North Carolina

HERMAN P. MILLER
Special Assistant, Office of the Director, Bureau of the Census

THEODORE W. SCHULTZ
Charles L. Hutchinson Distinguished Service Professor of Economics, University of Chicago

I. THOMAS STONE
Research Associate, Program in Social Psychiatry, Cornell University

Contents

Contributors   v

Preface   ix

Part 1: DEFINITION AND MEASUREMENT OF POVERTY   1

   1. Poverty from the Civil War to World War II
      by Oscar Handlin   3
   2. Population Change and Poverty Reduction,
      1947–1975 *by Robert J. Lampman*   18

Part 2: SOCIAL ATTITUDES, SOCIAL ORGANIZATION,
     AND POVERTY   43

   3. Poverty and Social Organization
      by Harold A. Gibbard   45
   4. Poverty and the Individual *by I. Thomas Stone,*
      Dorothea C. Leighton, and Alexander H. Leighton 72

Part 3: SPECIAL CASES OF POVERTY   97

   5. Poverty and the Negro *by Herman P. Miller*   99
   6. Poverty in Appalachia *by Donald A. Crane and*
      Benjamin Chinitz   124
   7. Poverty and Resource Utilization
      by Joseph L. Fisher   150

Part 4: APPROACHES TO THE ELIMINATION OF POVERTY   163

8. Public Approaches to Minimize Poverty
     by Theodore W. Schultz   165

9. Unemployment and Poverty *by Harry G. Johnson*   182

10. Strategies in the War Against Poverty
     by Otto Eckstein   200

11. Ends and Means in the War Against Poverty
     by Robert J. Lampman   212

     Index   231

Preface

Within recent years much has been written and even more has been said about poverty in the United States. President Lyndon B. Johnson has proclaimed "war" on poverty and Congress has passed legislation and made appropriations for the purpose of eliminating, or at least ameliorating, poverty. Many individuals and institutions in communities widely dispersed throughout the United States have become engaged directly or indirectly in the effort to eradicate poverty.

Yet despite all the writing, talking, and activity there has been no systematic attempt to place before the American public a carefully reasoned statement of the nature of poverty in the United States, the extent to which it exists, its causes, and its consequences. It is only on the basis of an understanding of these aspects of poverty that sound attitudes toward poverty can be developed, constructive programs to eliminate or ameliorate poverty can be formulated, and suitable methods of measuring the success of such programs can be devised.

This book, it is hoped, will help to fill that need. It consists of a series of papers presented at the West Virginia University Conference on Poverty amid Affluence, held in May, 1965, on the University Campus in Morgantown, West Virginia.

Poverty is not a novel problem. It has existed since ancient times. It has been present in many different types of cultures in many different parts of the world. It is today far more prevalent in many other countries than in the United States. Yet poverty as it exists in the United States today has certain aspects and characteristics that are not clearly understood. Indeed, some of them have not yet been carefully defined.

To some, it must surely seem strange that poverty can still be found in the United States. The United States is generally considered to be very rich. Although technically precise methods of measuring and comparing incomes and levels of living in different countries are not available, even our imperfect methods of measuring and comparing them indicate very clearly that, relative to the population of other countries, the population of the United States as a whole receives a high income and enjoys a high level of living. The gap between per capita income in the United States and in most other countries is impressively large. Two decades of almost uninterrupted prosperity in this country have served to keep it that way, despite the more rapid rate of economic growth that some of the less-developed countries have experienced since World War II. Figures on per capita consumption of various types of goods and services often used as indices of material well-being suggest the same conclusion.

But despite the overall abundance of material goods in the United States and the generally high and increasing level of living that abundance has made possible, there are still families, communities, even some entire regions that are poor. When poverty is an exceptional condition, as it is in the United States today, the reasons for poverty, the attitudes of society toward the poor, the attitudes of the poor toward themselves and society, the possibility of ameliorating poverty, and the nature of the programs that may be adopted for that purpose are surely very different from what they are in a country where poverty is a general condition and only a relatively small number of families possess wealth or receive incomes sufficient for them to enjoy a comfortable level of living.

The very definition of poverty may be different in a rich, relatively well-developed country from what it is in a poorer, relatively underdeveloped country. As time passes and economic growth occurs, the definition of poverty, as well as social attitudes toward poverty, may undergo progressive change. Perhaps less obvious, but equally true, is the fact that the very conception of a "war" on poverty, and the general public acceptance of such terms as "the poverty problem" and "the poverty program," can themselves be properly understood or explained only in the light of the general affluence of the United States and the prevalent material well-being of the population. Where, except in a rich country, is it possible even to dream that a program of social action may be developed for the purpose of eliminating poverty (or at least reducing it to negligible proportions), that this program can be carried out within the framework of the existing social, political, and economic institutions, and that it can be expected to yield significant results within a relatively short period of time?

It is for these reasons that the title "Poverty amid Affluence" was considered most appropriate for the Conference from which this book has resulted. The central purpose of the Conference was the achievement of a better understanding of the nature of poverty in the United States today and possible approaches to its mitigation.

A group of eminent social scientists and public leaders were invited to present papers at the Conference. The expectation that each paper would make a significant contribution toward the objective of the Conference was fulfilled, as demonstrated by the reception the papers were accorded when they were presented, and the vigor and level of the discussion that followed each presentation. Not all of the questions raised in the papers have been answered in conclusive fashion, but even in those cases where better answers must yet be sought, important issues have been clarified.

While the Conference was still in progress many requests were received for copies of the papers, and subsequently many additional requests were received both from those who had attended the Conference and from others who had heard about it. This book will make them available in more convenient form.

It is not possible to list here the names of all who helped in the planning and organizing of the Conference or in the preparation of this book for publication. The whole-hearted cooperation and efficient performance of many members of the staff of West Virginia University contributed to the success of the Conference and made my job as Conference Chairman and Editor relatively easy and very pleasant. Special mention must be made, however, of Paul A. Miller, President of West Virginia University, who freely gave encouragement and support for the project when it was needed, John F. Golay, Provost of the University, Ernest J. Nesius, Vice President for the West Virginia Center for Appalachian Studies and Development, and George E. Kirk, Conference Director. Acknowledgment must also be made of the financial assistance provided to the Conference by Resources for the Future, Inc. Finally, I should like to express my appreciation for the cheerful and patient editorial cooperation of Jane Olson, for the Yale University Press.

L. F.

Morgantown, West Virginia
July 15, 1965

Part 1: Definition and Measurement
of Poverty

1: Poverty from the Civil War to World War II

by Oscar Handlin

Since the end of World War II, the conceptions of poverty and of social responsibility for it have changed so radically that the situation of the past has become almost irrelevant. Earlier eras are so remote from our own that they scarcely offer a model against which present action can be appraised, or even an analogy that will throw light on current problems. An examination of the views and practices of the past is valuable, if at all, simply because it reveals a contrast so sharp that it illuminates the distance we have come in a relatively brief period.

EARLY ATTITUDES TOWARD POVERTY

No doubt the citizen of 1965 would most like from the historian some indication of secular trends. How much poverty was there in the past? Has it been declining or increasing? To these questions there are no easy answers. Something, but not much, is known about the distribution of incomes.[1] But to relate that data

1. Varying viewpoints are presented by John R. Commons, *History of Labour in the United States, 1896–1932,* III (New York: Macmillan, 1935), pp. 51–96; E. Levasseur, *American Workman* (trans. T. S. Adams, ed. Theodore Marburg, Baltimore: Johns Hopkins Press, 1900), pp. 276 ff.; Gabriel Kolko, *Wealth and Power in America* (New York: Praeger, 1962), chs. 1, 3; Simon Kuznets, *Shares of Upper Income Groups in Income and Savings* (New York: National Bureau of Economic Research, 1953); Wesley C. Mitchell, et al., *Income in the United*

to costs and standards of living is a difficult task. Once the question is reframed—what percentage of the population had enough income for a decent style of life?—the problem shifts outside the realm of quantitative measurement and into that of perception and conception. What was "enough"? What was "decent"?

Here I shall attempt to deal with the problem on that level: to describe and account for the understanding of poverty which prevailed in the United States between the 1860s and the 1930s. Thus this essay is an exercise more in intellectual and social, than in economic, history.

Americans of 1965 inherited from a much earlier period a traditional conception of poverty to which they clung despite radically changing social conditions. The views that lingered tenaciously through the latter half of the nineteenth century rested upon ideas that originated in a much earlier period and were largely unrelated to the contemporary economy. They embraced deeply rooted assumptions about inequality and dependency.

Americans understood the self-evident truth that all men were created equal; but they did not draw from it the inference that equality of conditions should prevail in their society. "It is best for all," Lincoln explained in 1860, "to leave each man free to acquire property as fast as he can. Some will get wealthy. . . . A law to prevent a man from getting rich . . . would do more harm than good" so long as "the humblest man" had "an equal chance to get rich with everybody else."[2] Since individual abilities differed, it was to be expected that the rewards would be distributed along a spectrum between the least and the most successful. That some should be poor was no more surprising than that others should be wealthy. The historical conditions of settlement, the Puritan belief in calling and in the recognition of visible saints, and the speculative environment of an expanding economy all contributed to the acceptance of the actuality of inequality and therefore of poverty.

States 1910–1919 (New York: Harcourt, Brace, 1921); and W. S. Woytinsky, *Employment and Wages in the United States* (New York: Twentieth Century Fund, 1953).

2. Abraham Lincoln, "Speech at New Haven, March 6, 1860," *Life and Writings,* Philip Van Doren Stern, ed. (New York: Modern Library, 1942), p. 592.

Linked to this view was an equally traditional conception of dependency, the central assumption of which was the belief that society consisted of a cluster of households, each a self-contained economic unit capable of supporting its own members. It followed that only persons who were not, properly speaking, members of any household needed assistance. That category included orphans, the aged without children, and those prevented by some infirmity from sustaining themselves in their own households. In English as well as in early American practice, the community accepted responsibility for relief of these persons. The preferred course was to normalize their situation by locating them in some existing household; and that was generally possible through the apprenticeship of children or the indenture of servants. When that was not feasible the community could extend outdoor relief to the needy in their own homes, but it did so grudgingly and as a temporary expedient, assuming in these cases that dependency was the product of some momentary misfortune.[3]

However, by the nineteenth century and in some places indeed earlier, the facts belied this assumption. There were people in growing numbers permanently in need of assistance which the society did not recognize as due them. The initial response was the judgment that the household incapable of supporting its members did not really exist; the individuals who asked for aid were to be accommodated either in punitive workhouses or in philanthropic almshouses. Down to the end of the nineteenth century, in many places, the dependent faced a cruel dilemma: a request for help was an invitation to the destruction of the family. The community assumed no responsibility for those who wished to preserve family ties, for it assumed that every household would be able to sustain its own members.[4]

3. Marcus W. Jernegan, *Laboring and Dependent Classes in Colonial America* (Chicago: University of Chicago Press, 1931), pp. 175 ff., 189 ff.; David M. Schneider, *History of Public Welfare in New York State 1609–1866* (Chicago: University of Chicago Press, 1938); Alice Shaffer, Mary W. Keefer, and Sophonisba P. Breckinridge, *Indiana Poor Law* (Chicago: University of Chicago Press, 1936), p. 59.

4. Robert W. Kelso, *History of Public Poor Relief in Massachusetts* (Boston: Houghton Mifflin, 1922); David M. Schneider and Albert Deutsch, *History of Public Welfare in New York State 1867–1940* (Chicago: University of Chicago

The destitute who were not members of a household and had the physical capacity to sustain themselves were excluded from the community, at first simply by warning them away. That easy solution was not so readily available in the nineteenth century, a circumstance which led to prolonged concern about the problem of "settlement" and about the limits of communal obligations. In the 1870s and 1880s, the same uncertainty as to the extent of communal responsibility lay behind the anxiety about the tramp problem. Actually, soup kitchen philanthropy motivated by humanitarian sentiments mitigated the severity of the abstract position which refused to recognize the existence of men who could work but were not members of a settled household. Whatever the lack of logic of it, some provision was made for the emergency relief of the destitute and some social services were extended to those who, by the letter of the law and by the traditional view, were not entitled to it.[5]

INFLUENCE OF INDUSTRIAL CHANGE

This basic configuration of ideas was ever less relevant to social actualities after 1865. Well before the Civil War, a fundamental transformation of the economy had begun and the process of change accelerated steadily in the half century that followed the conflict. The new conditions complicated the application of the older ideas; yet the intellectual adjustment was slow.

When the Civil War broke out, the United States was already deeply involved in the expansion that would continue down to the 1920s. The most radical manifestation was territorial, as the continental possessions of the United States filled up in the decades to 1890, when Frederick Jackson Turner described some aspects of that process. But expansion also took other forms—a rapid in-

Press, 1941), pp. 35 ff.; Martha Branscombe, *Courts and the Poor Laws in New York State, 1784–1929* (Chicago: University of Chicago Press, 1943), pp. 74 ff.

5. Margaret Creech, *Three Centuries of Poor Law Administration* (Chicago: University of Chicago Press, 1936), pp. 42 ff., 134 ff.; Branscombe, *Courts and Poor Laws in New York,* pp. 83 ff., 100 ff.; Leah H. Feder, *Unemployment Relief in Periods of Depression* (New York: Russell Sage Foundation, 1936); Commons, *History of Labour,* III, chs. 11, 12; Schneider, *Public Welfare in New York, 1609–1866,* pp. 45 ff.; below, n. 19.

crease in population, a steady rise in the gross national product, and the elaboration of social institutions. Much of the expansion of the post-Civil War decades was urban. Cities had grown as the rest of the society had through the whole period of American settlement, of course; but after 1865, the main thrust of development was urban. Moreover, the types of cities that appeared in this period were modern in the size of their industrial proletariat, in the impersonal relationship of their inhabitants to the modes of production, and in the detached individualism of their communal life.

These aspects of expansion were related to industrialization. The rising level of production was a measure of the diffusion of large-scale manufacturing activities. By the Civil War, the factory was already familiar in some sections of the nation. In the postwar decades, it spread from textiles and other consumer goods to heavy industry where large-scale rationalized units were characteristic and where a good deal of managerial attention went to savings in labor costs. These branches of manufacturing depended upon the availability of a large pool of surplus labor, existing on a marginal level and susceptible to the recurrent shocks of economic fluctuations.[6]

The assumption that expansion was the overall direction of American historical development generated a calm acceptance of the business cycle. Looking back from 1865, Americans could recall the commercial setbacks of 1837 and 1857. Persuaded that there was a regularity to these phenomena, they regarded such fluctuations with some equanimity and they did not perceive until too late that the depressions of 1873 and 1893 were different in kind in their effect upon the population. The panics of those years were not merely signals of speculative collapses; their effects extended into the whole system of production and they rendered helpless large elements of the population for which prevailing social arrangements made no adequate provision. Not until 1929 would the impact of these differences be felt—and then only slowly and reluctantly.[7]

6. See, e.g., David Brody, *Steelworkers in America* (Cambridge: Harvard University Press, 1960), chs. 1, 2.

7. Samuel Rezneck, "Distress, Relief, and Discontent during the Depression of 1873–78," *J. Pol. Econ., 58* (1950), 494 ff.; Feder, *Unemployment Relief*, ch. 3.

By the 1890s, a large sector of the industrial labor force lived so close to destitution that any fluctuations in employment endangered its existence. Precisely how large a percentage fell into that sector is not known; there are only fragmentary impressions based on the number who actually applied for relief.[8] Yet many more households which did not turn to charity could be counted self-supporting only by stretching the concept; they survived by accepting the harshest conditions of life. The urban housing of the 1880s and 1890s would seem unimaginable to the present-day slum resident; expenditures on clothing were minimal; and, although food prices declined in those decades, the standards of nutrition were low.[9]

Although the percentage of the total population which lived under the conditions of poverty is difficult to estimate, the poor were certainly visible. But the dominant social attitudes of the period refused to acknowledge any communal obligation toward such people. Their distress did not constitute a claim against their neighbors.

The sight of the helpless was expected to move individuals to acts of private benevolence and, by extension, to occupy philanthropic voluntary associations. The primary responsibility for the relief of suffering rested upon charitable impulses of this sort and even these were to be yielded to with caution lest the beneficiaries of good will be corrupted by dependence. Rigid tests were to exclude the unworthy, though they occasionally caused the deserving to suffer. That men and women actually starved in the great cities was known; while deplorable, that fact was not enough in itself to shake the old conceptions of responsibility.

At the end of the century, a sympathetic observer could lament the plight of a family starving to death in New York City without any sense of surprise that such events should occur.[10] By then, the

8. Nathan I. Huggins, "Private Charities in Boston, 1870–1890" (Ph.D. thesis, Harvard University, 1962).

9. "A West Side Rookery," *Greenwich House Publications*, II (1906); Helen Campbell, *The Problem of the Poor* (New York: Fords, Howard & Hulbert, 1882), pp. 111 ff.; Commons, *History of Labour*, III, chs. 6, 8; Levasseur, *American Workman*, pp. 393 ff.; below, n. 22.

10. James Huneker, *New Cosmopolis* (New York: C. Scribner's, 1915), pp. 169–75.

states and municipalities were deeply involved in relief, particularly in periods of depression, but on a scale so limited and with such serious gaps as to leave many unprotected. In any case, the only condition of which society took cognizance was that of want at the level of starvation.

Significantly, the vigorous reform movements that agitated much of the nineteenth century had not, until the 1890s, addressed themselves squarely to the problems of poverty. The optimism that prevailed in some decades had nurtured a long view of progress; time would lead to a gradual amelioration of the condition of mankind and the difficulties of the moment lost their critical character in the long extended dimension. Meanwhile the poor, while remaining poor, could grow in moral grandeur. "In this class," William Ellery Channing had explained, "may be found those who have withstood the severest temptation, who have practiced the most arduous duties, who have confided in God under the heaviest trials, who have been most wronged and have forgiven most; and these are the great, the exalted."[11]

Socialists and other utopian thinkers from Thomas Skidmore to Henry George were not so acquiescent. But they looked forward to a total transformation of the social system and accepted the existing evils as evidence of the need for a change. They therefore expected no interim improvement, rather an actual worsening of conditions. Without the use of his remedy, warned George, "the evils arising from the unjust and unequal distribution of wealth" would "grow greater and greater, until they sweep us back into barbarism by the road every previous civilization has trod."[12]

By contrast, the exponents of social Darwinism regarded the adverse living conditions of the poor as a providential means of eliminating the unfit and advancing the positions of the fittest. "The socialist or philanthropist who nourishes them in their situation and saves them from the distress of it is only cultivating the distress which he pretends to cure." The system of nature, argued William Graham Sumner in the 1880s, was competitive and rewarded men according to their ability. "If we try to amend

11. William Ellery Channing, "Honor Due to All Men," *Works,* III (Boston: J. Munroe, 1841), p. 305.
12. Henry George, *Progress and Poverty* (New York: J. W. Lovell, 1882), p. 489.

it, there is only one way in which we can do it. We can take from the better and give to the worse. We can deflect the penalties of those who have done ill and throw them on those who have done better. We can take the rewards from those who have done better and give them to those who have done worse. We shall thus lessen the inequalities. We shall favor the survival of the unfittest, and we shall accomplish this by destroying liberty."[13]

There was, paradoxically, a keen sense of communal responsibility for such social disorders as criminality, prostitution, poor housing, and intemperance, which were often linked to poverty. But the thrust of remedial efforts, whether by reformers or conservatives, stressed the capacity of the individual to improve himself by acts of his own will while accepting the persistence of poverty as a given and unalterable fact of life. Helen Campbell in 1882, for instance, understood that "our poor are fast becoming our criminal class, and more and more it is apparent that something beyond preaching is required to bring order out of the chaos which threatens us." She advocated a religious awakening to revive spiritual values and turn the needy people into "quiet, steady workers," who would adjure drink, be educated for industrial labor and use their limited incomes effectively. Legislation could eliminate unfit homes and permit builders to construct profitable but cheap houses on sanitary principles. Training would show the women of the poor how to improve their famly diets by baking their own graham bread instead of wasting money on ribbons and needless finery.[14]

No one, however, regarded the existence of a large population destitute to the point at which it had no assurance of support and perpetually on the margin of starvation as a challenge to immediate action. That population, isolated in its own cultures in the industrial quarters of the large cities and in rural pockets throughout the country, was expected to improve itself, but not to disappear.

13. William Graham Sumner, *The Challenge of Facts* (New Haven: Yale University Press, 1914), pp. 22, 23, 25, 52; and "The Abolition of Poverty," *Earth-Hunger and Other Essays* (New Haven: Yale University Press, 1913), pp. 228 ff.

14. Campbell, *Problem of the Poor*, pp. 5, 23, 114, 219 ff.

The traditional belief that only starvation or the threat of it was a valid basis for social intervention limited the perception of the extent of poverty in the United States down almost to the end of the nineteenth century. Significantly this democratic nation was less responsive to the problem than most European countries at comparable stages of industrial development. The reasons are important.

A large proportion of the poor were either immigrants or Negroes and were therefore considered groups apart, toward which society did not bear full responsibility. The foreign-born had come of their own volition; they could go back if they wished; and they were better off than they had been in the places of their birth. The exclusion, by law, of newcomers likely to become a public charge created the assumption that those admitted had no claim upon communal assistance. As for the Negroes, a costly Civil War had liberated them; they were now to prove that they were worthy of their freedom.[15]

A narrowing concept of community action dulled the awareness that poverty existed among the native white population also. Since aid was primarily a subject of voluntary philanthropic action, anything done for the poor was testimony to the goodness of the hearts of the charitable rather than the fulfillment of an obligation. The United States was almost by definition the land of opportunity and any failure to take advantage of those opportunities was personal. There were acres of diamonds in each man's garden; each was responsible for finding them. Failure was the result of laziness, wickedness, or lack of ability. The appearance of eugenic theories which accounted for dependency by congenital defects supplied the decisive element in this explanation.[16]

15. See, e.g., Edith Abbott, *Historical Aspects of the Immigration Problem* (Chicago: University of Chicago Press, 1926), pp. 651, 682, 685, 847.

16. Richard L. Dugdale, *The Jukes* (New York: G. P. Putnam, 1877); A. H. Estabrook, *The Jukes in 1915* (Washington, D.C.: Carnegie Institution of Washington, 1916); H. H. Goddard, *The Kallikak Family* (New York: Macmillan, 1912); Oscar C. M'Culloch, "The Tribe of Ishmael," National Conference of Charities and Correction, *Proceedings*, XV (1888); Amos G. Warner, *American Charities: Study in Philanthropy and Economics* (New York:

The existence of empty land on the frontier and of open opportunities in the expanding cities provided just enough cases of success, of rags to a modest competence if not to riches, to lend plausibility to these assumptions.[17] Insofar as they considered the problem in any general economic context, Americans took for granted a frame of reference of scarcity. There was no radical break with classical European social theory in this respect. But Americans could take pride in their exceptionalism. In the Old World, corrupt institutions and the lack of opportunity depressed the population in a hopeless poverty, of which the swarms of beggars were the visible evidence. In the United States, the Biblical injunction—"The poor always ye have with you"—remained valid; but the poor were the unworthy, unwilling or unable to better themselves. That the facts of the matter, even in the nineteenth century, contradicted this complacent view did not weaken its hold on the minds of the dominant groups in the society.

In the 1890s signs of doubt appeared, but they were as yet not focused enough to alter the habitual attitudes toward poverty. Talk about the closing of the frontier and about the need for conserving natural resources reflected an uneasiness about the future and strengthened the assumption of scarcity. These forebodings cast doubt on the fate of American exceptionalism and therefore called attention to the potential menace of poverty; the United States might become like the other nations in the beggary of its population.[18]

The poor from this perspective were the dangerous classes in society. Already the tramp problem literally terrified many communities.[19] Now, as Jacob Riis called attention to *How the Other Half Lives,* it became clear that the menace of disease and dis-

T. Y. Crowell, 1894), pp. 88 ff.; James and Katherine M. Ford, *The Abolition of Poverty* (New York: Macmillan, 1937), p. 27.

17. For social mobility and the ideology of success, see Stephen A. Thernstrom, *Poverty and Progress* (Cambridge: Harvard University Press, 1964); Kenneth S. Lynn, *Dream of Success* (Boston: Little, Brown, 1955).

18. See, e.g., Frederick Jackson Turner, *Frontier in American History* (New York: H. Holt, 1920), pp. 293 ff.

19. E.g. Charles L. Brace, *Dangerous Classes of New York* (New York: Wynkoop & Hallenbeck, 1872); Josiah Willard Flynt, *Tramping with Tramps* (New York: Century, 1899). See also Robert H. Bremner, *From the Depths:*

order lurked in every community.[20] Mingled with the compassion with which the more fortunate regarded them was the suspicion that the poor were a source of contagion. That the accounts of even sympathetic observers were loaded with pejorative adjectives in the effort to win support for the work of converting or redeeming the unfortunate, did not diminish the dread in which the poor were held.

Charles Booth's pioneering study of the poor of London was widely read in the United States for it seemed to foreshadow the shape of things to come. But, significantly, it had no counterpart on this side of the Atlantic; Americans did not seem to wish a close-up view of the culture of poverty in their midst. Instead they gained their glimpses of it in a series of disconnected assessments of discrete social problems—slums and housing, immigrant assimilation, criminality, dependence, and the like.[21]

Of these, the most influential was Amos G. Warner's analysis of charity in 1894. This study had an empirical basis. But its major concern was to categorize the causes of poverty. Warner was able to classify the poor into two primary groups: those whose difficulties originated in "misconduct" and those who fell because of "misfortune," the latter being by far the larger. Insofar as he recognized that not all need was a product of such misconduct as drunkenness, laziness, and the lack of will power, Warner escaped some of the inhibiting effects of the traditional assumptions about the nature of poverty. But he was still on familiar ground in considering the poor, when not culpable, simply victims of misfortune; they remained, from that point of view, worthy objects of charity.[22]

The Discovery of Poverty in the United States (New York: New York University Press, 1956), pp. 142 ff.

20. Jacob A. Riis, *How the Other Half Lives* (New York: C. Scribner's, 1890); Bremner, *From the Depths,* pp. 68 ff.

21. Robert W. DeForest and Lawrence Veiller, *Tenement House Problem* (New York: Macmillan, 1903); Robert A. Woods, *City Wilderness* (Boston: Houghton Mifflin, 1898); and *Americans in Process* (Boston: Houghton Mifflin, 1902); Jacob A. Riis, *The Children of the Poor* (New York: C. Scribner's, 1902; first published 1892); also Roy Lubove, *Progressives and the Slums* (Pittsburgh: University of Pittsburgh Press, 1962), pp. 117 ff.

22. Warner, *American Charities,* pp. 27 ff., 37; also A. M. Simons, "A Statistical Study in Causes of Poverty," *Amer. J. Soc., 3* (1898), pp. 615 ff.

Robert Hunter's *Poverty* (1904) marked a more important intellectual break. By linking it with income level he arrived at the conclusion that poverty was socially created. Efforts to determine the distribution of incomes and the costs of living went back to the speculations of Matthew Carey and Hezekiah Niles in the nineteenth century. They grew more important in the 1890s as a result of the refinement of statistical procedures and of the growing use of such data in shaping public policy. Local welfare agencies, state bureaus of labor statistics, and Congressional investigating committees had assembled a good deal of information on the subject by the time Hunter wrote.[23]

By distinguishing between the paupers and the poor, Hunter drew attention to the fact that the problem of poverty was not coterminous with the problem of relief. While he still made a ritual condemnation of the "voluntarily idle and vicious" and acknowledged that "there is unquestionably a poverty which men deserve, and by such poverty men are taught useful lessons," he went on to argue that "the mass of the poor" were "bred of miserable and unjust social conditions, which punish the good and the pure, the faithful and industrious, the slothful and the vicious, all alike." Industrial society put obstacles in the way of self-support that might be too great even for the most determined individual.[24] Furthermore the poor in that sense were far more numerous than Americans realized; more than 10,000,000 families lacked the annual income of $460 in the north and $300 in the rural south that Hunter considered the boundary of poverty. Above all, poverty was "procreative"; its conditions tended to perpetuate themselves from generation to generation and threatened to grow worse with time.[25]

Important and innovative as this work was, it still clung to some traditional American attitudes. Hunter, for instance, set the poverty line well below the then current estimates of the minimum family income necessary for a "decent" standard of living ($600–700 in Massachusetts). He thus located the poor in an intermediate

23. James Leiby, *Carroll Wright and Labor Reform: The Origin of Labor Statistics* (Cambridge: Harvard University Press, 1960); Bremner, *From the Depths,* pp. 71 ff.

24. Robert Hunter, *Poverty* (New York: Macmillan, 1904), pp. 62, 338.

25. Ibid., pp. 47 ff., 191 ff.

position between the least adequate style of life and dependence upon relief.[26]

More important, the remedial action Hunter proposed followed the familiar reform lines: the establishment by government of minimum standards of working and living conditions and the creation of opportunities so that the most worthy could advance. Within a social order the dominant characteristic of which was scarcity, there seemed no alternative to measures which encouraged the ablest to shed their poverty, for there was no way of distributing an income—the totality of which was insufficient—that would avoid the deprivation from which some suffered. It is suggestive that shortly after the publication of his book, Hunter became a socialist, as if in recognition of the inadequacy of these palliatives and of the necessity for a total overturn of the social system.[27]

In the thirty years after the publication of Hunter's book the problems of poverty received increasing attention. The appearance of a corps of professional social workers in whose thinking environmental factors were important called attention to the social costs of deprivation; and the emphasis of progressive reform shifted perceptibly to a greater concern than earlier with the lot of the underprivileged elements in society. Nevertheless the advocated techniques of amelioration reflected the persistence of the old assumption that inequalities of condition and some degree of want would remain in a productive system in which goods continued to be scarce. Insurance could protect the individual and the community against the loss of earning power through age, incapacitating illness, and unemployment; and minimum standards of wages, housing, and working conditions would encourage the efficient utilization of labor. But want would not disappear. The abolition of poverty meant the abolition of dependency and demanded the gradual "development of a social milieu which will educe latent abilities and train them." Poverty was a kind of pathology: "personal incapacity expressed in shiftlessness, thriftlessness and criminalism is . . . in large part the product of an environment which elicits or encourages socially undesirable

26. Ibid., pp. 51 ff.
27. Ibid., pp. 338 ff.; Bremner, *From the Depths*, pp. 151 ff.; David A. Shannon, *Socialist Party of America* (New York: Macmillan, 1955).

habits." The cure would come in time through alterations in the environment.[28]

The New Deal, in which twentieth-century progressivism culminated, expressed this point of view. The depression had dramatically exposed the reality and extent of poverty; in 1934, one-fourth of the nation had ceased to be self-supporting and in an exceptionally vulnerable city like Butte, Montana, 76 per cent of the families were on relief. A succession of FERA and WPA studies showed the degree to which dependency overwhelmed people stranded by economic disorders over which they had no control and against which they could not prepare. The New Deal was sensitive to the needs thus revealed; but its program still assumed that poverty was an inevitable and incidental feature of the American social system. Franklin Roosevelt spoke eloquently of the needs of the one-third of the nation that was ill-housed, ill-clothed, and ill-fed. At the same time much of his program for recovery involved the manipulation of planned economic scarcities. The concepts of full employment and of the universal diffusion of adequate minimum incomes which are basic to present-day concepts of poverty were not widely heard until the Second World War.[29]

The depression did have a less direct, but more consequential, intellectual effect. Its length and the hardships it entailed shattered the belief that such fluctuations in the productive system were self-correcting irregularities, inevitable in an expanding economy. With that belief went the faith in American exceptionalism and in the universal access to opportunity in the United

28. Jacob H. Hollander, *Abolition of Poverty* (Boston: Houghton Mifflin, 1914); Ford and Ford, *The Abolition of Poverty*, pp. 99, 186 ff.; Clarke A. Chambers, *Seedtime of Reform: American Social Service and Social Action, 1918–1933* (Minneapolis: University of Minnesota Press, 1963), pp. 1 ff., 27 ff., 59 ff., 85 ff.; Bremner, *From the Depths*, pp. 46 ff., 125 ff., 249 ff.

29. Ford and Ford, *Abolition of Poverty*, pp. 28–32, 163, 164; Chambers, *Seedtime of Reform*, pp. 183 ff.; Schneider and Deutsch, *Public Welfare in New York*, pp. 293 ff.; Irving Bernstein, *The Lean Years* (Boston: Houghton Mifflin, 1960), pp. 287 ff., 456 ff., 475 ff.

States. Poverty became not the lot of those who fell behind in a race open to all, but a threat that might overwhelm anyone. The inequality in the distribution of the world's goods therewith became far less tolerable than formerly.

Meanwhile, probing, although as yet not widely heeded, questions had been raised about the basic premise of scarcity. The economist Simon Patten had speculated about the nature of a society in which the essential commodities were abundant; and occasional social engineers and technocrats had outlined patterns of organization framed within the entirely new assumption that enough—however defined—would be available for the whole population.[30] At the same time, within industry and outside it, doubts had been raised about the proposition that the least costly labor force was the most economical; and evidence had accumulated about the degree to which poverty was wasteful in lowering the efficiency of workers.[31] But these challenges to the accepted traditional point of view remained abstract until the tremendous outburst of productivity after 1939 created a new set of conditions within which poverty acquired its present meaning.

30. Daniel M. Fox, "Simon Patten, Moralist of American Abundance" (Ph.D. dissertation, Harvard University, 1964).

31. Ford and Ford, *Abolition of Poverty*, pp. 167, 274; Samuel Haber, *Efficiency and Uplift* (Chicago: University of Chicago Press, 1964).

2: Population Change and Poverty Reduction, 1947–75

by Robert J. Lampman[1]

In order to direct attention to the essential characteristics of poverty in the United States, we must ask certain questions. What is the composition of that part of the American population which is poor? What is the process by which the size and composition of the poor population changes from year to year and decade to decade? What is the likely size and shape of the poverty problem in the years to 1975? The underlying reason for all such inquiry is to learn what policy measures hold greatest promise for maintaining and accelerating our historic rate of poverty reduction. But before attempting to find the answers to these questions, consideration will be given to the definition of poverty.

SETTING THE POVERTY LINE

President Johnson and his Council of Economic Advisers (CEA) have started with an admittedly crude definition of poverty as less than $3,000 (at 1962 prices) of total money income for families

1. The author is pleased to acknowledge valuable counsel on the topic of this paper from W. Lee Hansen and Burton A. Weisbrod, at the University of Wisconsin, and assistance on Table 2.9 from Peter Durkee, at the University of Washington.

and $1,500 for unrelated individuals. Using that definition, it can be estimated that 20 per cent of American families and 45 per cent of unrelated individuals, making a total of 35 million persons, were poor in 1962.

The scope of the poverty problem, the time and effort required to reach the goal of eliminating it, and, to a lesser extent, the remedies that should be emphasized all depend upon the original definition of the term. Hence, although it should not be thought of as an end in itself, the definition of poverty deserves careful attention. Poverty is a discrepancy between needs and resources —or between needed and actual consumption—and it remains at bottom a matter for judgment as to where to set the line separating the poor from the nonpoor. The CEA method can be said to be based on the concept that the basic consumption needs, or a minimally acceptable level of consumer satisfactions, could be met by the typically situated family with $3,000 or more of total money income. This method then yields a hypothetical estimate: if all families had the same needs or desires and the same resources other than total money income, then 9.3 million families would have been poor in 1962.

A smaller hypothetical number could be said to be poor if either a lower total money income, or $3,000 of consumption expenditures or $3,000 of personal income (which includes such nonmoney income as home-produced food and imputed rent) were used as the standard for need. It should be noted that the shift from money income to either consumption expenditures or personal income is tantamount to a lowering of the poverty line just as surely as is adopting a lower money-income line. This is so unless one interprets the CEA standard of $3,000 as connoting a standard of $3,000 in consumption expenditures. If that is what is meant, then it is appropriate to make, as some critics have, a series of downward adjustments in the 9.3 million families estimate by accounting for nonmoney income, spending of savings, borrowing, receipt of gifts, and even potential consumption of assets.

On the other hand, one could, as a matter of judgment, raise the standard by, for example, raising the total money income line, or by selecting a higher level than $3,000 of consumption or personal income. To get back to more neutral ground, one could set the line in terms of disposable personal income plus and minus interpersonal gifts and plus capital gains and free public services, all averaged over a period of several years.

The poverty line could be drawn to define a family as poor unless it has one of a stated set of combinations of income and net worth, e.g. $2,500 of personal income and $5,000 of net worth, or $3,000 of personal income and zero net worth, with further variation by age. The logical extension of this reasoning is to capitalize future income or to convert net worth to annuity value. Needs could be measured not by a single money income line of $3,000 for families of any size (two or more), of all age and sex compositions, in all residential and occupational situations, in varying needs of health care, child care, and varying special obligations toward relatives or others, but by various income standards for various combinations of these factors.

The possibilities for variation are infinite, and complete realism in accounting for all differences in needs and resources is beyond reach. The case method of detailed description of individual family situations is a valuable addition to, but is no substitute for, demographic analysis. Such analysis, when aimed at causal factors or at changes over time, will not necessarily be helped by a great number of separate classifications. In practice, analysis is limited by presently available data.

Hence, here we shall use as our reference point the total money income line, because it is the only one for which time series by relevant demographic characteristics are available. However, it is helpful to know the directions in which our understanding of poverty is biased by the particular poverty line in use, and we will comment on adjustments for family size, income variability, and other factors where appropriate.

COMPOSITION OF THE POOR IN 1962

Who are the poor? This question can be answered in a variety of ways, but perhaps the most meaningful is by reference to broad policy alternatives. How are the poor families and poor persons situated with reference to employment and hence to policies which affect the number and quality of jobs? How are they divided with reference to what might be called "handicapping characteristics"

and hence to policies which will raise one group's incomes relative
to that of others? Finally, how are the poor divided as to geographic location and hence to programs that are aimed at certain
areas?

TABLE 2.1. SELECTED CHARACTERISTICS OF
POOR FAMILIES, 1962*

SELECTED CHARACTERISTICS	PER CENT OF ALL POOR FAMILIES
Total	100ᵃ
Earners in family	
None	30
One	46
Two	18
Three or more	4
Labor force status of head	
Not in civilian labor force	44
Unemployed	6
Employed	49
Age of head	
14–24 years	8
25–54 years	42
55–64 years	15
65 years and over	34
Children under 18 years of age in family	
None	52
One	16
Two	12
Three or more	20

*Poor families are those with a total income in 1962 of less than $3,000.
a. Detail may not add to 100 per cent because of rounding.

Source: *Economic Report of the President, 1964* (Washington, D.C.: Government Printing Office, 1964), adapted from Table 4, p. 61, and Table 7, p. 71.

RELATIONSHIP TO THE LABOR MARKET

A glance at Table 2.1 shows that the dominant part of the contemporary poor are closely related to the labor market: 70 per cent
of the poor families have at least one income earner, 54 per cent of
the family heads are in the labor force, and 57 per cent of them
are in the prime working ages of 25 to 64 years. Relatively few

(6 per cent) are what is technically defined as "unemployed" at any given time, and only 15 per cent are unemployed at any time during the year. (It helps to understand how poverty can exist in spite of a low rate of unemployment to know that at least 10 million employees receive a wage of less than $1.50 per hour, and many farmers and other self-employed persons, who are rarely counted as unemployed but are sometimes underemployed, earn low entrepreneurial incomes. It should also be noted that some of those not actively seeking employment would be doing so if employment opportunities were available.)

The impression that most of the poor are in the labor force, and hence would benefit by higher employment levels and economic growth, is heightened by adjustment of the poverty income line for family size and by counting the number of *persons,* rather than *families,* in poverty. The difference this method of figuring would make is indicated in the bottom panel of Table 2.1, which shows that 48 per cent of all poor families have children, and 20 per cent of them have three or more children. This suggests that the majority of poor persons are in families with children, and that most poor children are in families with one or both parents in the labor force (at work or seeking work).

By use of the straight $3,000 income cut-off we estimate that 11 million children live in poverty; or to put it another way, almost one-third of poor persons are children. By adopting a set of poverty lines that take into account the size of family, we find that children constitute well over one-third of the poor population. Table 2.2 shows that 72 per cent of poor persons are in families of three or more persons and 36 per cent are in families of six or more persons.

The recent study by Mollie Orshansky, of the Social Security Administration, based upon a set of 248 income cut-offs for families of different size and age-sex composition, with a lower cut-off for farm residents, concluded that 44 per cent (15 million) of the poor in 1963 were children. Thus $6.6 billion of the $11.5 billion by which the poor as a group fall short of the poverty income line would be required to raise families with children above the poverty line.[2] Also significant was the finding that the poor population's

2. "Counting the Poor: Another Look at the Poverty Profile," *Social Security Bull.* (January 1965).

TABLE 2.2. DISTRIBUTION OF LOW-INCOME PERSONS BY FAMILY SIZE, BASED ON MINIMUM INCOME VARYING WITH FAMILY SIZE, 1963

	Total no. of families	FAMILY SIZE						
		1	2	3	4	5	6	7 or more
All consumer units (millions)	58.6	11.2	15.3	9.8	9.4	6.3	3.2	3.3
All persons (millions)	187.2	11.2	30.6	29.4	37.6	31.5	19.2	26.4
Minimum income for each family size[a]		$1,261	$1,785	$2,296	$2,742	$3,148	$3,527	$4,088
Number of low income units (millions)	11.1	4.1	2.5	1.3	.9	.8	.5	1.0
Number of low-income persons (millions)	31.5	4.1	4.9	3.8	3.5	4.0	3.1	8.1
Low-income persons as per cent of all persons in each family size	16.8	37.0	16.0	13.0	9.0	13.0	16.0	31.0
Per cent of total low-income population in each family size	100.0	13.0	15.0	12.0	11.0	12.0	10.0	26.0
Per cent of total population in each family size	100.0	6.0	16.0	15.0	20.0	17.0	10.0	15.0

a. Income cut-offs were selected on a basis similar to the one used in the author's study, *The Low-Income Population and Economic Growth*, Joint Economic Committee Study Paper No. 12 (Washington, D.C.: Government Printing Office, 1959).

Source: Bureau of the Census, *Income of Families and Persons in the United States, 1963*, P–60, No. 43 (Washington, D.C.: Government Printing Office, 1964), p. 60.

tie to the labor market is tighter than is suggested by our Table 2.1. One striking point made is that at least 5.7 million of the 15 million poor children were in families whose heads had a regular full-time job in 1963.[3] Counting children also has the effect of reducing within the ranks of the poor the relative importance of the aged and heads of families not in the labor force. The relative

3. Ibid., pp. 18–20.

importance of the aged in the ranks of the poor is further diminished when account is taken of assets holdings. The effect goes the
other way when account is taken of poor unrelated individuals,
70 per cent of whom are women, 52 per cent of whom are aged, and
66 per cent of whom are nonearners. Keeping these points in mind,
and also remembering that some aged persons are in family units
headed by a younger person, I estimate that one-fourth to one-fifth
of the poor are aged persons.

HANDICAPPING CHARACTERISTICS

The leading characteristic which distinguishes the poor from
the nonpoor population is limited educational attainment: 61 per
cent of poor family heads have no more than eight years of schooling (see Table 2.3). This percentage would fall somewhat if the
adjustment for family size were applied, because it would reduce
the importance of aged heads, who tend to be least educated.
However, we know there is also a disparity of educational attainments for young people. While 32 per cent of all persons 16 to
24 years of age in 1960 had not graduated from high school, 45 per

TABLE 2.3. SELECTED "HANDICAPPING" CHARACTERISTICS OF
POOR FAMILIES, 1962

SELECTED CHARACTERISTIC	PER CENT OF ALL POOR FAMILIES
Total	100
Education of head	
8 years or less	61
9–11 years	17
12 years	15
More than 12 years	7
Sex of head	
Male	75
Female	25
Color of family	
White	78
Nonwhite	22

Source: *Economic Report of the President, 1964* (Washington, D.C.: Government Printing Office, 1964), Table 4, p. 61.

cent of those whose fathers had incomes under $5,000 had not graduated.[4]

Aside from limited education, the principal handicapping characteristics in our market-oriented society are old age (discussed above), disability, female sex, and nonwhite color. The heads of most nonaged poor families are neither disabled, female, nor nonwhite. The relative importance of nonwhites among the poor is somewhat understated by Table 3, since it does not take into account the fact that nonwhites are disproportionately nonfarm residents and, moreover, often have to pay more for the same quality housing than do whites. It also appears that, while nonwhite families are only 22 per cent of all poor families, nonwhite children make up one-third of all poor children.[5]

WHERE ARE THE POOR?

Most of the poor are urban dwellers, and most of those, in turn, live in metropolitan communities, that is, areas with populations of 250,000 or more.[6] A significant minority live in rural nonfarm

TABLE 2.4. SELECTED RESIDENTIAL CHARACTERISTICS OF
POOR FAMILIES, 1962

SELECTED CHARACTERISTIC	PER CENT OF ALL POOR FAMILIES
Total	100
Residence of family	
Rural farm	16
Rural nonfarm	30
Urban	54
Regional location of family	
Northeast	17
North Central	25
South	47
West	11

Source: *Economic Report of the President, 1964* (Washington, D.C.: Government Printing Office, 1964), Table 4, p. 61.

4. *Poverty in the United States,* House of Representatives, Committee on Education and Labor, 88th Congress, 2nd Session (April 1964), p. 278.
5. Ibid., p. 31.
6. Ibid., p. 159. Also see *Poverty in Rural Areas of the United States,* Agricultural Economic Report No. 63, U.S. Department of Agriculture (November 1964).

settings, but only a small minority are farm residents. (Whether the 16 per cent figure cited in Table 2.4 overstates or understates the true importance of this group is highly controversial.)

Almost half the poor live in the South. However, relatively few of the poor are located in what can be identified as isolated "pockets of poverty," like the Ozark plateau or the cut-over region of the Upper Great Lakes (the total population of the latter region was only 1.3 million in 1960). The state having the largest absolute number of poor is Texas, which had 7 per cent of the nation's poor in 1960; the next highest ranking states were New York and California (see Table 2.9, below).

YEAR-TO-YEAR CHANGE IN SIZE OF THE POOR POPULATION

In 1962 there were 9.3 million families in poverty; by 1963 the number was down to 9.0 million. How did that reduction take place? Answers to that question are important for gaining predictive control over the rate of reduction. Some insight into the process of poverty reduction is afforded by a special tabulation of the Census sample survey that shows incomes of families for two successive years. Estimates derived from that tabulation are shown in diagram form in Figure 2.1. It appears that approximately 70 per cent of those families with money incomes under $3,000 in 1962 were also present and poor in 1963. About 6 per cent (400,000) of the 1962 poor families were dissolved by death or otherwise, and about 23 per cent moved to a higher income class. Most of the latter group moved to income classes only slightly above $3,000, and most of them had an income average for the two years of under $3,000. The other side of the process is that the 1963 poor group was largely (70 per cent) made up of the families who were poor in 1962. It includes some (about 23 per cent) who descended from above-poverty income levels and a small number (about 7 per cent) who came out of newly formed and immigrant families. The net reduction by 300,000 in the number of poor families is explained by the facts that (1) the number of poor families dissolved exceeded the number of poor families newly created by approximately 200,000 and (2) the number of families rising out of poverty to above-poverty income levels exceeded the

FIGURE 2.1. CHANGES IN POVERTY 1962–63 (MILLIONS OF FAMILIES)

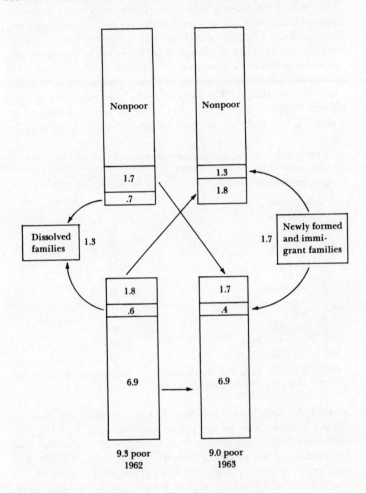

Source: *Economic Report of the President, 1965* (Washington, D.C.: Government Printing Office, 1965), Table 20, p. 165.

number descending from above-poverty to poverty income levels by about 100,000.

The exits from poverty reflect temporary movements in the incomes of many from one year to another, owing to unemployment, illness or disability, part-period incomes of families formed during the year, and the risks of enterprise for many of the self-employed. They also reflect more permanent movements up the occupational and income ladder as people become more productive with added experience on the job. The extent to which the rate of exits from poverty depends upon these and other factors is indicated in Table 2.5, which shows variation in the persistence of poverty by

TABLE 2.5. THE PERSISTENCE OF POVERTY, 1962 TO 1963

SELECTED CHARACTERISTICS	PER CENT IN POVERTY IN 1962 ALSO IN POVERTY IN 1963
All families	69
Age of head	
14–24	62
25–34	55
35–44	53
45–54	63
55–64	71
65 and over	80
Color of head	
White	67
Nonwhite	76
Nonworking head	83
Female head	76

Source: *Economic Report of the President, 1965* (Washington, D.C.: Government Printing Office, 1965), Table 19, p. 164.

selected characteristics of families. The rates of exits appear to be highest among those in the prime working ages, reflecting the experience factor, and among those unemployed in the 1962 base year, reflecting the temporary nature of their lack of work. The persistence of poverty is greater than average for nonwhites, for families headed by women, and by persons not in the labor force, and by those in the South.

But just as there are many who exit out of poverty, another slightly smaller group slides back into poverty every year. Pre-

TABLE 2.6. TRENDS IN POVERTY: DISTRIBUTION AND FREQUENCY OF LOW-INCOME CONSUMER UNITS, BY SIZE OF UNIT, 1947, 1957, 1961, 1962, 1963

	NUMBER IN GROUP (MILLIONS)					NUMBER OF LOW-INCOME UNITS* (MILLIONS)					INCIDENCE OF LOW INCOME (PER CENT)				
	(1)	(2)	(3)	(4)	(5)	(6)	(7)	(8)	(9)	(10)	(11)	(12)	(13)	(14)	(15)
	1947	1957	1961	1962	1963	1947	1957	1961	1962	1963	1947	1957	1961	1962	1963
Size of consumer units															
1 person	8.1	10.3	11.2	11.0	11.2	4.1	4.4	4.4	4.2	4.1	51	43	39	40	37
2 persons	11.7	14.3	15.2	15.0	15.3	2.7	2.5	2.7	2.4	2.5	23	17	18	16	16
3 persons	9.6	9.5	9.8	9.8	9.8	1.8	1.2	1.2	1.1	1.3	19	13	12	11	13
4 persons	7.4	8.8	9.2	9.4	9.4	1.5	1.0	1.1	1.1	.9	20	11	12	11	9
5 persons	4.2	5.5	5.9	6.1	6.3	.9	.8	.8	.8	.8	21	15	14	12	13
6 persons	2.2	2.9	3.3	3.4	3.2	.7	.7	.6	.6	.5	32	24	18	17	16
7 persons or more	2.3	2.6	2.9	3.3	3.3	1.0	1.0	1.0	1.0	1.0	44	38	34	31	31
Totals of consumer units	45.3	54.0	57.5	58.0	58.6	12.7	11.6	11.8	11.2	11.1	28.0	21.5	20.5	19.2	18.9
Total persons	144.6	168.3	180.3	185.3	187.2	37.6	32.2	32.7	32.6	31.5	26	19	18	18	17

*Low-income units defined as those below variable minimum incomes for the several family sizes with $2,000 (1947 prices) for a family of 4 as a base.

Source: Data for 1947 and 1957 are obtained from the author's Joint Economic Committee Study Paper No. 12, *The Low Income Population and Economic Growth*, op. cit. Data for 1961, 1962, and 1963 are derived from Bureau of the Census, *Current Population Survey*, P-60 series, op. cit.

sumably, the newly unemployed, older family heads, and the ill and disabled are most important among those retreating into poverty. Thus, it is important not only to increase the number of exits from poverty but to bolster the defenses against backsliding into poverty.

Table 2.6 presents the changes from year to year in the poor population in a different way. This table, which is based upon the poverty lines adjusted for family size as in Table 2.2, reveals that between 1947 and 1957 the groups of various family sizes changed in such a way as to bring about an increase in the number of poor consumer units and poor persons. The greatest increase in numbers of consumer units over the 10-year period occurred near the extremes of the family sizes where the frequency of poverty was unusually high—families of one person, two, five, and six (compare columns 1 and 2). The shift into these particular family sizes would have had the effect of raising the total number of low-income persons if no other changes had taken place. However, the frequency of low income fell dramatically, by one-third or more, for three, four, and five-person families and less dramatically for other family sizes, causing the number of low-income persons to fall from 26 to 19 per cent (compare columns 11 and 12). While the number of large families increased in the total population, the number of such families in the poor population fell, partly due to an increase in number of workers per family.

Between 1957 and 1963 the change in family size also worked to bring about an increase in the number of poor persons, and this time the demographic change was less offset by incidence changes. While small families increased by less than 10 per cent, the families of five and seven or more increased by more than 20 per cent. The startling result is that the number of poor persons was 32.2 million in 1957, 32.7 million in 1961, 32.6 million in 1962, and 31.5 million in 1963. In other words, the absolute numbers of persons in poverty, when the poverty definition takes account of variation in family size, was virtually unchanged from 1957 through 1963. If the poverty line was set higher for nonfarm than for farm residence (this is a debatable procedure), then the absolute number of poor might seem to be increasing during this period.

Adjustment for family size also gives rise to doubts about the

TABLE 2.7. ESTIMATES OF PERCENTAGE OF FAMILIES, CONSUMER UNITS, AND PERSONS IN POVERTY,
SELECTED YEARS, 1929–63

	PER CENT OF FAMILIES, CEA METHOD ($3,000 total money income, 1962 prices)	PER CENT OF CONSUMER UNITS, OBE METHOD ($3,000 personal income, 1954 prices)	PERSONS (PER CENT) LAMPMAN METHOD Total money income	Personal income	SOCIAL SECURITY METHOD
1929	—	59	—	—	—
1935–36	—	63	—	—	—
1941	—	47	—	—	—
1947	32	35	26	—	—
1957	23	26	19	13	—
1961	21	25	18	—	—
1962	20	24	18	—	—
1963	19	—	17	—	18

Sources: Column 1. *Economic Report of the President, 1964* (Washington, D.C.: Government Printing Office, 1964), Table 3, p. 59.
Column 2. Department of Commerce, *Survey of Current Business*, April 1964, Table 13, p. 11.
Columns 3 and 4. See Tables 2.2 and 2.5.
Column 5. Mollie Orshansky, "Counting the Poor: Another Look at the Poverty Profile," op. cit., Table 1, p. 11.

rate of poverty reduction in recent years. The CEA method shows that poor families fell from 32 per cent in 1947, to 23 per cent in 1957, and to 19 per cent in 1963, a fall of almost one percentage point per year. However, by reference to a variable income cut-off, ranging around $2,742 (1962 prices) for a family of four persons (see Table 5), we find that persons in poverty fell from 26 per cent in 1947 to 19 per cent in 1957, to 17 per cent in 1963 (see Tables 2.6 and 2.7), a fall of only half a percentage point per year, and a very slight fall from 1957 to 1963.

CHANGE IN THE POOR POPULATION, 1947–62

Over a period of years the number and composition of the poor population changes as a result of births and deaths, differential growth of groups having different susceptibility to poverty, migration and shifting among groups, and differential change in the incidence of poverty within the several demographic groups. A rather broad look at this process of change is presented in Table 2.8, which shows the change from 1947 to 1962, and projects the change to 1970 and 1975 (see below for discussion of projection). While the overall incidence of poverty fell from 32 to 20 per cent from 1947 to 1962, it fell unevenly among different groups, some increasing and some decreasing in relative importance in the total population, with the result that the poor population had a quite different composition in the two years. Demographic change was working both for and against reduction of the national poverty rate: working for it was the movement off the farms (where poverty incidence was high) to higher-income occupations and industries, to the West, and into high-income states.

The numerous demographic changes working against poverty reduction included disproportionate increases in no-earner families, not-in-labor-force family heads, young heads, nonwhites, and families with three or more children. The fully proportional growth of the population in the South, the poorest region, may also be said to have worked against poverty reduction.

Some unusual changes in incidence should also be noted. The much smaller than average decreases included the categories of the no-earners, the not-in-the-labor-force heads, the young and the old, the female heads, and those on farms. The result of demographic change combined with changes in incidence rates can be seen in the changing composition of the poor. The no-earner families increased in importance, from 16 to 30 per cent of all poor families. Related to this was the rise of incidence rates among families with heads who were elderly or women, or who were not in the labor force. There was also a moderate increase in the relative importance of nonwhites and large families. On the other hand, farm residents fell in importance, from 30 to 20 per cent.

The poor were more concentrated in the poorest region, the South (up from 43 to 47 per cent), and in the West, partly because of the relatively high growth of population in these regions, and partly because of the relatively slow fall of incidence. The incidence of poverty fell more sharply in the rich states than in the poor states, generally speaking, with the result that the range of difference was wider in 1959 than in 1949. The poorest state, Mississippi, had 70 per cent of its families in poverty in 1949, when the richest state, Connecticut, had 20 per cent in poverty. In 1959 the incidence rates were 52 for Mississippi and 9 for Connecticut.

A further inquiry into the effect of population change is shown in Table 2.9, which records changes on a state-by-state basis between the two most recent census years. It shows, for example, that Mississippi, the state having the highest incidence of poverty in both years, had an absolute decline in population, that it experienced a net out-migration equal to 20 per cent of its 1950 population, that it reduced its numbers in poverty at the same rate as the nation, that it had about 3 per cent of the nation's poor in both years, but rose in rank from 14th to 12th among the states in absolute number of poor families.

By contrasting the 13 poorest and the 13 richest states, we find that population increases were greatest in the richer states. The poorest states had an average population gain of 13 per cent while the richest states gained 23 per cent on the average. Some of the change is due to the fact that the poorest group had an average rate of out-migration of 7 per cent, whereas the richest group had an in-migration of 6 per cent. In spite of this, the poorest group had a slightly larger share (36 per cent and 34 per cent) of the nation's poor in 1959 than in 1949. Part of the answer to the puzzle is that the rate of reduction of poverty was greater in the

TABLE 2.8. NUMBER OF FAMILIES AND INCIDENCE AND COMPOSIT[...]
WITH PROJECTI[...]

| | NO. OF FAMILIES (MILLIONS) | | | | PER CENT CHANGE | | |
	1947	'62	'70	'75	1947–62	1962–70	196[...]
All families[b]	37.3	47.0	52.5	57.1	26	12	[...]
Earners in family							
None	2.2	3.8	4.2	4.6	68	10	[...]
1	21.9	21.1	25.3	27.4	—4	20	[...]
2	9.9	17.0	17.7	19.2	73	4	[...]
3 or more	3.3	5.1	5.3	5.8	56	4	[...]
Labor force status of head[c]							
Not in civilian labor force	5.5	8.4	9.1	9.9	52	8	[...]
Unemployed	1.2	1.7	1.9	2.1	49	12	[...]
Employed	31.9	36.9	41.5	45.1	16	12	[...]
Age of head							
14–24 years	1.8	2.5	4.9	5.8	39	96	1[...]
25–54 years	25.0	30.4	32.4	35.2	22	6	[...]
55–64 years	6.1	7.3	8.2	8.7	19	11	[...]
65 years and over	4.4	6.8	7.0	7.4	54	3	
Children under 18							
None	16.2	18.8	21.1	22.6	16	12	[...]
1	8.9	8.7	10.6	11.6	—2	22	[...]
2	6.4	8.5	9.5	10.5	33	12	[...]
3 or more	5.7	10.9	11.3	12.4	92	4	[...]
Sex of head							
Male	33.5	42.3	47.3	51.4	26	11	[...]
Female	3.8	4.7	5.2	5.7	26	11	[...]
Color							
White	34.2	42.4	47.3	51.3	24	11	[...]
Nonwhite	3.1	4.6	5.3	5.8	46	15	[...]
Residence							
Farm	6.5	3.2			—51		
Nonfarm	30.8	43.8			42		
Region							
Northeast	10.1	11.7	12.7	13.4	15	9	1[...]
North Central	11.5	13.3	14.7	15.7	15	11	1[...]
South	11.5	14.2	15.9	17.3	23	12	2[...]
West	5.1	7.7	9.3	10.8	51	21	4[...]

a. The incidence of poverty is measured by the per cent that poor families with a given characteristic are of all families having the same characteristic.

b. Detail may not add to totals because of rounding.

c. For the years 1947 and 1962 labor force status is for April survey week of 1949 and March survey week of 1963.

d. The projections of the per cent of families with incomes under $3,000 in 1970 and 1975 are based on the assumption that incomes at this level generally will rise 2.5 per cent per year. This amounts to a determination of how many

POVERTY, BY SELECTED FAMILY CHARACTERISTICS, 1947, AND 1962,
R 1970 AND 1975

	INCIDENCE OF POVERTY[a] (PER CENT)				NO. OF POOR FAMILIES[d] (MILLIONS)				PER CENT OF POOR FAMILIES WITH CHARACTERISTIC			
	'47	'62	'70	'75	1947	'62	'70	'75	1947	'62	'70	'75
2	20	16	14		11.9	9.3	8.4	8.0	100	100	100	100
3	76	65	60		1.8	2.8	2.7	2.8	16	30	33	33
5	20	15	14		7.7	4.3	3.8	3.8	64	46	46	46
0	10	8	7		2.0	1.7	1.4	1.3	17	18	16	15
0	8	6	5		.3	.4	.3	.3	3	5	5	5
1	50	40	36		3.4	4.1	3.6	3.5	28	44	49	46
9	34	27	25		.6	.6	.5	.6	5	6	7	8
8 (25)	12	9	8		7.9	4.6	3.3	3.6	66	49	44	47
5	31	24	21		.8	.8	1.2	1.2	7	8	15	14
7	13	10	9		6.7	3.9	3.2	3.4	56	42	39	41
2	19	15	14		2.0	1.4	1.2	1.3	17	15	15	16
7	47	37	33		2.5	3.2	2.6	2.5	20	34	31	30
6	26	20	18		5.8	4.9	4.2	4.1	53	52	51	51
0	17	14	12		2.7	1.5	1.5	1.4	25	16	18	17
7	13	10	9		1.6	1.1	1.0	.9	15	12	12	11
2	17	13	12		1.8	1.9	1.5	1.5	16	20	18	19
0	17	13	11		10.0	7.0	6.1	5.7	84	75	74	71
1	48	41	38		1.9	2.3	2.1	2.2	16	25	26	29
9	17	13	12		9.9	7.3	6.2	6.2	82	78	76	76
7	44	36	33		2.1	2.0	1.9	1.9	18	22	24	24
6	43	36	32		3.3	1.5			30	16		
7	18	14	12		8.4	7.7			70	84		
6	14	10	9		2.5	1.6	1.3	1.3	20	17	15	15
0	18	14	13		3.4	2.4	2.1	2.0	27	25	25	23
9	32	26	24		5.6	4.5	4.0	4.2	43	47	48	48
8	15	11	10		1.4	1.1	.9	1.1	10	11	12	13

families in 1962 had incomes which, if increased 2.5 per cent per year for 13 years, would equal $3,000. This method yields estimates of the numbers of families that will be poor in 1970 and 1975 which vary with the breakdown selected.

Sources: *Economic Report of the President, 1964* (Washington, D.C.: Government Printing Office, 1964), Table 7, p. 71; and House of Representatives, Committee on Education and Labor, *Poverty in the United States* (Washington, D.C.: Government Printing Office, 1964), Table 23, p. 273.

TABLE 2.9. CHANGES IN POVERTY 1949–59, BY STATE, WITH STATES LISTED BY INCIDENCE OF POVERTY IN 1949

	POVERTY INCIDENCE		CHANGE IN NUMBER OF FAMILIES (PER CENT)	NET MIGRATION (PER CENT)	CHANGE IN NUMBER OF POOR FAMILIES (PER CENT)	PER CENT OF NATION'S POOR*		RANK IN NUMBER OF POOR FAMILIES	
	1949	1959				1949	1959	1949	1959
	(1)	(2)	(3)	(4)	(5)	(6)	(7)	(8)	(9)
All States	—	—	17	—	−30	100	100	—	—
Mississippi	1	1	− 2	−20	−32	3	3	14	12
Arkansas	2	2	− 5	−23	−34	2	2	18	18
Alabama	3	4	8	−12	−31	3	3	11	11
Georgia	4	9	15	− 6	−31	4	4	8	10
South Carolina	5	3	13	−10	−24	2	2	22	19
Tennessee	6	5	11	− 8	−27	3	4	9	9
Kentucky	7	6	5	−13	−30	3	3	12	14
North Carolina	8	7	16	−10	−22	4	4	7	5
Louisiana	9	8	19	− 2	−22	3	3	15	15
Oklahoma	10	12	4	−10	−35	2	2	21	21
Florida	11	15	79	+57	+ 5	3	4	17	8
Vermont	12	21	5	−10	−46	—	—	46	46
West Virginia	12	11	− 4	−23	−29	2	2	27	27
Virginia	14	16	22	− 6	−24	3	3	16	16
Missouri	15	17	7	− 3	−34	3	3	10	12
Maine	16	22	8	− 1	−45	1	1	35	37
Texas	17	13	21	+ 1	−20	6	7	2	1
South Dakota	18	10	4	−13	−16	1	1	38	36
New Mexico	19	20	39	+ 7	−22	1	1	37	38
Arizona	20	25	71	+41	−10	1	1	36	34
Kansas	21	23	12	0	−38	1	1	28	28
Nebraska	22	18	6	− 9	−30	1	1	31	31
North Dakota	23	14	3	−18	−24	—	—	40	39

State									
New Hampshire	24	41	14	−52	0	—	—	43	45
Iowa	25	19	4	−25	−9	2	2	26	22
Colorado	26	28	30	−32	+12	1	1	33	32
Idaho	27	26	12	−34	−1	—	—	41	41
Minnesota	28	24	12	−28	−3	2	2	25	24
Indiana	29	29	15	−35	+2	2	2	19	20
Delaware	30	36	40	−31	+20	—	—	47	47
Rhode Island	31	34	11	−41	−4	—	—	39	40
Montana	32	27	14	−27	−1	—	—	45	42
Wisconsin	33	30	14	−36	−2	2	2	24	25
Pennsylvania	34	33	10	−39	−5	6	5	3	4
Maryland	35	40	31	−34	+14	1	1	29	29
Oregon	36	32	12	−36	+1	1	1	32	33
Utah	37	43	23	−38	+1	—	—	42	43
Ohio	38	38	19	−32	+5	4	4	5	7
Wyoming	39	35	16	−30	−1	—	—	48	48
Washington	40	39	16	−34	+4	1	1	30	30
California	41	44	41	−25	+30	5	6	4	3
Massachusetts	42	47	10	−48	0	2	2	20	26
Nevada	43	46	77	−14	+45	—	—	49	49
New York	44	45	12	−39	+1	7	6	1	2
Michigan	45	37	20	−24	+3	8	3	13	13
Illinois	46	42	13	−31	+1	4	4	6	6
Dist. of Columbia	47	31	12	−36	−20	—	—	44	44
Connecticut	48	49	28	−45	+12	1	1	34	35
New Jersey	49	48	25	−36	+1	2	2	23	23

*Blanks in Columns 6 and 7 indicate less than .5 per cent.

Sources: Except for data on net migration, all data are derived from the 1950 and 1960 Censuses of Population. Net migration as a percentage of 1950 population derived from Bureau of the Census, *Current Population Reports*, Series P–25, No. 227, op. cit.

TABLE 2.10. ESTIMATES OF COMPONENTS OF CHANGE IN POPULATION BETWEEN 1950 AND 1960, BY REGIONS

REGION	NET INCREASE (millions) (1)	NET INCREASE (per cent) (2)	BIRTHS (millions) (3)	DEATHS (millions) (4)	NET TOTAL MIGRATION (millions) (5)	RATIO OF BIRTHS TO DEATHS (6)	NATURAL INCREASE AS PER CENT OF TOTAL NET INCREASE (7)
U.S.	28.0	18.5	41.0	15.6	+2.66	2.6	—
New England	1.2	12.8	2.2	1.0	+.02	2.2	100
Mid-Atlantic	4.0	13.3	7.0	3.3	+.31	2.1	92
East North Central	5.8	19.2	8.4	3.2	+.70	2.6	90
West North Central	1.3	9.5	3.6	1.5	−.82	2.4	161
South Atlantic	4.8	22.6	6.2	2.0	+.65	3.1	87
East South Central	.6	5.0	3.1	1.1	−1.46	2.8	333
West South Central	2.4	16.6	4.3	1.3	−.59	3.3	125
Mountain	1.8	35.1	1.7	.5	+.56	3.4	66
Pacific	6.1	40.2	4.4	1.6	+3.29	2.8	46

Source: Columns 1–5, Bureau of the Census, *Current Population Reports*, Series P–25, No. 227, op. cit. Column 6 is derived by dividing column 3 by column 4. Column 7 is derived by subtracting column 4 from column 3 and dividing the difference by column 1.

TABLE 2.11. GAIN OR LOSS FROM MIGRATION BY REGIONS, 1955 TO 1960

REGION	TOTAL POPULATION 5 YEARS OLD AND OVER 1960 (MILLIONS)	IN-MIGRANTS (MILLIONS)	OUT-MIGRANTS (MILLIONS)	NET MIGRATION (MILLIONS)	NET MIGRATION (PER CENT)
New England	9.4	.4	.5	− .05	− .6
Middle Atlantic	30.6	.9	1.3	− .5	−1.6
East North Central	32.0	1.4	1.8	− .4	−1.2
West North Central	13.6	.7	1.1	− .4	−2.9
South Atlantic	23.0	1.8	1.3	+ .5	+2.0
East South Central	10.6	.6	.9	− .3	−2.8
West South Central	14.9	.9	1.0	− .2	−1.1
Mountain	6.0	.9	.7	+ .2	+4.1
Pacific	18.8	2.0	.9	+1.1	+5.7

Source: Bureau of the Census, U.S. Census of Population: 1960, *Lifetime and Recent Migration, Final Report,* PC(2)—2D, Washington, D.C.: Government Printing Office, 1961.

richer states. The table suggests but does not provide clear proof that interstate mobility contributed to the nationwide reduction of poverty.[7] We do not know, for example, whether it was poor or nonpoor people who moved out of Mississippi and out of the New England states. Nor can we tell for sure whether Texas would have risen to the rank of having the most poor people if it hadn't had an influx of population. (More information on migration among regions is supplied in Tables 2.10 and 2.11.)

The future of the geographic distribution of poverty is, of course, related to the present distribution of poor children: 56 per cent are found in the South, 20 per cent in the North Central region, 13 per cent in the North East, and only 11 per cent in the West. The average number of children per family for these regions, respectively, is 2.8, 2.4, 2.2, and 2.4.[8]

TABLE 2.12. NUMBER OF CHILDREN EVER BORN PER 1,000 WIVES
IN THE UNITED STATES, 1960

AREA	INCOME UNDER $3,000	INCOME OVER $3,000
Total United States	2,869	2,347
White	2,767	2,321
Nonwhite	3,362	2,753
Rural farm	3,464	3,182
South	3,216	2,426

Source: United States Committee on Education and Labor, *Poverty in the United States,* op. cit., Table 51, p. 300.

The reduction of poverty will depend upon changes in the differential in birth rates between poor and nonpoor. The number of children ever born per 1,000 poor wives is a fourth higher than for the nonpoor (see Table 2.12).

There are no available data on death rates by income class, but both infant mortality and general mortality rates are higher in

7. It appears from one calculation that the number of poor would have been about the same if all states had had identical rates of population growth in the decade. We applied 1959 incidence rates to hypothetical populations by state and found 9.3 million families would have been poor.

8. *Poverty in the United States,* p. 295.

lower-income occupations, regions, and educational classes. However, differentials in both birth and death rates by class have been narrowing in recent years.

It is also important to know that we have been making progress on the educational front. Since 1950 the median level of educational attainment of the total population has risen from 9.3 to 11.4 years in 1962. The progress for nonwhites has been especially rapid, not so much for the population as a whole but certainly for the young: young nonwhites aged 20 to 24 had 9.2 years of schooling in 1950 as against 12.1 years for all those aged 20 to 24; by 1964 the nonwhite young had 12.1 years of schooling as compared to 12.5 for all those aged 20 to 24.

PROJECTING THE POVERTY RATE FOR 1975

In the future some of the factors that have worked for the reduction of poverty are not likely to continue. For example, the rate of improvement in educational attainment will not be sustained; neither will the rate of movement off the farm. On the other hand, we foresee the arresting of a number of the demographic factors that have slowed poverty reduction in the recent past. Aged family heads will only increase by 9 per cent between 1962 and 1975, while the total population will increase by 21 per cent; families with three or more children will increase by only 14 per cent, but the youngest family heads will increase by 132 per cent (see column 7 of Table 2.8). One result of the changing composition of the total population in the decade ahead is that the composition of the poor is not likely to change radically by 1975 (see the last column of Table 2.8).

Projecting the number of families who will be in poverty in 1975 is, of course, a hazardous undertaking. Table 2.8 shows the result of one method, specifically one which assumes that the 1975 population would have the same incidence of poverty in each demographic group as obtained in 1962 but which also assumes that family incomes will rise by 2.5 per cent per year. This yields an estimate that is slightly different for every demographic grouping, ranging from 7.7 to 8.6 million families but centering around 8 million, which would be 14 per cent of all families (see column 16). Another method is simply to project the average postwar rate of decrease, extending the line from 32 per cent of families in poverty in 1947 to 19 per cent in 1963 to, say, 10 per cent in 1975.[9]

Both these methods are very crude, but they give sobering results to anyone who might think poverty is going to disappear in a short time. They challenge us to find ways to encourage favorable movements among the demographic groups, e.g. from unemployed to employed, and to encourage rapid falls in the incidence of poverty within groups. The Table 2.8 forecast, for one example, is that a third or more of the aged, the women heads, and the non-whites, and a fourth of the Southern families will still be poor in 1975. At the same time that we aim at a high rate of poverty reduction, we should look for ways to close the poverty-income gap, which is now about $12 billion and which should be down to $9 billion, or about one per cent of GNP by 1975.

The first steps in selecting strategic weapons in a war on poverty must be identifying the poor's relationship to the labor market, their handicapping characteristics, and their geographic location. They also require understanding the process by which people move out of and back into poverty and the process by which the total population's susceptibility to poverty changes as the composition of the population changes. The next and more difficult steps are determining the relative gain in poverty reduction from alternative measures.

9. W. H. Locke Anderson in his "Trickling Down: The Relationship between Economic Growth and the Extent of Poverty among American Families," *Quart. J. Econ.*, 88, No. 4 (November 1964), 511–24, offers some interesting reasons why this estimate may be too optimistic. His reasons have to do with the frequency of incomes near to and far below the $3,000 line among the present and past poverty populations. On the other hand, Lowell E. Gallaway supports the case for a forecast of the lower levels of poverty; see his "The Foundations of the 'War on Poverty,'" *Amer. Econ. Rev.*, 55, No. 1 (March 1965), 122–30.

Part 2: Social Attitudes,
Social Organization, and Poverty

3. Poverty and Social Organization

by Harold A. Gibbard

Poverty is both an economic and a social condition. The poor not only do not live as well as people with more adequate means; the general thesis of this paper is that many of them also live differently in ways which the lack of income does not wholly explain. The organizations and informal groups to which the poor belong often have distinctive characteristics. The outlook of the poor on the world is often at variance with the outlook of other segments of society.

I take social organization to be an inclusive term referring to all the ongoing relationships within a society. A society is organized into such units as informal groups, formal associations, social strata, and communities. Each of these has its own internal organization. In turn, smaller units often exist within larger units. For example, within a factory informal work groups come into existence; many associations draw their memberships from a single class or race; communities embrace systems of stratification. Further, the different units, be they gangs, churches, or races, have external relations with other such units.

This inquiry into the life styles of the poor focuses on four aspects of social organization: family structure, the schools and education, other formal-association memberships, and "street-corner" groups. They are best understood when placed in the context of the larger organization of the society.

THE SOCIAL CONTEXT OF POVERTY

Two aspects of this larger organization have a special relevance. The first is the community setting of poverty. Poverty involves different experiences in an urban slum from those in a coal community or an Appalachian farm hamlet, even though poverty may be equally acute in all three and the problems of breaking out of it equally difficult. The differences begin with the physical setting itself, the cramped living space in the city, and the frequent changes of residence.

Consider the contrasts between the urban and the Appalachian rural communities. While some small Appalachian settlements have geographic clusters of families in dire poverty interspersed amid families that are fairly well off, other communities are relatively homogeneous. True, no Appalachian settlement is wholly without social distinctions, and the people are sensitive to differences of wealth even when they must be described as varying intensities of poverty. Yet status distinctions are softened by personal contacts, and in some places social distinctions are tempered by the fact that the same external influences, a good growing season or orders for coal, affect them all. In the city slum, the unfavorable lot of the people is underscored by the surrounding economic contrasts. No matter how limited their movements about the city, slum residents cannot shut out the awareness that they occupy a low position in the community.

There are other differences too. For example, the community setting affects income opportunities. We shall note later that in some of our larger cities there are relatively more jobs for uneducated women than for uneducated men. One result is a population of drifting men; another is the female-based household, a form of organization that is rare in the coal communities or agricultural settlements of Appalachia. A further difference is that urban poverty is more likely to be complicated by race or nationality. There are racially mixed rural communities in the Old South and places of mixed Anglo-Mexican settlement in the Southwest. But many small places are homogeneous in population type as no large city is. Indeed, in some Appalachian hamlets kinship ties interrelate most of the people.

Second, poverty exists within a context of social stratification. So long as the social system provides for economic and status inequalities, some of the people will be outranked by nearly everybody else. In turn, so long as norms are rooted in class subcultures, some people will appear degraded in the eyes of others. The present attack on poverty is not an attempt to end economic and status inequalities per se, but to open up new opportunities for the most disadvantaged so that their lives may be bettered.

The inequalities enmeshed in the American social system are tied to distinctions of race, national origin, and religion. It is well known that Negroes are grossly overrepresented among the unemployed and the poor. The current racial revolt and the resistance it has met from some segments of the population are testimony to the persistence of race as a factor governing the distribution of economic opportunities, political power, and social standing. But Negroes do not stand alone as objects of discrimination. Puerto Ricans are caught in a web of limited job opportunities, unemployment, poverty, and dependency. While other ethnic groups now encounter fewer discriminations, restrictions based on national origins have not wholly disappeared. So long as the social system presses any class of people into the lower social and economic strata of the society, many of its members are going to live in poverty.

Before turning to the smaller units of social organization, it is perhaps well to state the usual caution. The poor are many sorts of people: city-dwellers, many living in slums, new arrivals from Puerto Rico or Mexico, Negroes, migrant agricultural workers, sharecroppers, the folk in some of the hollows or ridges of Appalachia, and others. Some of these are growing categories; others are declining. We shall concentrate on the urban slums and, where the data are available, on rural Appalachia. Each description, however sweeping, will apply to only some of the poor, and no generalizing to the total low-income population is intended.

FAMILY PATTERNS AMONG THE POOR

In virtually all sectors of American society the family is a unit of major psychic and social importance. The values attached to it and the functions it is expected to perform give it a central place

in American social life. The family is expected to provide for the
flow of emotion among its members; it is the principal institution
for the protection and rearing of children; it persists as the consuming unit for items such as shelter, food, and television. Established family patterns yield in one way or another to unemployment and poverty. It is natural to begin an examination of the
micro-organizational aspects of poverty with the family.

Every household is, virtually by definition, a consuming unit.
At the minimum, it provides a common shelter for its members.
Universally, food and shelter make the first claims upon the resources of a people: the lower the income, the higher the proportion of it that goes into these necessities. Families in poverty thus
use more of their resources within the home and, in turn, consume
relatively more of their goods together than do higher-income
families.

This does not mean that all the poor occupy the same kind of
dwelling space or eat the same sorts of foods. The poor are not
one kind of population, but many. Still, two patterns of family
organization are so prevalent among them as to be identified as
working-class or lower-class types: the patriarchal family, dominated by the authority of the husband-father; and the female-
based household, which has no regular adult male.

In the patriarchal family, consisting of husband, wife, and
children, the roles of husband and wife are quite specific and more
sharply drawn than in high-income families. The male is the
chief wage-earner and controls the purse. The husband-father's
authority is assumed, and on occasion may be asserted by force.
While the father may be final arbiter in practically all matters, it
is the mother who rears the children and is the housekeeper too,
and she does not expect her husband to share in the household
tasks when he returns from work. The wife may seek a job if the
household needs her earnings. Husband and wife share few interests, and their marriage is less a companionship than in middle-
class families. Children, though valued and welcome, have less
importance than in higher-income families and are subordinate
to their parents, who do not sacrifice for their education and future
careers to the extent expected in other populations. Marriage
often takes place at an early age, especially for girls. There is wide
variation in the stability of lower-income patriarchal families, and

desertion, which may be temporary, is not uncommon. Usually it is the male who leaves, and the wife-mother is left to care for the children.[1]

This pattern, with local variations, is found in all parts of the country. A variation in some Appalachian settlements is that the family is tied into a larger kinship system. Beech Creek, in eastern Kentucky, is a settlement of self-sufficient, subsistence, family farms spaced along the main stream and its branches, hemmed in by steep hills. James S. Brown has described its family and kinship forms.[2]

The conjugal family is the most important single group in Beech Creek. The husband is expected to be dominant. Most marriages are within the same or nearby neighborhoods, and the families are bound together in extended kinship relations. Groups of two, three, or four families, usually close relatives, are particularly solidary. Known locally as "family groups," these clusters have a territorial bond; their members visit together and sometimes eat together; they may carry on some cooperative farming; they have recognized leaders, often an older father or mother. Tension sometimes arises at marriage, for it may require a shift of loyalty from one extended family to another. Kin ties commonly develop on the husband's side.

This family and kinship pattern persists in the geographic isolation of the mountains where the economic base is simple agriculture. It could not be expected to survive industrialization, which puts the extended family to a severe strain everywhere in the world.

What happens to the patriarchal family organization when the husband, who is normally the breadwinner, loses his job and family receipts shrink? In the Great Depression of the 1930s, when a quarter or more of the labor force was unemployed, millions of families faced an abrupt loss of income. Unemployment was to stretch out over months and years, producing income crises allevi-

1. A good, representative account of "conventional" working-class family organization is included in Ruth Shonle Cavan's *The American Family* (3rd ed. New York: Thomas Y. Crowell, 1963), Ch. 7.
2. James Stephen Brown, "The Conjugal Family and the Extended Family Group," *Amer. Soc. Rev., 17* (June 1952), 297–306. The data on the Beech Creek family are drawn from this source.

ated only by public works and direct relief. How did the family fare in this situation?

Several studies of the effects of the depression on the family together document that adjustments were neither simple nor uniform. Yet the studies brought forth some recurrent themes: role adjustments of the male worker who could no longer be the main breadwinner; lowering of the husband's status, because of the loss of his earning power, and loss of his authority within the home; and the projecting of frustrated ambitions onto the children. While the loss of income put some stress on most families, those for whom unemployment and dependency were familiar and recurrent experiences found their family life little changed by the depression. Among the families for whom unemployment was new and peculiarly threatening, the impact on family solidarity was governed in part by the adaptability of the family. But more than anything else, the resiliency of the family rested on the relations of the family members to each other before the depression. Closely knit families tended to draw more closely together; those in which relations were already strained were likely to deteriorate still further.[3]

Unemployment may have a different character today. A system of unemployment insurance, and of supplemental unemployment benefits for workers in some of the largest manufacturing firms, not only provides income for a period but it also stands as a recognition that unemployment is the result of the workings of the economy, and so may soften the emotional blow that an earlier generation experienced at the loss of a job. The studies of the depression families were good ones in their day; they should be repeated now, with their major findings serving as hypotheses for the new studies.

One of the themes that might be pursued is the change in family

3. See Robert Cooley Angell, *The Family Encounters the Depression* (New York: Charles Scribner's, 1936); Mirra Komarovsky, *The Unemployed Man and His Family* (New York: Dryden Press, 1938); Ruth Shonle Cavan and Katherine Howland Ranck, *The Family and the Depression* (Chicago: University of Chicago Press, 1938); Samuel A. Stouffer and Paul F. Lazarsfeld, *Research Memorandum on the Family and the Depression* (New York: Social Science Research Council, 1937).

organization which follows when the wife becomes the family breadwinner. It is widely noted that family decision-making shifts; the family becomes more matriarchal. But beyond that, what are the effects on the unity or solidarity of the family? In a West Virginia mining settlement near Morgantown, a number of wives are working to support their families and unemployed husbands. One informant close to these people reports that some of the men have difficulty in adapting to this reversal of roles. In another West Virginia community, long plagued by high unemployment, it is informally reported that the coming of a garment factory, which provided jobs for women, was followed by a severalfold increase in the divorce rate. The basic hypothesis has to be that the reversal of roles brought on by unemployment of the husband results in a weakening of conjugal ties.

Another theme is mutual aid among both immediate family members and more distant relatives. Do brothers and sisters help one another in crises? Is there a stronger commitment to the welfare of relatives among the disadvantaged than in the higher class levels, or are there just more occasions when help is needed? From more than one rural section of West Virginia have come reports that parents leave childern with grandparents or other relatives while they go to Ohio to work. Parents are not abandoning their children; they return to them often, and will come and get them when the out-of-state jobs appear secure. The evidence suggests that a class pattern of mutual aid rooted in economic circumstances exists among the poor.

So far we have been examining families wherein it is normal for husband, wife, and children to be present and to fulfill expected roles. At a lower socioeconomic level, another family pattern is to be noted. In the slums of many of our larger cities are scores of households in which there is no male head. James B. Conant, in *Slums and Suburbs,* tells of a slum which, he says, might be in any of several cities he has visited: "The inhabitants are all Negroes and with few exceptions have entered the city from a state in the deep South any time within the last month to the last three years. . . . In one neighborhood, by no means the worst I have seen, a questionnaire sent out by the school authorities indicated that about a third of the pupils came from

family units (one hesitates to use the word 'home') which had no
father, stepfather, or guardian."[4]

The female-based slum households include a few wherein the
widowed mother, once a part of a "conventional" family, is carrying on. Two other patterns, though, are more common. In the first,
the husband contributes but little to the family group, is often
away for a short time, and is sometimes away for weeks or months.
There may be a marriage, or just a common-law arrangement. In
the second pattern, the woman may have a temporary mate from
time to time and live without a mate in the intervening periods;
she provides the continuity in the household.

Matricentric households, particularly of the latter type, are
frequently extended families, commonly including a grandmother
and one or more aunts, and the children of more than one mother.
Some of these households have an impressive stability; the women,
as a rule, are extremely loyal to their children and committed to
their welfare. Many of the children do not know who their fathers
are. These families are not "broken" in the usual sense, in which
it is the norm for both parents to be present.

Matriarchal households are more commonly found among Negroes than among whites, not only in city slums, but also in the
rural South. E. Franklin Frazier notes that the pattern had its
origin in slavery, when the mother was the dependable member
of the family.[5] Let it be clear, though, that the female-based household is not exclusively a Negro family form.

The explanation of the female-centered family is complex. It
includes sex norms and the sense of being cut off from the approval
of the larger community. The most potent influence in support
of this pattern, however, is a characteristic of the urban labor
market. Among the poorly educated and unskilled, women may
be more employable than men. In New York City, the garment
industry and domestic services open up many jobs for women,
some of them low-paying, to be sure, but fairly stable. Many men,
on the other hand, have only sporadic jobs, or are permanently
unemployed. The consequent reversal of economic roles makes

    4. Conant, *Slums and Suburbs* (New York: McGraw-Hill, 1961), p. 18.
    5. E. Franklin Frazier, *The Negro in the United States* (New York: Mac-
millan, 1949), p. 320.

more difficult a normal family function for men and reduces the family's need of them.

While data on the number of individuals who move out of such a family background into a more conventional style of life are lacking, it is all too plain that the female-centered family pattern is in some measure self-perpetuating. The boy who spends his most formative years with no father in the home does not experience the sex-based division of labor that characterizes both the patriarchal working-class and the more equalitarian middle-class family. The adult-male models he sees at close range enter only periodically and unreliably into his life. These adult males are without regular jobs or regular families and are often on the loose in their neighborhoods. Until he himself can join a street group, the boy's principal close ties are with women.

Girls growing up in a matricentric household at least have a stable relationship with adults of their own sex. They may indeed come to hope for a man and family of their own, yet they know that their mothers find men unreliable and untrustworthy. The girls' life circumstances are such that many of them tend to marry men who are unstable husbands, as were their own fathers, and the family cycle is thereby repeated.

The female-based household is only one family pattern among the very poor. How general is it? Unfortunately, the census figures on female-based families provide no clue, since they include homes broken by death and divorce. Apparently the matricentric family is very common among the welfare recipients in some of the larger cities. One estimate places female-based child-rearing units as between 25 and 40 per cent of all households in slum areas of the larger cities.[6] The pattern is found occasionally in some towns and cities of West Virginia. There is no ground for the complacent view that this is only a deviant form among outcast people. If the pattern is to be attacked as not providing fair life chances for the children growing up within it, the target must be the transforming of the boys into employable young men. Our thesis is that the female-centered household is a response to the absence of dependable, job-holding men. With the problem identified, what

6. Walter B. Miller, "Implications of Lower-Class Culture for Social Work," *Social Serv. Rev., 33* (September 1959), 225–26.

is its solution? It will surely be slow and difficult. Can the schools help?

In all Western societies, the school stands alongside the family as a unit of organization in which almost everyone participates at some stage of his life. In most of the societies of the world, and certainly in the newly developing countries, the value placed on education is rising rapidly. The functions that schools are called upon to play in the present American society are both basic and numerous, but two are especially relevant here. First, schooling is increasingly a requirement for employment. The number of jobs for high school graduates has been rising in recent years; those for nongraduates are declining. A second function is as an avenue of escape from the handicaps of a limiting environment. Under favorable conditions, education is a ladder by which boys and girls rise above the levels of their parents. Through it they gain access to new life styles, learn to participate more fully in the political and social life of their communities, and leave poverty behind. These two functions both assign to schools the task of lifting children into better occupational and social levels.

How well are the schools succeeding in this task? The blunt fact is that neither in measured intelligence nor in achievement scores do children of the poor, as a class, measure up to the attainments of the children of higher-income and better-educated parents. In some large-city schools the pupils represent a fair economic range, but in others, nearly all pupils are drawn from the low-income levels.[7] The trend appears to be toward more rather than less class segregation because of the continuing move of the more successful families to the suburbs. The pupils in the lower-class schools in some parts of the country are very likely to be either Negroes or Puerto Ricans—that is, youngsters who would face handicaps in later life even if their schooling were the best.

The quality of schooling everywhere depends on two inter-

7. See Robert J. Havighurst, "Urban Development and the Educational System," in A. Harry Passow, *Education in Depressed Areas* (New York: Teachers College, Columbia University, 1963). This paper draws together several earlier works by the same author.

acting sets of influences: those centering in the schools themselves and those inhering in the abilities and aptitudes of the pupils. Many lower-class schools do not educate their pupils well, for reasons that lie both in the schools and in their student bodies.

First, some slum schools have high rates of teacher turnover. A study of Chicago public school teacher careers reveals that teachers normally are first assigned to the poorest neighborhoods, where vacancies are the most numerous, and are moved on to "better" schools as soon as possible.[8] This pattern results simultaneously in the staffing of these schools with the least experienced teachers and in staff instability. It is also widely suspected that, in many cities across the country, teachers who for one reason or another are out of favor with the school authorities are assigned to slum schools.

Second, slum schools have to contend with a constant change in their student bodies. Conant makes this comment:[9]

> Often the composition of a school grade in such an area will alter so rapidly that a teacher will find at the end of a school year that she is teaching but few pupils who started with her in the fall. I recall the principal of one school stating that a teacher absent more than one week will have difficulty recognizing her class when she returns. This comes about because mothers move with their offspring from one rented room to another from month to month and in so doing often go from one elementary school district to another.

Such pupil turnover handicaps both the school and the pupils. Education cannot proceed in disconnected bits and pieces.

A third handicap is the disproportionate amount of school time taken up with discipline. When even the best teachers spend as much as half their time in activities other than instruction and the poorer ones three-quarters or more, schools in fact become caretaker institutions more than educational establishments in the middle-class sense.

Fourth, many depressed-area children begin school unprepared and unequipped to cope with it. They have limited vocabularies,

8. Howard S. Becker, "The Career of the Chicago Public School Teacher," *Amer. J. Soc.,* 57 (March 1952), 470–78.

9. Conant, op. cit., p. 18.

and their language is different in style from that of the teachers. Having grown up in very crowded homes, they have learned how not to listen. Many are unfamiliar with books and pencils. Because they have had few toys and few if any trips beyond their home neighborhoods, the child's world of the first primer is alien to them. The cultural discontinuity between home and school is so wide as to make early failure all too likely.

Fifth, the slum child is quite likely to face school as something brought on by the process of growing up, not as an impatiently awaited adventure. The middle-class child is pointed toward school from his early years, and he looks forward to it, is ready for it, is motivated to succeed. The slum child is not likely to have any understanding of what school could mean in his life. He may have no concept of his own advancement, of readying himself for a respected place in the larger society. The school alone may have to provide the child with the incentive to learn and it does not always succeed.

For these reasons, and others as well, one can hardly expect high pupil achievement in the lowest-income schools. While the students are not all alike, such schools record for their pupils both below-mean IQs and below-mean achievement ratings. Moreover, within low-income schools, the evidence reveals a clear tie between the economic position of the pupil's family and his test scores.

When pupils from contrasting elementary schools enroll in the same junior high school, where they are presumably subjected to the same grade norms, the difference in their performance may be striking. Havighurst compares the eighth-grade (junior high) course grades of pupils from a middle-class and a lower-class school in "River City" (population 45,000) in a group of basic subjects.[10] The pupils that had attended the middle-class school recorded 45 per cent A grades, just 10 per cent D grades, and no failures. In almost diametric contrast, those from the lower-class school had no As, just 10 per cent Bs, and 44 per cent failures. Their rate of dropout is higher and, of those who stay, some soon fall behind a year.

Havighurst makes the lower-class school itself an issue.[11] The pupils from lower-class schools, he contends, do not achieve as

10. Havighurst, op. cit., p. 31.
11. Ibid., pp. 30–33.

well as they would if enrolled in either a mixed or a middle-class school. The explanation, he says, is that the "academic climate" in a school affects the attitudes and goals of the pupils. His second finding is related: the same pupils have lower educational aspirations in lower-class schools than they would have in mixed or middle-class schools. He goes on to note that the lower-class schools develop less talent than the higher-ranking schools would from the same pupil population, and so contribute to talent waste. Further, the lower-class school "reduces the democratic quality of our society" by failing to make its contribution to the upward mobility of the most handicapped members of the society.

It must not be assumed that all the children of the poor do badly, even in the most economically segregated schools. These children, too, differ from one another in basic ability, in preschool development, and in motivation—a significant variable. In a study into the relations of social class to educational attitudes and participation, in Manhattan's Lower East Side, Cloward and Jones, on the basis of nearly a thousand interviews, reached two significant findings. First, among the lower and working classes, the importance attached to education is affected by occupational aspiration. "The point is not, as has been so often suggested, that low income people fail to perceive the importance of education as a channel of mobility, but rather that their level of occupational aspiration influences their evaluation of education much more than is characteristic of the middle-class person."[12] Second, education is viewed more positively when family members participate in the schools by visiting them or taking part in PTA activities. Cause and effect are doubtless intertwined here.

Rural schools

Are rural schools any different? Much of Appalachia is rural and much of it is depressed. How good are the schools in this setting of rural poverty?

Per pupil expenditures in rural Appalachia are much below national means. In 1963–64, the mean current expenditure per pupil in daily average attendance was $455 in the nation as a

12. Richard A. Cloward and James A. Jones, "Social Class: Educational Attitudes and Participation," *in* Passow, op. cit., p. 215.

whole. The average in both Kentucky and West Virginia was $300, or only two-thirds as much. In Kentucky, per pupil costs have long been lower in the depressed mountainous eastern counties. In West Virginia, every county falling within a state metropolitan statistical area is above the state average. In the rural counties there is only a rough relation between per pupil expenditures and other economic indices. Yet the county with the lowest mean family income in 1960 perhaps not surprisingly also has the lowest per pupil expenditure in the state.

In eastern Kentucky school districts, the scores made by students on the High School Senior Achievement Tests in 1960 averaged much below those elsewhere in that state. Where only county districts are compared—they tend to be more rural than the independent districts—69 per cent of eastern Kentucky districts and 31 per cent of other districts in Kentucky had mean scores below 80 (100 is the national norm). No eastern county averaged as high as 100, and only one averaged in the 90–99 range.[13] Only a minority of the east Kentucky youth reached performance levels that average pupils achieved elsewhere. It may be assumed that the same pupils would have done better in a more favorable setting.

In his strong prose, Harry M. Caudill describes the educational deficiencies of the eastern Kentucky region:[14]

> Unfortunately the region's poor schools and the limited cultural facilities have produced whole crops of high school graduates who are poorly prepared when compared with students who have been educated in good public or private schools elsewhere. Despite twelve years in elementary and high school, a majority of the proud young graduates are scarcely literate. They have read little outside their pallid textbooks and have made no real effort in composition. The mathematics classrooms have long been the "sideline" domain of the football and basketball coaches. Physics, chemistry, calculus, algebra, and geometry have been so neglected that

13. Mary Jean Bowman and W. Warren Haynes, *Resources and People in East Kentucky: Problems and Potentials of a Lagging Economy* (Baltimore: The Johns Hopkins Press, 1963), pp. 240–41.

14. Harry M. Caudill, *Night Comes to the Cumberlands* (Boston: Atlantic-Little Brown, 1963), p. 335.

in some institutions they have practically vanished. Latin and
foreign languages, too, disappeared from many curricula during or soon after the Second World War and few students can
comprehend a word in any foreign language. Shakespeare and
the other poets and playwrights, old and new, are mysterious
citadels whose walls few of them have attempted to breach.

He reports that on the College Qualifying Test, designed to
measure both cultural background and scholastic achievement,
in 1960 the students of Virginia and Tennessee averaged 80 per
cent. In Kentucky outside the plateau, the averages were 55 to
65 per cent, but in a number of eastern Kentucky coal counties
the average was 17.5 (the dropouts are not included here). In
eastern Kentucky, and in the state as a whole, there is a positive,
if loose, relationship between pupil performance and per pupil
expenditures.[15] Poorly supported schools and poor pupil per-
formances go together.

Doubtless some of the same factors operate in rural Appalachia
as within the urban slums. Uneducated parents, a highly restric-
tive home and community environment, youngsters insulated from
the aspirations of the urban middle class, a school climate in which
learning is not always directly rewarding, and the unavoidability
of employing teachers who are not properly certified are all too
common. Where present, these circumstances make it difficult for
rural depressed-area schools to fulfill their democratic mission of
readying youngsters to fit effectively into tomorrow's world.

New approaches to education

In this era, when concern is fixed on the education of economically and socially disadvantaged children, some hope may be
drawn from a new development. We are beginning to hear that
the teaching of deprived children may call for new skills. Teacher
education is now geared largely to helping the new graduates
work with good students in schools oriented to middle-class values.
It leaves them ill-equipped for the school of the slum, either urban
or rural.

15. Bowman and Haynes, op. cit., p. 241.

Early in 1965, Senator Gaylord Nelson (D. Wisconsin) proposed as an amendment to the President's school aid proposals that a National Teacher Corps be established.[16] After college graduation, the members would be given three months of intensive training, and then, in groups of five, they would be assigned to a city slum. Further in-service and summer study would be expected of them, and they would be paid by the federal government. After two years, they would receive the Master of Arts in Teaching, and would be specially qualified for teaching in city slum schools.

At almost the same time, the University of Kentucky announced a special academic program to train teachers for schools in Louisville slums and for the depressed eastern counties.[17] The curriculum is to have a strong behavioral science emphasis.

It is encouraging to note the growing recognition of the need for different training skills for teachers in low-income schools. Much remains to be done, but headway is being made on these and other problems, too. Three critical points in the education of the disadvantaged, and some of the steps now being undertaken to meet them, are here singled out for comment: entry into first grade; the time of dropout; and the schooling of adults with educational deficiencies.

Deficient in language development, variety of experience, appreciation of the value of education, and in motivation, children of the slums and depressed rural areas are not prepared for the school programs in the first grade. The preschool movement which is spreading across the country is one attempt at a solution. Preschools are designed to reach the child at an age when basic patterns are acquired. Nursery and kindergarten programs, in the pattern of those directed by Martin Deutsch for slum children in the public schools and day-care centers of New York, are being set up in many cities and some rural depressed areas. In all these programs of preschool enrichment there is a strong verbal emphasis. Children learn that objects have names and properties that can both be sensed and identified. Objects new to the deprived children are brought into their experience. Thus, in any of the three "pilot" programs conducted near Charleston, W. Va.,

16. *New York Times,* Feb. 14, 1965, p. E7.
17. Ibid., p. 52.

by West Virginia University's Appalachian Center, children may learn the feel and smell and taste of an orange. They tell what they see, and so add to their grasp of language. They learn to stand in line, to wash their hands after toileting, to say "please" and "thank you." Thus they have new experiences, come to handle language better, and learn the rudiments of how to live with others.

One impressive feature of the Appalachian Center program is that it is family oriented. Mothers are encouraged to attend these schools, not so much to help the teachers as to learn such things as simple rules of health and even how to hold scissors. If the function of the preschool program is to help the child surmount the handicaps of a limited home life, it surely makes sense to try to bring new standards into the home and family at the same time. Gains made by the preschools in narrowing of the discontinuity between home and school can thereby be solidified and extended.

At the time of this writing, Operation Head Start is being developed across the country within the Economic Opportunity program, to provide preschooling for impoverished children during the summer before they begin the first year of school. While a summer program may be too short to accomplish much, it nevertheless is a step in the right direction and may prove helpful in preparing youngsters for the first grade.

School dropouts are another educational concern. It is not simply that the potential talent of dropouts is being lost to society, but also that dropouts are likely to constitute a special problem in a world where the need for specialized training and skills is growing apace. Those without sufficient education will run a high risk of becoming the dependents of the next generation.

The school dropouts come predominantly from poor families. In communities where poverty is widespread the dropout problem is proportionately greater than in richer communities. Using the percentage of sixteen- and seventeen-year-olds not in school as a measure of the rate of school dropout, the West Virginia county which in 1960 had the highest rate of male unemployment, 17.1 per cent, also had the highest rate of resident dropouts, 47.3 per cent. This county was also next to lowest in median family income. Of the twenty-one counties with 10 per cent or more male unemployment in 1960, sixteen had a higher rate of dropouts than the state average. In contrast, of the six counties with not over 6 per cent male unemployment, none had a rate of dropout as high as the state average. Systematic data on the financial status of the actual families of the dropouts are not at hand.

Apart from reasons of cost of attending school—this may not be crucial to the family until after high school graduation—school dropouts apparently have two main causes: first, a relatively high level of education is not linked to the aspirations of the pupil; and second, the pupil is encountering failure in school—to leave is to escape failure. Because many dropouts give up long before they actually withdraw, the problem calls for a three-pronged attack. We must make sure that no pupil leaves for financial reasons; the provision of the Economic Opportunity program which provides for part-time jobs for young people while they continue in school is a contribution to this end. We must help children to acquire reasonable aspirations for their adulthood and to see the role of education in their attainment. This is a task for all the educational facilities of the community: schools, library, press, radio and TV, youth workers, and others. And we must help in overcoming school failures. If education is felt to be purposeful, the rate of failures is likely to decline.

But more is needed. Some professional educators believe that behind many school failures is a lack of reading ability. Behind that, too often, is a more basic deficiency in language skills, and here preschool programs and in-school and summer remedial reading programs may make a contribution. The students of West Virginia State College, at Institute, are offering special tutoring in reading, in out-of-school hours, to children living in the hollows; they report that the youngsters respond eagerly to this bit of personal aid and attention. If schooling can somehow be made rewarding to the children of the poor, both immediately and in terms of their aspirations, the problem of school dropouts may diminish.

School failures and dropouts point to a third critical phase in education, namely the redeeming of adults who have had so little education as to be severely handicapped in the labor market. Adult education programs are no novelty in the United States, but today they are being given new emphasis. Along with retraining and other forms of vocational education are a host of programs in basic education for adults, some carried on under the initiative and auspices of state and local school authorities. Now a new thrust is being given in at least two federal programs. The Manpower Development and Training Act, under the "basic education" amendment (December 1963), now provides that workers may receive up to twenty weeks of basic education—reading, writing, language skills, and arithmetic—to ready them to enter into vocational training. Thus, women training for office work will be taught spelling, grammar, and punctuation; carpenters' helpers will learn fractions. Second, under the Economic Opportunity Act, like provision is made for basic education in conjunction with vocational training in several programs. The Act also authorizes adult basic education independent of vocational education, within community action programs. This education is aimed at persons eighteen years of age or over whose inability to read or write the English language impairs their ability to get jobs commensurate with their real potential. The tough question is whether such basic education is too little or too late.

FORMAL-ASSOCIATION MEMBERSHIPS

Sooner or later the family and the school enter into the experiences of virtually all Americans. Plainly membership in no other organization is so all-inclusive. What about the poor? Do other organizations touch their lives, providing a vehicle for activities and personal contacts? The church is one; the evidence is that the lowest-income members of our society have few or no memberships outside the church.

Reporting on the corn-belt community to which he gives the pseudonym *Elmtown*, Hollingshead reported a few years ago[18] that his Class V persons—those of lowest rank in prestige structure—

> are almost totally isolated from organized community activities. A few men claim membership in veterans' organizations, but they neither pay dues nor attend meetings. Workers in

18. A. B. Hollingshead, *Elmtown's Youth* (New York: Science Editions, 1961), p. 119.

the Mill belong to the union. . . . Since they do not participate in organized community affairs, hours off the job and
during periods of unemployment or layoff are spent the way
the person chooses without too much interference from neighbors. Leisure is expended in loafing around the neighborhood,
in the downtown district, along the river, and at home. Their
social life consists of informal visits between neighbors, gossip,
petty gambling, visits to the cheaper theaters, going to town,
drinking in the home or public taverns, with now and again
a fist fight.

Survey data gathered in scattered communities throughout the
country indicate that voluntary group memberships are not so
frequent for the population as a whole as are sometimes assumed.
The surveys all show a direct relationship between family income
and memberships. The National Opinion Research Center in 1955
asked a national cross-section of adults: "Do you happen to belong
to any groups or organizations in the community? If *yes,* which
ones?" Of the whole sample, 64 per cent reported no memberships;
only 16 per cent reported two or more.[19] But in the under-$2,000
income level, 76 per cent had no voluntary organization memberships, and only 7 per cent had two or more. Where the education
was 0–6 years, 83 per cent had no organizations; when the inter-
viewer rated the level of living as very low, 92 per cent were without such memberships. Occupational data tell the same story.
As one might expect from the above, Negroes have fewer memberships than whites.

This class pattern may be superimposed on a pattern based on
the degree of urbanism. Predominantly metropolitan counties,
those with a city of 50,000 or more, have a higher rate of memberships than urbanized counties with a city of 10,000 to 50,000,
while counties with no town of 10,000 have the lowest rates.

19. These and the following data are drawn from Charles R. Wright and
Herbert H. Hyman, "Volunteer Association Memberships of American Adults:
Evidence from National Surveys," *Amer. Soc. Rev., 23* (June 1958), 284–94. See
also Mirra Komarovsky, "The Voluntary Associations of Urban Dwellers,"
Amer. Soc. Rev., 11 (December 1946), 686–98; Morris Axelrod, "Urban Structure
and Social Participation," *Amer. Soc. Rev., 21* (February 1956), 13–18; and
Wendell Bell and Maryanne Force, "Urban Neighborhood Types and Participa-
tion in Formal Organizations," *Amer. Soc. Rev., 21* (February 1956), 25–34.

Within each of the three types of counties, the urban and rural nonfarm areas are much alike; the urban patterns are diffused out into the suburban and nonfarm rural areas. But the rural farm is below the nonfarm in all three. The lowest ranking of all, then, are the lowest-income people in farm settings.

The poor not only have fewer memberships than their more prosperous townsmen, they also have different memberships. Komarovsky (1946) notes that New York male unskilled workers, if they belonged to associations at all, joined "social and athletic clubs," then later in life a fraternal lodge. Obviously, they would not join professional societies or country clubs. Church memberships furnish another example. It has been shown repeatedly that the sect-type churches draw most of their followers from the lowest-income and economically most insecure members of society.[20]

What is the effect of the loss of one's job and particularly of sustained unemployment on group participation? The classic study on this theme, Bakke's *Citizens without Work*,[21] comes from the 1930s, at a time when unemployment may have been viewed differently from today. New Haven's jobless three decades ago tended to reduce their participation in virtually every form of group activity except chatting at the corner store, the gas station, or on the street. While 119 persons from a sample of 200 participated in clubs before unemployment, only 61 did after. Visits with family and friends were reported by 132 before losing their jobs, only 58 so reported after.[22] There was even some falling off in church attendance; the common explanation was that one was expected to contribute money. Since churches tend to be rather homogeneous with respect to their members' community status, it is perhaps not surprising that several of the unemployed, after prolonged joblessness, transferred from a downtown church to another whose members were in circumstances more like their own.

20. See, for example, Liston Pope, *Millhands and Preachers* (New Haven: Yale University Press, 1942), and Walter R. Schmidt, "Class Denominationalism in Rural California Churches," *Amer. J. Soc.*, 44 (January 1944).

21. E. Wight Bakke, *Citizens without Work: A Study of the Effects of Unemployment upon the Workers' Social Relations and Practices* (New Haven: Yale University Press, 1940). This is a companion to the same author's *The Unemployed Man*.

22. Ibid., p. 14.

The low rate of formal memberships among people in poverty is perhaps simply explained as a lower-class life style, but life styles, too, are to be explained. Two obvious factors are the narrow range of interests and sophistication among the poorly educated and costs of participation in group activities, such as dress, travel, and dues. Another set of factors may be found in the dynamics of groups. Any group that brings members face to face in similar roles tends to be homogeneous, and in low-status groups this homogeneity may narrow the range of possible leadership. The value of a leadership of equals in voluntary groups is suggested by the results of efforts to mobilize the poor in community action. When such groups are staffed by educated professional and business people, low-income persons too often become intimidated by their alien, superior style and, feeling insecure and inferior, they withdraw.[23]

In contrast are the longstanding Chicago Area Projects. These neighborhood projects, fostered to help combat delinquency in some of the lowest-rent sections, have been organized around local leadership, including in one instance a man who had served time in prison. There is general agreement that having persons from the neighborhoods in the key offices has contributed much to the success of these projects. The difficulty is that while voluntary groups, including even the settlement house and the religious mission, succeed best if indigenous members at least share the functions of leadership, the lower classes produce few leaders for the tasks involved.

STREET-CORNER SOCIETY

Unlike urban life where formal associations serve as vehicles of personal contacts, rural life is characterized by informal personal contacts. These contacts are not indiscriminate, of course, even in the smallest semi-isolated ridge or hollows settlements of Appalachia. Recall the role of kinship in the patterning of relations in Beech Creek in eastern Kentucky. Age, sex, personal traits and interests, and subtle status distinctions all have their effects.

How different is the pattern among the urban poor? City slum

23. Mobilization for Youth, *A Proposal for the Prevention and Control of Delinquency by Expanding Opportunities* (New York, 1961), pp. 324–25.

residents do indeed have many quite clearly structured personal relationships within their neighborhoods. Both informal groups and semiformalized "clubs" abound in lower-class areas and are a vital part of their social organization. This is particularly true of ethnically or racially homogeneous neighborhoods, and except during periods of transition, most low-rent areas are highly homogeneous.

The slum inhabitants spend much of their time out of doors. Women gather in small groups on doorsteps or on the sidewalk, or where they exist, in yards. Some lean out of windows to watch or join in conversations. Men also gather on the street or at established meeting places, such as a tavern; boys have their own street corners or customary indoor meeting places. The informal groups have fixed memberships, though some may also have floating or marginal memberships.

The groupings that characterize urban low-class society consist of members of the same age and sex. Far more so than in the higher economic levels, they continue as one-sex groups beyond adolescence and into adulthood. Some of the groups form when the members are in their early teens, or even younger, and stay together right into adulthood. Physical proximity provides the basis for the initial social contact. Then, as the family moves about the neighborhood, the contact may be maintained. Men retain their membership even when they marry. William F. Whyte, in his account of Cornerville,[24] says that in the urban slum

> it is easy to overlook the distinction between married and single men. The married man regularly sets aside one evening a week to take out his wife. There are other occasions when they go out together and entertain together, and some corner boys devote more attention to their wives than others, but, married or single, the corner boy can be found on his corner almost every night of the week.

These peer groups are the primary psychic forces in the lives of those over twelve or thirteen[25]—the groups to which the mem-

24. William Foote Whyte, *Street Corner Society* (Chicago: University of Chicago Press, 1943), p. 255.
25. Walter B. Miller, "Lower Class Culture as a Generating Milieu of Juvenile Delinquency," *J. Soc. Issues, 14* (1958), 14.

bers give their primary loyalty and whose approval they most cherish. In them the individual has a meaningful affiliation and a feeling of acceptance. While peer groups characterize all strata of our society, in the higher socioeconomic levels they tend not to be so all-embracing. For example, they tend not to supersede the family in the loyalty and affection of the youth. Not so in the lowest-class world; here the peer group is vital precisely in the measure that the family is unable to provide such basic satisfactions as rewarding activity or emotional response. The female-centered household is especially vulnerable in this respect; it fails to meet the needs of the boy in his teens. The school fails also. A Negro teacher told Dr. Conant: "We do quite well with these children in the lower grades. Each of us is, for the few hours of the school day, an acceptable substitute for the mother. But when they reach 10, 11, or 12 years of age, we lose them. At that time, the 'street' takes over. In terms of school work, progress ceases; indeed many pupils begin to go backward in their studies."[26]

Many lower-class groups are precisely structured. Organized around key members or leaders, the group gives each member his own position. The complex of member roles ordinarily has a high stability, though the groups do change, of course; some members drop out, perhaps temporarily during a period of courtship, and others come in. Like more formally organized voluntary associations, these groups depend for their equilibrium on a continuity of leadership.

Some street-corner groups are essentially law-abiding. They may engage in sports, such as bowling or pool, or watch ball games; some may serve political machines. But many youth groups include in their activities pilfering and shoplifting, auto theft, "mugging," assault, and, though pretty well under control in most cities, the gang fight or rumble. To be added now is the use of narcotic drugs. All these activities are supported in a delinquent subculture which not only sanctions them but undergirds them with their own set of values. Toughness and physical prowess, the smartness to outwit or outfox, the excitement of risk and danger, and the autonomy which says that "no one is going to push me around" may all be favored.[27] Although street-corner groups do not account for delin-

26. Conant, op. cit., p. 21.
27. Miller, "Lower Class Culture," loc. cit., p. 14.

quency, they do induct boys and girls into it. From the point of view of law enforcement the delinquent groups are deviant. Nevertheless, they can be understood as the product of a complex set of social circumstances not the least of which is poverty.

CULTURE AND THE CYCLE OF POVERTY

Certain social organization patterns recur in the ways of life of the lower class of American society: the patriarchal family or the female-based household; deficient school performance; limited memberships, mostly in organizations that do not provide equal contacts with people of other socioeconomic levels; regular and loyal participation in informal groups whose members are age and sex peers from one's own neighborhood. The relation of some of these patterns to irregular employment and poverty is close and direct; in other cases, the relation is tenuous though not absent. While not all the poor adhere to it, there may be said to exist, in urban America at least, a culture of poverty, which is dominant in the life style of a fairly stable population. Does this culture of the lowest socioeconomic segments of our society impede advancement into the mainstream of American life?

Poverty in itself is obviously not a final barrier to personal advancement. With few exceptions, immigrants to the United States were poor to begin with. Yet most of their descendents have risen above the economic floor and escaped the slums. Immigration, sometimes an act of desperation, has often been an act of ambition, a way to better one's own and one's family's lot, and was thus conducive to a spirit of upward mobility. Most immigrants settled in the slums, in poverty but not of it. Yet the descendents of some of the immigrants are still in the slums. Is it that poverty keeps its tightest grip on those for whom it has become a stabilized way of life?

Our basic question may be subdivided into three. First, do some aspects of lower-class culture *interfere directly* with the achievement of a better life? Let us be cautious about assuming that everything middle class is superior. Who is to say that clearly differentiated husband and wife roles, such as typify working-class families, are better or worse than the loosely differentiated roles that mark professional families? Is there any virtue in belonging to clubs rather than to street-corner peer groups? Is it better to be Episcopalian? To suggest that one way of life may not be superior to another in all respects is not to imply that all are equally desirable. A proper criterion is whether the way of life of the poor materially impedes their advancement. The evidence seems to indicate that it does. The female-based household does very little to orient the growing boy toward the adult world of work or to a concept of family organization in which he might have a stable role. It need hardly be said that regular employment is the prime requisite for cutting loose from poverty. In addition, the street group, while useful in providing psychic satisfactions for its members, inculcates in the growing boy values which too often are negative toward either education or "normal" adult responsibilities. Recall the teacher who observed that when the street takes over, the pupils may actually move backward in school.

The next question is whether the *discontinuity* between the culture of the poor and the culture that dominates the larger community can be readily bridged. Schools exist for all the people. Their functions include the strengthening of the democratic quality of our society by opening doors to new opportunities for the young. The problem of cultural discontinuity shows up first in the schools. There is no question that the deprived child starts school with a handicap rooted in the atmosphere and ethos of his home. Early failure in school, because he cannot bridge the two cultures, is more likely for the deprived child. If the school were to adapt to him, his confrontation with the problem of cultural discontinuity would be delayed until the deprived child leaves school to find his place in the adult world. Cultural discontinuity constitutes a real problem which limits the upward mobility of the poor and for which there is no ready solution.

A final question is whether residential patterns and variations in life style and status have given rise to *segregation of the poor* so as to isolate them from the norms and expectations of the larger community. There can be no doubt that such segregation exists, but the extent to which it walls off the lowest-income groups and keeps them from interacting with other groups in the population is not known. The surmounting of poverty requires that people see the vision of a better life for themselves and come to feel the possibility that they, too, can move upward. The different life that is perceived is so often viewed as far off and inaccessible. The need is to awaken the poor to more meaningful aspirations. Cloward and Jones found that the importance attached to education by both pupils and parents was tied closely to occupational aspirations. The consequence of segregation associated with poverty is that it impedes the assimilation of the norms and goals of the larger community and thereby serves to perpetuate poverty.

If poverty is to be eliminated from America it must be attacked on many fronts. The economy must be kept vigorous. The aspirations of the poor must be raised and ways of attaining them found. Good schooling and vocational training are mandatory. The goal we seek is the good life, which may take many forms; but whatever its style, let it be for all of the people.

4: Poverty and the Individual

by I. Thomas Stone, Dorothea C. Leighton, Alexander H. Leighton*

The anthropologist Oscar Lewis has provided what is perhaps the most graphic and widely known recent literature dealing with the effects of poverty on the lives of individual human beings. Lewis' studies[1] in depth of the life of the poor poignantly illustrate in minute biographical detail his contention that poverty in modern nations is often something more than a state of economic deprivation. It can also be a persistent way of life, passed down from generation to generation, which carries definite social and psychological consequences for those who are caught in it.

*This work has been conducted as part of the Cornell Program in Social Psychiatry and has been supported through funds provided by the Milbank Memorial Fund, the Carnegie Corporation of New York, the Ford Foundation, the National Institutes of Mental Health, and the Dominion Provincial Mental Health Grants of Canada. These bodies are not, of course, the publishers or proprietors of this report, and are not to be understood as approving, by virtue of their grants, any of the statements made or views expressed herein.

We wish to express our particular debt of gratitude to the late Allister M. Macmillan, who met with the councillors, studied the people of The Road, and helped draft the plan that played a part in the community's rehabilitation.

1. Three books by Oscar Lewis on this general subject are: *Five Families* (New York: Basic Books, 1959); *The Children of Sanchez* (New York: Vintage Books, 1963); and *Pedro Martinez* (New York: Random House, 1964).

Certain effects that poverty may have upon the character of an individual's social dealings and upon his psychological attributes make it a distressing and obdurate condition. The impact of poverty upon his health, both physical and emotional, puts him in a poor position to initiate change or to take advantage of opportunities. We intend here to point out and illustrate some of the debilitating consequences that poverty can have for the individual, to offer for consideration some ideas about how these consequences are related to poverty, and to describe how some amelioration was brought about among the inhabitants of one depressed community.

MATERIAL AND PHYSICAL FACETS

Our examples will be drawn from Stirling County, a rural area in the Northeast, where for 15 years we have been accumulating data in some depth on both comparatively affluent communities and economically depressed settlements and on the individuals who inhabit them.[2] To begin, we may note those features of some communities in the county that lead county residents and outside observers alike to designate them as "poor."

A passerby sees clusters of bedraggled houses dotted about an area of poorly drained, scrubby, often rocky terrain with a scattering of undersized trees among a general cover of weeds and bushes. Coming to this community from other settlements of neatly painted houses and well-tilled fields interspersed with blocks of thick woodlots, one is struck by the derelict appearance of the small frame houses, paintless, patched here and there with rough lumber, many covered with tarpaper, which stand starkly on their little treeless plots. The occasional large, better-built house looks time-worn, dilapidated, and rather abandoned. Now and then there is a small garden to help feed the family during the summer, but the thin soil does not support a large crop of either vegetables

2. Alexander H. Leighton, *My Name is Legion* (New York: Basic Books, 1959); Charles C. Hughes, M. A. Tremblay, R. H. Rapoport, and A. H. Leighton, *People of Cove and Woodlot* (New York: Basic Books, 1960); and Dorothea C. Leighton, J. S. Harding, D. B. Macklin, A. M. Macmillan, and A. H. Leighton, *The Character of Danger* (New York: Basic Books, 1963).

or trees. Paths lead from the road to the house and from the house to the scrubby woods behind, but rarely from one house to its neighbor.

On approaching and entering a house, one finds debris scattered about, both within and without. Inside is a small amount of rickety furniture in a dark interior whose only decoration may be a few sooty pictures or faded calendars.

The look of these neighborhoods reflects their economic situation: the characteristic subsistence pattern is sporadic employment at a variety of low-paying, unskilled jobs—usually very hard work for very little money. The people here may, for example, dig clams, but to do so must travel 20 miles or more to a suitable beach, dig at low tides in the cold wet sand, and camp near the beach in makeshift shelters to save the cost of transportation. Or they may do woods work if someone outside the community wants to have his pulp wood harvested. Both occupations are piecework —clams by the bucket and wood by the cord. Lacking capital they cannot exploit natural resources for themselves; they cannot afford a boat and fishing gear, a woodlot or a truck.

Other available jobs are mostly seasonal work for nearby farmers or odd jobs of almost any kind for people in neighboring communities. They are given these jobs when no one "better" can be found, and let go when the need for help is over. There is little in this employment picture to foster regular work habits or feelings of identification and loyalty to any particular type of work or to any particular employer. Neither is there much opportunity to develop skills. Their employers consider them unreliable, and they themselves have little incentive to do more than act in keeping with common allegations that they are chronic ne'er-do-wells and loafers.

In other words, the people here have little or no capital, poor credit, few skills of economic value, and low and irregular earned income. Stated more generally, one sees them in a *position of economic disadvantage*. The poor here as elsewhere display a lack of the motivational and technical resources necessary to achieve even the limited material well-being that their sociocultural milieu provides. As a direct consequence of this, inhabitants of the poor communities in the county contrast markedly with neighboring, more prosperous communities by virtue of their *substandard ma-*

terial style of life. This is apparent in such things as their poor and overcrowded housing, poor clothing and diet, and a dearth of the material conveniences that are commonplace in the county at large. Commonly the people look unhealthy—pale and pasty, not robust and vigorous. Many studies in other places have shown a strong association of poor health with poverty. Although we have not conducted physical examinations, we have collected health histories and interviewed the doctors who serve the area, and in such data we find complaints suggesting a considerable prevalence of chronic disease—high blood pressure, arthritis, peptic ulcer, and bronchitis—as well as chronic anxiety and depression. Not only is disease sometimes a by-product of poverty; it probably serves to perpetuate poverty either by actual disablement or by a considerable reduction in energy level and physical endurance.

But economic disadvantage and a substandard material style of life, which serve, in effect, to define poverty, provide only a partial synopsis of the characteristics common to the poor. Our picture of what poverty means to the individual in the sketch above is patently incomplete until we probe further.

SOCIAL FACETS

Social life in Stirling's depressed communities also contrasts markedly with the rest of the county.[3] Compared with others in Stirling County, inhabitants of these settlements generally show an ineptitude for establishing and sustaining stable collaborative social relationships. They have little social contact with surrounding less-disadvantaged populations, and social dealings among their own number tend to be marked by a lack of conventional restraints and amenities, by an emphasis on the immediate gratification of personal wants, and by overt expressions of antagonism.

Social characteristics of these sorts doubtless surprise and offend would-be employers. A man, for example, may be offered a well-paying job with the opportunity to acquire some marketable skill—as a mechanic, welder, or whatever. In spite of its obvious advantages, such a venture will often end in failure for him. He persists in periodically failing to appear for work while he devotes

3. Hughes, et al., op. cit., pp. 244–311.

a day or two to dispatching his accumulated earnings on a good
drunk, or he repeatedly engages in some other offensive behavior
which leads to his dismissal. A potential employer's opinions about
the unreliability of the individual, and people like him from his
community, are thereby strengthened. The employee, for his part,
will view the employer's treatment as arbitrary, unjust, overly
demanding, and exploitative, weakening any sense of obligation
on his part to future employers.

The roots of the social ineptness are multiple, and, like so many
features of life in a depressed community, are intermixed with its
results. Family composition, to begin with, is often irregular by
county standards: consensual or common-law marital arrangements are common; children often reside with their grandparents
or other relatives. Many household arrangements are found which
do not fit easily into a general classification such as, e.g., a man
living with his niece and their offspring, or a man living with his
daughter, his daughter's illegitimate children, and an illegitimate
daughter of his deceased wife.

Severe verbal, and often physical, abuse is a feature of life in
many families. One also finds household members who manage to
obtain some money spending it quickly for themselves, often on
liquor for their own consumption. Nonearners reap little benefit,
owing to the small sense of responsibility toward others in the
family group on the part of the earners.

Whether the family displays such extreme behavior or not, it
is uncommon for persons to take much interest in working together
to provide for the upkeep of the home, or for anything else beyond
the bare minimum of domestic necessities. The remaining in-
volvements between household members mostly take the form of
idling away leisure time. Few games, outings, or other forms of
household recreation and entertainment are in evidence. The
major exception to this is an occasional trip to town together by
the younger members to see a movie or visit a traveling carnival.

Nor is the pallor of social bonds within the family offset by
much in the way of viable social ties outside it. Dealings among
fellow members of the depressed communities show much the
same features. There is little direct economic collaboration among
the neighborhood residents, with the exception of occasional
lending between persons who visit each other. Whereas members

of bordering communities take part in formal associations, religious activities and church socials, and in the less formal gatherings for sewing bees, cards and other games, "social" suppers, sings, and showers, such social gatherings do not occur within the depressed communities. Informal visiting, which is the chief extrahousehold social activity, takes place in small groups that gather to idle or gossip, the group usually limited to close kin or near neighbors. Occasionally drinking parties bring people together but much drinking is carried on in isolation.

Chronic animosities divide individuals and families from much of the community, these hostilities finding expression in mutual avoidance and vituperative gossip, punctuated by occasional eruptions of physical violence. Petty thievery in the neighborhood is frequent. The depressed settlements are known for an unusually high frequency of reports to the police of actual or rumored illegal activities as well as reports to the welfare department about wifebeating, the maltreatment of children, and so forth. The stream of gossip circulating through these settlements serves to aggravate rather than control the hostilities common within them.

There is little participation in the activities of neighboring churches—an important focus for social life in the region. Few from the depressed settlements go to services and, should a group happen to attend any church social function, they generally clique together, self-consciously watching the proceedings for a time rather than taking an active part in them. There is almost no involvement in local politics or education, and the schools draw little interest on the part of older residents. What encouragement is given children to continue schooling is based on the money this brings into the home under a government allowance. Petty crime beyond the confines of the neighborhood is common, and outsiders are continually subject to belittlement and made the butt of jokes among the inhabitants.

PSYCHOLOGICAL FACETS

Intimately interlaced into the sort of social behavior which the poor in Stirling both confront, and perpetuate by their own acts, is a pervasive set of attitudes and expectations associated with their life experience. The child draws his first breath in a small, drafty, sparsely furnished wooden house already overpopulated with children whom no one really wants. His needs will be attended to after a fashion by somebody if he squalls long and loud enough. For a while the somebody will probably be his mother since she is nursing him. When she stops feeding him, his care is often relegated to his brothers and sisters, who may or may not take much interest in him. For a while he will have a bottle when he is hungry, and eventually he will find out how to drink out of a cup. It is quite exceptional that anyone will spend much time cuddling him or playing with him or teaching him how to do things. When he is able to get around by himself, he will trail the other children or play alone. During the day they all come and find some food in the house from time to time if they are hungry, while at night they join in whatever the family has for supper if they like it. No one is much concerned about proper nutrition, or about whether the children eat or not.

The man of the house is not around much and pays little attention to the children when there. He may or may not be the baby's father, and the man in this role may change from time to time. He may come home drunk or angry, in which case he may start a fight with someone (most often his wife), which the children witness and learn to keep out of. There will be loud arguments and fierce accusations of misbehavior of all sorts. A crude sexual vocabulary is learned at an early age, and its meaning is well comprehended.

The growing child has a hard time finding out what is expected of him, and what limits there are to doing as he likes. In general there are few rules and little enforcement. He is rarely praised or encouraged for anything, though he may be scolded or threatened at times for various misdemeanors which at other times will go unnoticed. Punishment and threats are employed inconsistently in alternation with displays of affection, depending largely on the mood of the parent. Discipline is generally brought to bear when his activities cause difficulty or inconvenience for adults in the house. The child receives little training in basic amenities, and there is scant attention to preparing him for the future. He has no clear rights to defend, nor must he observe the rights of other children in the family, though there are strictures regarding fighting with children from other families. Position in the family and sex are no guarantees of any special treatment. Catch-as-catch-can is about the only regular rule.

Naturally enough, the whole group of such families, the settlement in which they are clustered, is as little regulated as is the individual family. No one feels himself "in charge," and similarly no one feels subject to the control of others. The remote authority of the police who might put one in jail, or of the welfare officers who might cut off the relief allowance, is recognized but is limited in its effectiveness. If one can get away with petty antisocial acts, he will, thereby increasing his self-esteem and possibly his reputation with his peers.

When old enough the child goes to school, for if he does not attend his family will lose his share of the school allowance. Until recently he was likely to attend a one-room school, where he associated mostly with other children of the same kind. Due to the inadequacies of their preschool socialization and the low quality of the available teachers, his school experience did little to enhance his interpersonal skills or to enlarge his picture of the world. Nor did it develop his intellectual capacity to any great extent. After six to eight years of it he was ready to follow his parents' footsteps into an early marriage and a cat-and-dog, hand-to-mouth existence.

While such a child is, generally speaking, no less gifted at birth than any other baby with capacities for intellectual and emotional development,[4] so little has been done to develop his capacities that by the time he gets out of school he is stunted in these respects in much the same way as a chronically undernourished child will be physically stunted. Like a child with a squint who fails to develop vision in the squinted eye unless the good eye is covered so that the squinted eye learns to deal with visual stimuli, so these children fail to develop many of their innate capacities. The environment of children living in such impoverished circumstances has been recognized as commonly detrimental to their mental (as well as physical) development.[5]

4. Allister Macmillan and Alexander H. Leighton, "People of the Hinterland," *in* Spicer (ed.), *Human Problems in Technological Change* (New York: Russell Sage, 1952), p. 229.

5. Martin P. Deutsch, "The Disadvantaged Child and the Learning Process,"

The child develops a depressed and disparaging view of himself and his group that is reinforced by the attitudes he encounters when he goes to look for a job outside the community. In the limited goals of keeping from hunger, clothing himself, finding shelter, maybe finding a spouse, and having a little fun, it does not worry him much whether the means used should be hard work or taking from others.

The uncertainty of the disadvantaged child's position in life tends to give rise right from the start to an uneasiness that later on, in adulthood, expresses itself in a variety of ways: sometimes in somatic symptoms such as headache, restlessness, indigestion, vague aches and pains; sometimes in feelings of hopelessness or in easy discouragement; sometimes in fury and frustration that may vent itself in destructiveness of some sort. The unpredictability of other people makes the maturing individual loath to trust anyone, either in the community or outside. It prevents developing a sense of responsibility and reciprocal obligation.

Since these people are themselves "no good" and come from a "no good" community, both in their own eyes and in the eyes of outsiders, they never try very hard to make a place for themselves —it is hopeless from the start. They take no blame for this. Partly it is just the way life is, partly their health is not good enough for them to exert themselves, and besides other people have it in for them and prevent their getting ahead. To an outsider the resulting apathy, hostility, and suspiciousness may be apparent, but not the underlying anxiety, the depressiveness, the unreal image of the world and how it works.

We should stress here a point we shall return to shortly, namely, that we do not regard the social and psychological situation sketched above as an inevitable consequence of poverty per se. It can nevertheless be said with some assurance that it is quite likely to be found in association with poverty that strikes a whole community or neighborhood both severely and chronically. Although our illustrations have been drawn from poverty in a rural setting, the above portrait bears a notable similarity to what, for example, Lewis describes as common traits of the poor in urban settings, on

---

in A. H. Passow (ed.), *Education in Depressed Areas* (New York: Columbia University Press, 1963), pp. 163–79.

the basis of his own work in Mexico and that of others elsewhere in the world. Among the common features of poverty which Lewis sees exemplified in his Mexican materials[6] are

> a high incidence of alcoholism, frequent resort to violence in the settlement of quarrels, frequent use of physical violence in the training of children, wife beating, early initiation into sex, free unions or consensual marriages, a relatively high incidence of the abandonment of mothers and children . . . a strong present time orientation with relatively little ability to defer gratification and plan for the future, a sense of resignation and fatalism based upon the realities of their difficult life situation.

Haggstrom, in his summary of certain characteristics which are commonly cited in recent literature concerning the poor, paints a similar picture.[7] Spinley, summarizing the personality characteristics of a group of slum-dwellers in London,[8] also concludes:

> The individual shows a marked absence of a strict and efficient conscience, an unwillingness and inability to deal with disturbing or unpleasant situations, and a flight from these. He is unable to postpone satisfactions. . . . Relations with other people are coloured by negativism, distrust, suspicion, and excessive fear of ridicule, this last so strong that feelings of inferiority are indicated. He has marked aggressiveness which is permitted violent expression, and his attitude towards authority is one of hostility and rebellion. Emotional response and fantasy production are constricted and intellectual discrimination poor. His response to failure, frustration, or mishap of any kind is extrapunitive.

POVERTY AND ITS SOCIAL AND PSYCHOLOGICAL FACETS

The discussion up to this point may be summarized by stressing the apparent interplay among the physical, social, and psycho-

6. Lewis, *The Children of Sanchez,* pp. xxvi–xxvii.

7. Warren C. Haggstrom, "The Power of the Poor," *in* F. Reissman, et al. (eds.), *Mental Health of the Poor* (Glencoe, Ill.: The Free Press, 1964), pp. 205–23.

8. B. M. Spinley, *The Deprived and the Privileged* (London: Routledge and Kegan Paul, 1953), pp. 129–30.

logical characteristics of the poor that emerges in our observations. Their underdeveloped capacity for maintaining beneficial social relationships can be seen working to reinforce and perpetuate their generally impoverished condition and to deny them the inter- personal support necessary to achieve a sense of worth and well- being. This type of life situation fosters the development of cer- tain psychological characteristics, such as apathy, anxiety, depres- sion, hostility, and pessimism, which serve to reduce the capacity for establishing, maintaining, and learning how to engineer sup- portive social bonds. Thus all these facets of poverty are likely to combine into a "vicious," self-perpetuating cycle.

It should be apparent that our conception of the meaning of poverty to the individual includes features closely akin to the time-honored concept of anomy. A recent paper by McClosky and Schaar makes the point, however, that most people dealing with anomy have limited themselves to sociological explanations for the phenomena of the condition.[9] Taking psychological aspects of anomy as their field of enquiry, McClosky and Schaar report two extensive surveys, one in Minnesota (1,082 adults), the other national (1,484 adults), in which they collected data by means of a large battery of personality and attitude scales. Because their findings are congruent with our own observations, but result from such a different group of people and such different methods, they reinforce our conclusion that there is a significant reciprocal interplay between the social and psychological characteristics we have noted. Michael reports similar findings from the Midtown study.[10]

McClosky and Schaar[11]

> conceptualize anomy as a state of mind, a cluster of attitudes, beliefs, and feelings in the minds of individuals. Specifically, it is the feeling that the world and oneself are adrift, wander- ing, lacking in clear rules and stable moorings. The anomic feels literally *de*-moralized; for him, the norms governing be-

9. Herbert McClosky and John H. Schaar, "Psychological Dimensions of Anomy," *Am. Soc. Rev., 30* (1965), 14–40.

10. Stanley T. Michael, "Social Attitudes, Socio-economic Status and Psychi- atric Symptoms," *Acta Psych. et Neurol. Scand., 35,* 1960.

11. McClosky and Schaar, ibid., p. 19.

havior are weak, ambiguous, and remote. He lives in a norma-
tive "low pressure" area, a turbulent region of weak and fit-
ful currents of moral meaning. The core of the concept is the
feeling of moral emptiness.

In addition to scales for measuring the subject's anomy, other
scales define his cognitive functioning from several angles, his
emotional characteristics (inflexibility, anxiety, low ego strength,
generalized aggression), and his substantive beliefs and opinions.
Considering here only the portion of the samples scoring high in
anomy, this group ranked low on education, intellectuality, and
awareness; high on mysticism and acquiescence; high on inflexibility, manifest anxiety, stability-disorganization, and bewilderment;
high on guilt, alienation, status frustration, pessimism, political
futility; low on self-confidence, life satisfaction, dominance, social
responsibility; high on hostility, paranoia, intolerance of human
frailty, contempt for weakness; high on extreme beliefs (either
left or right) and misanthropy. A final test to determine the part
played by personality characteristics was to match 275 high-
anomics with 275 low-anomics on seven sociological variables
(education, age, size of community, occupational status, race, sex,
and region) and then compare their scores on the personality
scales. Matched thus, high-anomics continue to differ from low-
anomics as indicated above.

McClosky and Schaar conclude that "the principal source of
anomic feeling resides for some people in their social settings; for
others in their individual personalities; and for still others, in a
combination of the two. . . . Some social conditions combine with
personality to intensify the anomic response, while others combine
to diminish it."[12] They suggest that "an alternative and possibly
more useful approach [i.e. to the usual sociological explanation
of anomy] might be to regard anomy as a by-product of the socialization process—as a sign of the failure of socialization and of the
means by which socialization is achieved, namely, communication,
interaction, and learning."[13]

When people ranking high in the attributes of anomy are
congregated in small communities or neighborhoods, set some-

12. Ibid., p. 35.
13. Ibid., p. 39.

what apart from the rest of the society (as in the depressed communities of Stirling County), instead of being scattered over Minnesota or the United States and diluted with people of other kinds, the concentration of unfavorable influences is such that it is indeed an exceptional personality that can escape from chronic social and psychological incapacitation.

In considering how the various concomitants of poverty become linked to poverty itself, it is important to note that occasionally groups appear to show such reactions as a result of circumstances other than poverty. There are well-documented instances of culture contact, for example, where members of a subordinate society show these same psychological and social characteristics after being exposed to acculturative pressures from a dominant group.[14] It is claimed that culture contact may sometimes create conditions which prevent members of a group from sustaining or participating in a system of social relationships capable of providing for their major values and self-goals.

For example, among the Navahos of Fruitland, New Mexico, the consequences of wage work and an *increased* level of affluence included disruption of traditional patterns of economic assistance, breakdown of institutional and informal patterns of social control, deterioration of the processes of transmission of Navaho culture from old to young and of relationships among members of the kinship groups, attenuation of the pattern of ceremonial activities, and the emergence of rampant over-indulgence in alcohol. The Indians failed, at least for a time, to adjust to improved economic circumstances by assimilating a new social system, accommodating to wage work and their changed economic position. They did not learn quickly how to manage money wisely, how much liquor they could handle, the channels through which they could get welfare aid when economic assistance was needed, nor did they easily acquire the self-assurance necessary for dealing effectively with

14. A. Irving Hallowell, "Ojibwa Personality and Acculturation," *in* S. Tax (ed.), *Proceedings of the 29th International Congress of Americanists*, 1951–52. M. Felix Keesing, *Culture Change* (Stanford: Stanford University Press, 1953), pp. 84–85, 88; Margaret Mead, *The Changing Culture of an Indian Tribe* (New York: Columbia University Press, 1932); and G. D. Spindler, *Sociocultural and Psychological Processes in Menomini Acculturation* (Berkeley: University of California Press, 1955).

non-Navahos.[15] In such conflict, it is very likely indeed that an individual's sense of self-esteem and well-being will be fractured, leading to psychological incapacitation and socially dysfunctional behavior,[16] which will trigger the sort of vicious cycle described.

Such instances provide evidence that a group can suffer social and psychological breakdown for reasons other than poverty, and they also suggest the mechanism by which poverty itself may produce them. For their own self-esteem and sense of personal well-being, men are dependent upon their fellows in two ways. First, they assess their own position in life with reference to the standards of the groups of which they seek to be counted a part. Second, it is in collaboration with those who share such standards that they devise ways of meeting them. Individuals depend upon the support of others for carrying out the activities and winning the recognition necessary to realize these goals. Prolonged economic disadvantage and a substandard material level of living can easily lead to a group's loss of the capacity to achieve or maintain the standards upon which its members' sense of well-being and personal worth depend, which may suffer as a result, leading ultimately to the attitudes and behavior we have outlined.

The history of one of Stirling's depressed areas may serve again as an illustration. This settlement, which we shall call The Road, had existed for at least a century when it was first intensively studied at the beginning of the 1950s.[17] It was selected for study as an example of one of the most severely depressed neighborhoods in the county, a poverty-stricken group of 118 people living in 29 houses strung for two miles along a dirt road running inland from the coast. The Road had a reputation throughout the county as a group of mentally and morally inferior as well as impoverished people, and the community was known widely by a pejorative nickname.

Settlement of The Road was begun by French people who had migrated from 20 or more miles away into a predominantly

15. Tom Sasaki, *Fruitland, New Mexico* (Ithaca: Cornell University Press, 1960), pp. 175–93.

16. A. F. C. Wallace, *Culture and Personality* (New York: Random House, 1961), pp. 143–63; and Keesing, *Culture Change*, p. 89.

17. Macmillan and A. H. Leighton, op. cit.

English area, attracted by employment in shipyards at the coast and by the opportunity for hauling logs to the shipyards from an inland lumbering community. Not being concerned with farming, they settled on poor land which was cheap, was close to centers of employment at the coast, and was conveniently located for the profitable business of hauling timber.

So far as can be determined, these settlers came from normal farming families and represented surplus population, which their native farmlands could not support. As the economic situation continued good, French wives joined the men who had moved to The Road and families became established there. In time, however, the ties between the inhabitants of The Road and their remote relatives weakened. Intermarriage with the surrounding English-speaking Protestant population began to take place. Significant economic bonds with the English Protestants of the area increased. Proselytizing by Protestants appears to have weakened the Catholic faith, although it did not succeed in producing ardent converts. At the same time, except for their economic ties, the people of The Road remained socially rather isolated from their non-French cultural ambient. Cool feelings on the part of the English toward the French on The Road were apparently accentuated somewhat by the failure to win converts to the Protestant churches. Added to this, although The Road in time acquired the use of English and it became the major spoken language there, the lingering accent of the inhabitants both emphasized their distinctiveness and provided a source of amusement to the English.

The Road nevertheless remained an economically and socially viable community sustaining itself until the beginning of the present century, when the coastal shipbuilding industry collapsed and with it the trade in lumber. This resulted in a precipitous loss of the economic resources on which The Road depended. While this change in the economic situation also wrought hardship on surrounding populations, they were people with education, fluency in English, social connections, and capital resources which enabled them to move and otherwise adjust to the change. By contrast, the people of The Road were a small group, situated on poor land, without much capital or education, cut off from the French, and set apart by the English.

Suddenly the inhabitants of The Road found themselves economically deprived and disadvantaged, with what had made a good life for them no longer attainable. Their economic position, coupled with their other obvious differences, made them easy targets for disparagement as an inferior breed, a sentiment which continually confronted them in their dealings with outsiders, particularly in attempts to secure employment, and which they came to accept for themselves as part of their own self-image. The nature of their situation and their collective poverty rendered it impossible for them to draw support from one another in adjusting to the change that had taken place. Simple material survival necessarily became a major concern, and they were forced to seek out and take work that was not only arduous and low paying but in the eyes of others demeaning and indicative of personal incompetence.

All the available evidence indicates that The Road quickly began to display the social and psychological attributes of poverty we have discussed, and they were found to be persisting when The Road came to be studied intensively beginning in 1949.

It is worth observing that, within limits, poverty need not necessarily have these consequences. A man's poor material condition may not be associated with a loss of the capacity to carry on activities and win the recognition necessary to meet his standards of personal worth and well-being. There are many factors that can play a role in determining whether a low economic position will deprive persons of the requisite social support.

Depending on the culture of the group, it may be able to maintain a viable social system providing for the major self-goals of its members, even when in absolute terms its economic position is very low indeed. For example, a study of the Navaho Indians in 1940 showed a per capita income of $82, while the figure for the United States as a whole was $579. Even the lowest state in the nation—Mississippi—which was like Navaho country in that it was largely rural and had an important minority group, showed a per capita income two and a half times as large as the Navahos.[18] The Road was never so low economically as the Navahos, yet

18. Clyde Kluckhohn and Dorothea C. Leighton, *The Navaho* (Cambridge: Harvard University Press, 1946), pp. 25–26.

Navaho culture successfully accommodated this level, and the economic position of the Indians did not result in pervasive anomy, demoralization, or the kind of social and psychological debilitation we have described.

Similarly, the isolated poor individual within a successful group may still be able to participate in a social system that will provide him with some opportunities for self-fulfillment, so long as the capacity of the group as a whole to maintain the system is not seriously curtailed, and his acceptance as a participant in it is not wholly contingent upon his economic status. Taking this point a bit further, one finds poor families in some of the more affluent, homogeneous communities in Stirling, but their number is small. The resources of the community as a whole are able to support a well-integrated and effectively functioning social system in which the few economically disadvantaged individuals can participate. Here, even though their relative deprivation in economic terms is accentuated by the affluence of their neighbors, such poor people do not show the full effects of poverty we have detailed above. It is of course true that, in less rural and homogeneous communities, a person's ability to secure social support may be much more closely tied to his personal economic position.

Finally, in contrast to the poor people in some of Stirling's affluent settlements stand the few exceptional families of average-to-better economic position who reside in one or another of the depressed areas. Here, the poverty of the community as a whole has incapacitated the social system to such an extent that the affluent individual is not able, within the community, to find activities and earn recognition that will provide him with a sense of self-realization. If these individuals do not develop their social world beyond the boundaries of the community, or move out, they too tend to display the social and psychological attributes of poverty, *as a consequence of their membership in a community affected by poverty* and not because of any personal economic disadvantage.

Whatever the immediate source of the traits we have described, once developed in association with poverty they work against its alleviation even when new material resources or opportunities for economic self-improvement develop or are introduced. The vicious cycle continues. Apathy, disparagement, distrust, and hostility both support and are supported by behavior of a type that precludes effective responses to new opportunities which might serve to ameliorate an impoverished condition.

An attempt to organize a union at a lumber mill in Stirling further illustrates the point.[19] Potential members of the union all came from economically depressed circumstances, and most admitted the need for such an organization to raise wages and improve working conditions. Yet, as soon as the union was formed, distrust and suspicion from the members, directed at the organizer, spelled its failure. Throughout his attempts to form the association, the organizer was viewed as an exploiter, although long contact with him by a fieldworker provided only consistent evidence to the contrary. From the outset, the men wondered what he was planning to get out of the organization and accused him variously of trying to secure himself a lucrative salary from the dues, selling out to the company, and organizing some sort of a "communist" group. When it became necessary for him to seek an increase in union dues, this "proved" that he was out for personal profit at the expense of the men. Resulting lack of participation rendered the union unable to provide the very benefits that had been its goal and that the members desired.

REVERSING THE CYCLE: AN EXAMPLE

We do not contend that there are no mechanisms which can serve to reverse the enervating social and psychological effects of poverty. Rather, we emphasize that special attention is required for dealing with these effects if improved economic opportunities are to alter the position of the poor who display them.

Often individuals in a depressed population will seek a solution to their stressful circumstances by developing new standards that define worth and well-being in terms of what their situation permits them to achieve. Caught in a self-perpetuating cycle where their behavior and attitudes close avenues to meeting the standards the larger culture provides, such persons often seek a "deviant" solution. Delinquent gangs and what anthropologists refer to as "revitalization movements," like the ghost dance in some American

19. Seymour Parker, "Union Participation: A Study in Culture and Personality," Ph.D. dissertation, Cornell University, February 1955.

Indian tribes, usually get their start within depressed groups. Since such a partial solution is likely to run directly contrary to the goals of the larger society, it may reduce even further the possibility of effective social dealings between the group and its milieu. Because the behavior of the deviant group threatens the standards of the larger society, pressures will be brought to bear against the deviant solution. From the perspective of the larger society, the social problem continues; and the solution is not likely to prove ultimately successful even from the perspective of the deviant group.

Fortunately an alternative solution is also possible: the recent history of The Road demonstrates that, given the appropriate sort of stimulation, a disadvantaged group can overcome the hindrances imposed by self-defeating attitudes and dispositions and achieve the capacity for effective social action both within and outside the community, leading to a revived sense of well-being and worth. A number of events, which we were able to document, served to break or reverse the vicious cycle in effect on The Road for nearly 50 years.[20]

As an outgrowth of the first study of The Road,[21] a detailed program for possible improvement was drawn up by Macmillan, and school authorities became interested in implementing it. Early in the 1950s a man responsible for adult education in the area decided to conduct an experiment to see if improvement could be brought about. He defined his objective as that of improving the skills of the Road people so as to make them more employable, and he sought to accomplish this by establishing regular adult education classes at the settlement's one-room school. His initial tactic was to attract the adults of The Road to regular evening gatherings at the school by showing free movies. He obtained the collaboration of the schoolteacher, and they began by showing movies during school hours to the children, then sending them home with the report that there would be movies again in the evening, free for anyone who wished to attend.

Attendance at the first showings was reasonably good, and at the suggestion of the education agent the Road people elected a com-

20. Alexander H. Leighton, "Poverty and Social Change," *Scientific American*, *212* (May 1965), 21–27.

21. Macmillan and A. H. Leighton, op. cit.

mittee to select subsequent programs from the list of available films. He also gradually encouraged the showing of films with educational content, and began suggesting the possibility of adult classes in the school.

There was no electricity in the school and the first showings required that he bring along a portable generator. He pointed out that the school ought to be electrified if the evening programs were to be carried on properly and, further, that while the Department of Education was prepared to meet half the cost, the rest must be raised in the neighborhood. This suggestion was made partly because of the immediate practicalities, but it was also strongly influenced by his recognition that development of social organization, leadership, and experience in cooperation was a necessary preliminary to success in any more ambitious program. Courses could have been given in the school without electricity, but it seemed likely that they would get more attention if the place had been wired by community effort for this particular purpose. The risk was, of course, that the wiring project would fail from lack of interest, and judgment about the timing of this proposal was of vital importance. As it turned out, the project was a success: the people of The Road raised their share of the money and enough more to pay the electric bill for the suceeding year.

At this critical juncture, however, the project came to an abrupt end because the adult-educator was transferred to a different district. Such a collapse was so thoroughly in keeping with the Road's chronic attitudes of suspicion, apathy, and disparagement, and so completely matched the predictions of the project's opponents on The Road, that recovery seemed impossible, and prospects looked bleak for building a more integrated social system.

In the meantime, school officials had been endeavoring to hire a well-qualified teacher for the Road school, to remedy the fact that the position had been filled by teachers with only minimal qualifications for a number of years. A capable teacher was found, and she continued where the adult-educator had left off as a catalyst for activity on The Road. She maintained frequent contacts with the women and encouraged them to seek improved educational conditions for the settlement. In line with the program originally envisioned for improving conditions there, she took advantage of the fact that among the women there was some pre-existing interest in education, incipient leadership, and a measure of informal social cohesion. Evening bingo games were organized at the school, with prizes provided by the women, as a means of raising money to purchase new desks. One of the teacher's most important moves, however, was to stir up, at the suggestion of school authorities, the question of having the district admitted to the consolidated school of the region. Such admission meant transportation by daily bus for all children above the sixth grade to a town several miles away where educational opportunities were considerably richer and the way was clear for going on through high school. It also meant increased taxes for the district.

In spite of opposition on and near The Road, stemming from the necessity for increased taxes, the women in favor of the move, urged on by the teacher, campaigned in its behalf through the neighborhood with success. Supporters were brought out in sufficient number to a meeting of the district rate-payers to vote the measure through.

When the first group of Road children were thus admitted to the consolidated school, the staff noted that they were easily distinguishable from the other pupils because they stayed apart, and were silent and awkward in manner. Their clothing, too, was out of keeping with youthful fashions, and was often ill fitting, with trousers too big and coat sleeves coming only halfway to wrists.

At the end of five months the principal, noting one day at assembly that none of the Road children were in evidence, asked one of his assistants if they had given up. He was told that they were all still present, but had now blended with the rest of the student body. The speed of this adjustment was doubtless facilitated by the fact that each year the wave of new pupils entering the school included children from other rural areas who displayed varying degrees of difference from the clothes, manners, and language of the student majority. Thus the situation was not one of a large gulf between Road children and everyone else, but rather a continuum, with Road children at one extreme. It seems likely that these circumstances made it easier for the Road children to find places as part of the school group and to begin adjusting through a whole sequence of changes for which they found models at all stages and degrees among the strangers.

One may also suppose that the children began bringing new ideas about deportment, clothing, values, and motivation into the Road neighborhood. No doubt this was resisted and treated with ridicule at first, but as the number of children going to and from the central school increased (especially the older ones attending high school), they were able more and more to reinforce and support each other. There was thus opportunity for the development of a gradual but progressive impact that could never have been achieved by one or two people going out and coming back, whether adults or children.

Another development of major importance was the establishment of a work circuit that linked The Road to a city in Ontario. Its initiation had taken place, before the beginning of our study, when a family originally from The Road settled in this Ontario region and then wrote back asking some of their relatives to join them for a time to take advantage of comparatively lucrative employment in the city. By 1952 four people had responded and were living close to one another, engaged in the same type of unskilled work. On this basis a pattern developed whereby people from The Road would go to work in Ontario for six months or a year and then return home. The arrangement was such that on leaving The Road, they had assurance in advance that jobs would be available and that they would be moving in among people of their own kind, most of whom they knew. They apparently made a good impression as workers and, when they left, the employers were glad to accept a relative or friend as a replacement. The returnees to The Road expended their accumulated savings on paint, furniture, house construction, or a car.

In 1957 the movement reached a peak, with 21 people from The Road at the Ontario location, and by 1962 some individuals had made the circuit four or five times. Both men and women made the trip, married couples as well as single individuals. Some of the couples were newly married and chose this adventure as a means of acquiring a sum of money to start a home. It is evident, therefore, that the circuit served as an economic pump bringing money into The Road. Factors important in its success were the receiving friends at the Ontario end, the arranged job, and a prepared place to live. Fear of the unknown and apprehensions about being stranded among strangers in a strange place were thus reduced, and confidence in finding acceptable work and getting fair treatment from employers was established. The migrants were also beyond the sphere of their reputation as unreliable workers.

It is claimed by people on The Road, and others in the vicinity who know the neighborhood well, that among those who made the circuit the old habits of speech, dress, and deportment that had characterized the settlement had dropped away by the time they returned. The migrants arrived back home with a confidence in their ability to obtain more respectable forms of work and a marked unwillingness to take part in the traditional, low-status occupations of the neighborhood. They tended to deprecate many of their former habits, such as idleness, drunkenness, brawling, and unreliability in social dealings. They displayed a confidence and desire for dealing with outsiders on an equal footing, for living up to conventional codes of conduct, and living down the neighborhood's former reputation.

Throughout this period, economic opportunities in the local area were also improving, and the inhabitants of The Road were increasingly in a position to take advantage of them. New attitudes, supported by the improved economic circumstances of the neighborhood, led to a new look on The Road. Shacks gave way to new or refurbished dwellings as the men worked diligently to improve the looks of their places, while lawns and flower gardens replaced the earlier weeds and alders. This obvious improvement, coupled with the change in personal habits and deportment, signaled the change on The Road to the outside, and the old attitudes and prejudice directed against the neighborhood diminished.

It can be seen that the momentum for change building out of any one of these happenings would "feed back" and stimulate other events. The experiences of Road people away from home began to alter their outlook in a way that no longer supported the old attitudes that had promoted negative relations. The cycle, in effect, was reversed, with experiences and attitudes interacting in a way that led to the adoption of a whole new set of standards for conduct, subsequent alteration in the characteristic behavior patterns of the neighborhood, and positive social ties between the neighborhood and its surroundings. By 1962, not only was there a notable improvement in the Road's economic position and material style of life but the neighborhood had shifted from a disintegrated to a re-integrating social community, while the negative psychological characteristics of its inhabitants had subsided to a striking extent.

The notable improvement of The Road illustrates the importance of stimulating rewarding group action within the limits of existing social capacities, as a basis for the learning necessary to achieve development in disadvantaged groups. The social skills and attitudes of the people of The Road were gradually "shaped" in a positive direction. Both the improvements they were stimulated to seek for themselves and the means of achieving them were such that it was *necessary*, and at the same time *possible,* for the very rudimentary degree of social organization they possessed to mobilize sufficient group action to attain success. Their successes resulted in new experiences and new learning that made the attainment of further goals possible in the same way.

Conversely, the inhabitants of The Road were not encouraged to do what, for them, would have been impossible. Their response to overambitious suggestions would, in all probability, have been apathy or failure, and they would, of course, have learned nothing from them. Nor were the things they sought granted outright, without any effort or new activity on their part. If this had been the case it seems likely that nothing of ultimate value to them would have been accomplished.

The transformation of The Road serves to revive an optimism that the self-defeating reactions of individuals to life in such a depressed community can be altered. Even though the socialization of the children in such circumstances is faulty, peoples' attitudes and personality characteristics anomic, their training and skills very limited, and their material resources virtually non-existent, there is still the possibility that the downward trend and hopeless outlook can be overcome. They can be rehabilitated if only a chink in the forbidding wall of disparagement can be found through which can be beamed a large enough ray of confidence that they can help themselves so that it will seem worthwhile to make the effort. The location of the chink, and the constitution of the ray, will vary from one disadvantaged group to another. Familiarity with the people in the group and large measures of imagination and courage will help to identify them.

Once the start has been made, the whole catalogue of educational, cooperative, and organizational techniques devised in recent years for community development can be applied as they seem appropriate, letting group members' capacities and convictions about the usefulness of their own efforts determine both direction and speed of change.

An obvious corollary to this is that people engaged in community development need training not only in education, economics, construction, agriculture, arts and crafts, recreation, and so on but also in comprehending the social and psychological factors we have been describing and in knowing how to deal with them. The well-educated, well-paid middle-class worker may find considerable difficulty in relating to and communicating with people so different in outward characteristics from himself. It seems inescapable that some sort of field experience with depressed peoples is an absolutely essential precondition for successfully developing the receptiveness and self-confidence upon which a development program can be built. The model established by the Peace Corps for training volunteers to work in other nations can probably be adapted for domestic use with infinite benefit to the war on poverty.

Part 3: Special Cases of Poverty

5: Poverty and the Negro

by Herman P. Miller

So much has been said about Negro poverty these past few years that it is becoming increasingly difficult to say anything new or significant on the subject. It is common knowledge that Negroes are poorly housed, poorly educated, and discriminated against in many ways. It is also generally known that Negroes are over-represented in the bottom income groups, largely because they are either unqualified for the better jobs or because they often don't get them even when they are qualified. There would be little value in reciting once again the well-known facts about Negro disadvantage unless they could be put into an analytical framework which provides better insight into the historic causes of Negro poverty and the likely directions of future change. In attempting to do just that, I shall trace the role the Negro has played in the antipoverty program and explore the prospects for a narrowing of the economic gap between the races.

There are many who feel that a new day is dawning for the Negro in America. The passage of the Civil Rights Act, the enactment of the antipoverty program, the proposed expenditure of billions of additional dollars for education and training, and similar measures have raised hopes in some quarters that the day will soon come when the Negro and white worker will be able to compete for jobs on equal terms. However, some problem areas, in the absence of change, suggest caution rather than unbridled optimism regarding future prospects for a narrowing of the economic gap between whites and nonwhites.

Any objective evaluation of the economic position of Negroes in America would show that they have made tremendous progress. Negroes, once highly concentrated in sharecropping and farm labor, have now moved up to unskilled and semiskilled factory jobs. Appreciable numbers have even moved into white-collar employment. This change has raised the skills of the Negro labor force, it has increased their productivity, and it is in large measure responsible for the vast improvement in their level of living. If we take what is perhaps the single most important aspect of life that we attempt to measure, namely life expectancy itself, we find that the female Negro infant born in 1960 could expect to live 21 years longer than her mother born in 1920—a gain of nearly 50 per cent in life expectancy in the relatively brief span of 40 years.

Not only are Negroes living longer, they are also living far better than ever before. Negro housing, for example, may still leave much to be desired; but, the proportion living in dilapidated houses was cut in half between 1950 and 1960. The real incomes of Negroes have also shown a remarkable rise. Between 1940 and 1960 the wages and salaries of the average male Negro worker rose from about $1,000 to about $3,000 (both figures measured in terms of 1960 dollars). In other words, there was a threefold increase in Negro purchasing power during this period.

History is important for societies but it counts for little in the reckoning of most individuals. If a man tells his wife that she is three times as well off as her grandmother was at the same age, she is not likely to be impressed. She regards it as much more significant if her neighbor has three times as much income as she herself has *now*. It is with the present and future that most people are concerned, not with the past. And, in considering the present, our position relative to others is most important. The Negro's lot is improving but so is that of the white. The critical question in many minds is whether the gap between the races is narrowing.

Tom Kahn, who was Bayard Rustin's assistant in organizing the 1963 March on Washington, recently wrote:[1]

It takes a lot of running to stand still on the treadmill of this technologically advancing society. When you know you're

1. Tom Kahn, "Problems of the Negro Movement," *Dissent* (Winter 1964), p. 111.

running hard and everyone tells you you're moving at a fast
clip, and yet the scenery around you remains the same, the
most appropriate word to describe your reactions is . . .
frustration.

Yet, the fact is that the Negro has not been standing still and
the scenery around him has been changing most dramatically. He
has had tremendous increases in all aspects of life for which objective measures are available. The only reason many Negroes feel
they are standing still is that the whites too have had these gains,
and in many areas the gap between the races does not appear to
be narrowing.

ROLE OF THE NEGRO IN THE WAR ON POVERTY

The war on poverty has many causes, and it would be unwise
and incorrect to simplify too much. The high rate of unemployment for nearly a decade was undoubtedly a major factor in
initiating the new program, as was the threat of continued or
perhaps even increased unemployment caused by automation.
Nor can we forget the contributions of latter-day muckrakers like
Michael Harrington or the happy circumstance that we had an
action-minded President, who first proposed the war on poverty
in the fall of 1963. While all these factors are important—and
there were others too—I am inclined to agree with Nathan Glazer
that racial tension "is undoubtedly the chief reason why poverty
has become a major issue in this country."[2]

A casual glance at the statistics on poverty will show that 2.0
million of the 7.2 million poor families are nonwhite. On this
basis, one might conclude that nonwhites constitute only a small
fraction (about one-fourth) of the poor. Indeed, one astute scholar
who should and does know better came to this very conclusion not
too long ago. In a commencement address at Lincoln University
in 1964, Gunnar Myrdal said, "Though the Negro people account
for a disproportionately large number of the poor and the disadvantaged in the American nation, the poor among the Negroes
nevertheless constitute only a minority of the subdued 'under-
class' in the United States, perhaps 25 per cent or a little more

2. Nathan Glazer, "A Sociologist's View of Poverty," *Poverty in America,*
edited by Margaret S. Gordon (San Francisco: Chandler, 1965), p. 20.

depending on where the line is drawn."[3] A close examination of the facts will show that the Negro is much more prominent among the poor than this figure suggests.

The total number of poor families includes 1.5 million aged families, who today represent a more or less passive element among the poor. During the depression, the aged were very active as a pressure group for social reform. The movement that organized around Townsend was perhaps the most striking example of their activity. Although there still are some important pressure groups among them, the aged appear to be much less forceful and effective today than they were 30 years ago. If the aged poor are removed from the total, we find that nonwhites constitute one-third (33 per cent) of the poor under 65 years old. Even this number understates the importance of the Negro as a component of the poor, because it includes many persons who are only temporarily poor, and they are more likely to be white than nonwhite. An unpublished Census Bureau tabulation shows that about three-fourths of the nonwhite families with incomes under $3,000 one year are also likely to have incomes of the same amount the following year, as compared with only 60 per cent of the white families. On this basis, it seems likely that the proportion of chronically poor families that are nonwhite is likely to be closer to 40 per cent than to 28 per cent, as the raw unadjusted data show.

With these figures in mind, we can better appreciate the role of the Negro in shaping the new antipoverty program with its emphasis on education, training, and rehabilitation rather than money handouts. During the thirties, Negroes were largely tucked away in the rural South, where they worked for the most part as subsistence farmers or sharecroppers. Although their need then was as great as, and perhaps even greater than, that of other segments of the population, they operated largely as passive agents in the war on poverty waged at that time. During the depression the unions and their leaders sparked the drive against poverty. The target was income maintenance to combat the effects of unemployment. The unions organized the millions of unskilled workers; they marched, sang, and struck. They were the prime

3. Gunnar Myrdal, *Challenge to Affluence* (New York: Vintage Books, 1965), p. 178.

movers in obtaining passage of the social security laws that characterized the antipoverty measures of the depression.

Today it is primarily the Negro leadership that is focusing attention on the poor. Negroes have been particularly hard hit by the rapid economic changes in recent years. Unemployment rates for Negroes, especially Negro youth, have been painfully high for nearly a decade. For some years we suffered under the delusion that the next turn in the business cycle or a tax cut might clear things up; but it is quite apparent now that the dislocations for some segments of the population, the Negro in particular, are much deeper than that.

The recent riots in several major Northern cities suggest that there is a large dissident element among Negro youth that does not need government statistics to tell them they are being by-passed by society, as were their fathers and grandfathers before them. They are aware of the existence of job vacancies for delivery boys, bus boys, handymen, and other menial tasks, but they are not inclined to flock to them. Their attitude is summarized by Bayard Rustin, who stated recently, "To want a Cadillac is not un-American; to push a cart in the garment center is." [4] There is one major difference between these boys and their forebears: Negro youth today will not stand idly by. In all regions of the country, a revolution is in progress—a revolution that demands rights, dignity, and jobs.

This revolution may in large measure be responsible for the war on poverty today. President Johnson summed up the matter very neatly when he stated in his message on voting legislation: [5]

> The real hero of this struggle is the American Negro. His actions and protests—his courage to risk safety and even life—have awakened the conscience of the nation. His demonstrations have been designed to call attention to injustice to provoke change and stir reform. . . . And who among us can say we would have made the same progress were it not for his persistent bravery, and his faith in American democracy.

4. Bayard Rustin, "From Protest to Politics," *Commentary* (February 1965), p. 27.

5. House of Representatives, 89th Congress, 1st Session, "Message from the President of the United States Relative to the Right to Vote," March 15, 1965, p. 5.

The rural poor, the aged poor, and even the poor hillbillies in Appalachia and the Ozarks could not arouse the nation to their urgent needs. They continued to suffer indignities of body, mind, and spirit year after year in quiet desperation while they lived in hovels and their children were poorly educated. Action came only recently. It followed a prolonged period of marches, sit-ins, and other forms of protest by the Negro community. There is no reason to believe that the war on poverty and these protest activities are unrelated.

WHO ARE THE NONWHITE POOR?

The Council of Economic Advisers, in its study of poverty, used an income of $3,000 as the poverty line for a family of two or more persons and $1,500 for an individual living alone or with nonrelatives. The failure to take various factors such as size of family, age of family head, and farm residence into account was recognized as a serious shortcoming of the data at the time they were prepared; however, it was not then possible to make more refined estimates. As the data in Table 5.1 illustrate, it is now possible to do so, on the basis of the retabulation by the Department of Health, Education, and Welfare of the Census Bureau's statistics for 1963 using a flexible poverty line.

The basic procedure in preparing the revised estimates employed the use of an economy budget developed by the Department of Agriculture. This budget specifies in great detail the weekly quantities of foods needed by men, women, and children in various age groups in order to maintain nutritional adequacy. Using the quantities specified in the budget and food prices published by the Department of Agriculture, annual estimates were prepared for 124 different types of families classified by farm and nonfarm residence, age and sex of head, and number of children. These annual food costs were converted to incomes on the basis of assumed relationships between food expenditures and total income. Families of three or more persons were assumed to be in poverty if their income was less than 33 per cent of the cost of an economy food budget. In other words, the poverty line for these families was obtained by multiplying the cost of the food budget by a

TABLE 5.1. SELECTED CHARACTERISTICS OF NONWHITE FAMILIES
IN POVERTY STATUS IN 1963 BY ALTERNATIVE DEFINITIONS
(IN MILLIONS)

SELECTED CHARACTERISTICS	ALL FAMILIES	ECONOMY BUDGET[a]		INCOME UNDER $3,000[b]	
		Number	Per cent of total	Number	Per cent of total
Total	4.8	2.0	43	2.0	43
Residence					
Farm	0.4	0.2	62	0.2	79
Nonfarm	4.4	1.8	41	1.8	40
Region					
Northeast	0.9	0.2	27	0.2	26
North Central	0.9	0.3	30	0.3	32
South	2.4	1.4	58	1.4	59
West	0.6	0.1	21	0.1	19
Age of head					
14 to 24 years	0.4	0.2	60	0.2	63
25 to 64 years	3.9	1.5	39	1.4	37
65 years and over	0.5	0.3	53	0.4	73
Type of family					
Male head	3.7	1.3	34	1.3	34
Female head	1.1	0.7	71	0.7	73
Size of family					
2 persons	1.4	0.5	33	0.7	50
3–5 persons	2.2	0.8	38	0.8	39
6 or more persons	1.2	0.7	62	0.5	42
Employment status of head					
Not in labor force	1.1	0.8	65	0.8	72
Unemployed	0.2	0.1	53	0.1	43
Employed	3.5	1.1	35	1.1	34
Work experience of head in 1963					
Worked in 1963	4.0	1.5	37	1.4	36
Worked at full-time jobs	3.4	1.1	32	1.0	31
50–52 weeks	2.5	0.6	26	0.6	24
Worked at part-time jobs	0.6	0.4	68	0.4	70
Did not work	0.8	0.5	70	0.6	77

a. Economy level of the poverty index developed by the Social Security Administration by family size and farm vs. nonfarm residence, centering around $3,100 for a nonfarm family of four persons.

b. Interim measure used by Council of Economic Advisers—under $3,000 for families of two or more persons.

Source: Figures for all families and for number in "economy budget" column are taken from Mollie Orshansky, "Counting the Poor: Another Look at the Poverty Profile," *Social Security Bulletin,* January 1965, Table 8. Figures for number with incomes under $3,000 are based on unpublished data of the Bureau of the Census.

factor of three,[6] a reasonable relationship between income and
food expenditures based on data derived from the 1960 Survey of
Consumer Expenditures.[7] A ratio of 27 per cent was used for two-
person families; unrelated individuals were assumed to need 80
per cent of the requirement for a couple "on the premise that the
lower the income the more difficult it would be for one person to
cut expenses such as housing and utilities below the minimum for
a couple."[8] The estimates for farm families are based on the
assumption that they would need 40 per cent less cash income than
nonfarm families of the same size and type since many farmers
receive part of their food and most of their housing without cash
payment.

The dollar values used as the poverty line ranged from about
$1,100 for an elderly couple living on a farm to $5,100 for a nonfarm family with seven or more persons. A nonfarm family of four
persons was assumed to need $3,130, which allows about 70 cents
daily per person for an adequate diet, and an additional $1.40 per
person for all other needs—housing, clothing, medical care, transportation, etc. The poverty lines for other family types were designed to provide equivalent levels of living. Using these dollar
values, retabulations were made of the March 1964 Current Population Survey, in which the income reported for each family was
compared with the income "required" by that family. If the reported income was below the required amount for that family type,
the family was classified as poor. Families identified as poor on this
basis were then retabulated according to various characteristics.

There is little difference in the results produced by the two
different concepts of poverty—the flat $3,000 poverty line used
by the Council of Economic Advisers and the flexible poverty line
used by HEW. The overall number of nonwhite families classified
as poor is virtually identical and the distribution by various
characteristics is also much the same. The analysis will therefore
proceed in terms of the $3,000 criterion, since that will facilitate

6. Mollie Orshansky, "Counting the Poor: Another Look at the Poverty
Profile," *Social Security Bull.* (January 1965).

7. Helen Lamale, "Expenditure Patterns of Low-Consumption Families,"
1964 Proceedings of Business and Economic Statistics Section, American Statistical Assoc., p. 440.

8. Orshansky, op. cit.

the use of the voluminous 1960 Census data available on the subject.[9] Following are some of the highlights regarding nonwhite poverty suggested by these data.

Geographic distribution

Nonwhite poverty is a geographic problem to a much greater extent than is commonly realized. About one-half of all nonwhite families live in the South, where incomes in general, and for nonwhites in particular, lag far behind the rest of the nation. Nearly 60 per cent of the Southern nonwhite families are in poverty as compared with rates that are only half as high in the rest of the nation. Because nonwhite families are concentrated in the South, where they receive low incomes, about 70 per cent of all nonwhites in poverty are located in that region.

The Negro sharecropper, who once figured prominently in the ranks of the poor, has dwindled in absolute and relative numbers. At present, only about one-sixth of all Negro families in the South live on farms—about one-quarter of a million. Negro poverty today, even in the South, is much more concentrated in the cities and in rural hamlets than on the farms.

Negro poverty in the North and West is located almost entirely in the big urban centers like New York, Chicago, Philadelphia, and Detroit. Old age does not appear to be a major cause of Negro poverty. Much more important are family instability, unemployment, and low rates of pay.

According to any reasonable assumptions regarding rates of out-migration, over half of all Negroes will still be living in the South by 1980. The expected relatively high rates of out-migration are likely to be offset by the high fertility of those who remain. As a result, the geographic distribution of the Negro population does not shift as much as the figures on migration might suggest. In view of the intensity of feeling manifested by Southern whites on racial matters, it is hard to believe that Negroes in this region will receive to any great extent either the training they need or the opportunity to move into more promising jobs.

9. There are many different kinds of poverty—economic, cultural, spiritual, etc. Only economic poverty is considered here.

We are, however, living in an age of rapid change and must not dismiss the possibility of a vast upheaval that will change the whole political structure in the South. The possibility of this kind of transformation is far greater today than it was only six months ago. At the same time, the ingenuity of the Southern white in thwarting the political aspirations of the Negro should not be underestimated. Only time will tell how the position of the Southern Negro will change, but it would be well not to expect too much. The President has wisely cautioned that after the new voting bill is passed "the people of Selma . . . must still live and work together. And when the attention of the nation has gone elsewhere they must try to heal the wounds and to build a new community."[10] It is at this point that the real tests will come.

The family structure

The matriarchal structure of nonwhite family life is well known and its relation to poverty is obvious. There are proportionately more than twice as many broken families among nonwhites as among whites. The women who head these families, particularly among the nonwhites, start childrearing early, often under very difficult circumstances. They lack the training to get a good job, and they have the dual burden of being both mother and father to their children. Under these circumstances it is not surprising that families headed by women have a very high incidence of poverty and that a large proportion of the poor nonwhite families are of this type.

In the Northern states, only one-fifth of the nonwhite husband-wife families were in poverty as compared with three-fifths of the broken families. Because of the very difficult circumstances faced by families headed by women in the North, they constituted one-half of all poor nonwhite families in the region.

The generally lower incomes in the South, particularly for nonwhites, produced a higher incidence of poverty for married couples as well as for broken families. In the South, about half of the nonwhite married couples and about 80 per cent of the broken families were in poverty. These figures suggest that in the

10. "Message from the President of the United States Relative to the Right to Vote," op. cit., p. 6.

North a married nonwhite couple stands an excellent chance of having an income above the poverty line; nonwhite married couples in the South and broken families in all regions are much less likely to have an adequate income.

Employment status related to income

Although psychological factors are often stressed in discussions of nonwhite poverty, about one million families—half the total classified as poor—were headed by full-time workers. About 600,000 of these families were headed by a person who worked full-time throughout the year, and 400,000 were headed by full-time workers who experienced some unemployment. Nearly half of these workers were employed as laborers or as service workers (domestics, janitors, gas station attendants, porters, etc.); another large block worked as semiskilled factory workers. These facts suggest that low wages and unemployment account for much of the poverty for nonwhites, as they do for whites. Retraining might get some of these low-paid family heads into more lucrative types of employment. For the great majority, however, it is not at all clear how they will be brought above the poverty line without some form of wage or income subsidization.

Increases in the coverage and the amount of the minimum wage are often suggested as antipoverty tools for the low-paid worker. Although this technique has understandable appeal, there is by no means unanimity of opinion—even among liberal economists —that it will do the job. Sar Levitan, an eminent authority in this field, wrote recently that there is a "need for exercising caution in considering any further increases in minimum wages over the next few years, assuming the continuation of recent trends in overall productivity and consumer prices." He expresses some concern about the disemployment effects of an increase in the minimum wage at present and concludes that there is a question "whether the low paying jobs would exist at all if minimum rates were raised above levels justified by the productivity of the affected workers."[11]

11. Sar A. Levitan, *Programs in Aid of the Poor* (Kalamazoo: W. E. Upjohn Institute, 1965).

OCCUPATIONAL GAP BETWEEN THE RACES

One of the important reasons for Negro poverty and discontent today is the Negroes' failure to move into the better-paying jobs in any large numbers. While none can deny that the Negro worker has gained in employment during the past 50 years in an *absolute* sense, he has not moved ahead relative to the white worker. It is of some significance therefore to examine the patterns of occupational change in the past to see what must be done if the Negro worker is to bridge the occupational gap.

Census data show that by 1910 the white labor force had already completed much of the transition from agriculture to industry. In the decennial census taken that year, only one-fourth of white workers were employed in farming; another one-fourth worked in white-collar jobs; and the remaining half were more or less equally divided among craftsmen, factory operatives, and non-farm laborers or service workers (see Table 5.2). In that same year, the Negro labor force was split 50–50 between farming and nonfarm work. The farmers were, of course, largely Southern sharecroppers or laborers working and living under the most miserable conditions, even by contemporary standards. Those who were not working as farmers were employed largely as service workers (i.e. domestics, waiters, bootblacks) and as nonfarm laborers largely on railroads and construction gangs. Relatively few (only 5 per cent) had even risen to the point of semiskilled factory work, and even fewer (only 3 per cent) worked as craftsmen or white-collar workers.[12]

The next fifty years witnessed a dramatic movement out of agriculture for both whites and Negroes. The proportion of white workers dropped from 28 per cent at the turn of the century to only about 7 per cent at present. In the case of the nonwhites the shift away from farming was even more dramatic. The 50 per cent estimate for 1910 dropped to only 10 per cent. The frequent cry of some economists for greater mobility as a solution to rural poverty has certainly been heeded by the Negro. He has shown tremendous mobility and energy in search of economic oppor-

12. Dale Hiestand, *Economic Growth and Employment Opportunities for Minorities* (New York: Columbia University Press, 1964), p. 42.

TABLE 5.2. PERCENTAGE DISTRIBUTION OF WHITE AND NEGRO LABOR FORCE, BY OCCUPATIONAL FIELD, 1910–60

	1910 WHITE	1910 NEGRO	1920 WHITE	1920 NEGRO	1930 WHITE	1930 NEGRO	1940 WHITE	1940 NEGRO	1950 WHITE	1950 NEGRO	1960 WHITE	1960 NEGRO
All sectors	100.0	100.0	100.0	100.0	100.0	100.0	100.0[a]	100.0[a]	100.0[a]	100.0[a]	100.0	100.0
Nonfarm	72.0	49.6	76.0	53.4	80.6	63.9	82.3	66.6	81.6	79.5	92.7	88.7
White-collar sector	23.8	3.0	27.8	3.6	33.0	4.6	35.7	6.0	39.9	10.2	46.5	15.4
Professional and technical workers	4.8	1.4	5.3	1.5	6.5	2.1	8.0	2.7	8.6	3.4	12.2	4.7
Proprietors, managers, and officials	7.4	.8	7.4	.8	8.3	1.0	9.0	1.3	9.8	2.0	11.5	2.3
Clerical and sales workers	11.6	.8	15.1	1.3	18.2	1.5	18.7	2.0	21.5	4.8	22.8	8.4
Manual and service sector	48.2	46.6	48.2	49.8	47.6	59.3	46.6	60.6	47.7	69.3	46.2	73.3
Skilled workers and foremen	13.0	2.5	14.5	3.0	14.2	3.2	12.2	3.0	14.4	5.5	13.8	5.7
Semiskilled workers and operatives	16.1	5.4	16.8	7.3	17.2	9.4	19.0	10.3	20.3	18.3	17.8	20.7
Laborers	14.3	17.4	13.4	20.8	11.7	21.6	6.1	14.3	5.0	15.7	4.4	14.1
Service workers	4.8	21.3	3.5	18.7	4.5	25.1	9.3	33.0	8.0	29.8	10.2	32.8
Farm	28.0	50.4	24.1	46.6	19.4	36.1	16.7	32.8	11.1	19.0	7.3	11.3

a. Sum of items does not equal 100 per cent because some failed to report an occupation.

Source: Dale L. Hiestand, *Economic Growth and Employment Opportunities for Minorities* (New York: Columbia University Press, 1964), p. 42.

tunity, often against overwhelming odds. The displacement of
Negroes from farming has largely been absorbed by the manual
and service trades, although in recent years, opportunities for
nonwhites in white-collar employment have been growing in importance.

A close examination of the decennial census data provides
better insight than we have had before into the way the transformation of the Negro labor force took place. In each decade,
as new industries and occupations developed, it was the white
worker who moved in first. According to one analysis, "White
workers capture the newly growing fields in which labor resources
are scarce, pay levels are good, prospects for advancement are
bright, the technology is most advanced, and working conditions
the most modern."[13] They leave in their wake jobs in the older
industries that are less desirable because the pay is not as good,
nor are the prospects for advancement. Moreover, many of the
jobs left behind by the whites are in industries dominated by an
old technology, which, when replaced, would be likely to require
reduced manpower.

Thus, in every decade, the newest and best opportunities available to the Negroes were often quite vulnerable. The jobs deserted
by the whites were invariably better than the ones at which
Negroes were employed at the time, but they were, nonetheless,
not the jobs with the bright futures. This pattern of occupational
change is, as we shall see, of great significance in assessing the
prospects of the Negro. It suggests that if the Negro is ever to
approach occupational equality with whites he must seek out and
somehow gain admittance to the "frontier area of occupational
expansion." If he continues to get only jobs that the white has
left over, he may never bridge the occupational gap. Indeed some
would argue that if the Negro follows the traditional pattern of
occupational mobility, he may find himself in a tighter and tighter
job squeeze because the employment that would have normally
been handed down to him is being automated.

It must be granted on the basis of the empirical evidence that
the absolute employment position of the Negro worker has improved considerably in the past fifty years. But, has the relative

13. Ibid., p. 114.

gap between whites and Negroes changed? In the work previously referred to, Hiestand constructed an occupational index that permits this type of comparison to be made.[14] He first separated the white and Negro workers for each year into seven occupational groups: professional, managerial, clerical and sales, skilled, semi-skilled, unskilled, and agriculture. A weight was then assigned to each occupation roughly indicative of the relative earning power for that kind of work. The actual weights used were the median incomes reported in the 1950 Census for workers who were employed throughout the year. A weighted index for each year was then constructed by multiplying the proportion of workers in each occupation by the weight and summing the results for all seven occupation groups. This operation was performed separately for white and Negro men and women. The ratio of the Negro to the white index computed for each year shows the relative occupational position of Negroes to whites.

In the case of men, the index shows no significant change between 1910 and 1940. There was some slight improvement in the relative occupational position of Negro men during the past twenty years; but this is entirely due to their movement out of the South. Indexes which have been constructed on a state-by-state basis show that there were very few significant changes in the occupational distribution of Negro males relative to whites in the past twenty years.[15]

The relative occupational distribution of Negro women relative to whites also was about the same in 1940 as it was in 1910. As in the case of the males, there appears to have been some improvement in the relative occupational position of Negro women during the past twenty years, but this change also may be primarily due to their movement out of the South with its very limited opportunities for Negro employment, rather than to any general upgrading of the kinds of jobs open to Negroes.

The weight of the evidence therefore indicates that although there has been considerable occupational improvement for Negro workers during the past fifty years in an absolute sense, the posi-

14. Ibid., p. 51.
15. U.S. Senate, *Hearings before the Committee on Labor and Public Welfare on Bills Relating to Equal Employment Opportunities* (Washington, D.C.: Government Printing Office, 1963), p. 323.

tion of Negroes relative to whites has not changed much. Having established these facts, we may now turn to an examination of their meaning, particularly with respect to assessing their significance for future trends in Negro employment (and income). Here we must tread with care because, as so many forecasters have discovered to their regret, past is not necessarily prologue.

FUTURE POSSIBILITIES

It seems clear from the data that the gap between whites and nonwhites will not be narrowed if the traditional patterns of occupational change are maintained. In order to catch up with the whites, Negro workers will have to be propelled into promising new jobs in new industries instead of drifting into the old jobs in the dying industries, as in the past. This change will come about for Negroes only if two conditions are met. They must obtain the education and training required for the new jobs, and the barriers to their entry into the better-paying fields must be lowered. The prospects that both of these conditions will be met in the near future are not very good. It is unrealistic to talk about bridging the occupational gap in the modern world when one-fourth of the Negro youth in their early twenties have not gone beyond the eighth grade and over half have not completed high school. There is not much that people with so little education can be trained to do in our complex economy.

Moreover, there is little evidence that society is willing to make the huge investments in education and training that are required if the Negro is ever to be able to compete on equal terms with the white in the labor market. Most attempts to provide effective school integration have met with hostility and "foot-dragging." Even in the prosperous North there has been more lip service than action in the improvement of the quality of education in deprived areas. Now at last we are beginning to talk seriously about pouring billions of additional dollars into education in low-income areas. It remains to be seen, however, if the money will in fact be appropriated and if it will result in better education.

Finally, we come to just plain discrimination, which may be the hardest of all obstacles to overcome because it is so deeply imbedded in our culture. As previously noted, about 60 per cent of the Negroes still live in the South and, according to any reasonable assumptions regarding rates of out-migration, over half of them will still be in that region by 1980. In view of the intensity of feeling that has been manifested by the Southern whites on racial matters, it is hard to believe that in the foreseeable future Negroes in this region will receive to any great extent either the training they need or the opportunity to move into the more promising jobs.

In the face of these and many other factors, there is little reason to be optimistic about the possibility of narrowing the occupational gap between the races in the near future. There are, however, offsetting forces that provide some hope. At present, there is probably less discrimination against Negroes than at any previous time in our history. It is also likely that discrimination will tend to decrease with time because of the strong pressures being exerted by the federal government. These efforts should create new opportunities for Negro employment in federal, state, and local governments, in private companies doing contract work for the federal government, and in other companies that will be under social pressure to liberalize their employment practices.

At the same time that the prospects for Negroes to obtain skilled employment have been increasing, the attitudes of some Negro leaders have been undergoing a change. Historically, the civil rights movement has focused attention largely on efforts designed to publicize the plight of the Negro and to promote integration. This emphasis led to the March on Washington, demonstrations, sit-ins, picketing, and other activities that were instrumental in promoting passage of the civil rights and antipoverty legislation. More recently it was the drive for voting rights in Selma, Alabama, that captured the headlines and the public imagination. In the background, however, there are signs that attention in some quarters is now shifting to other areas such as the fight for better jobs, education, and housing, with only secondary emphasis on questions like integration. This attitude was clearly expressed by Bayard Rustin when he said recently, "We have got to lift the school problem from integration to that of quality schools; which has to include, we say, integration secondarily."[16]

16. "The Negro Revolution—Where Shall It Go Now?," *Dissent* (Summer 1964), p. 282.

This is not to say that the fight for rights and political power is being abandoned. On the contrary, recent events suggest that they are being intensified, if anything. At the same time, however, there seems to be a growing recognition of the need to develop the skills and other qualities that are needed by Negro workers in order to take full advantage of the job opportunities that may arise. As Nathan Glazer has pointed out very effectively in a recent article, the legislative gains that have been made by Negroes in the past few years make it possible and perhaps even necessary for contemporary leaders of the civil rights movement to return to the fundamental policies outlined by Booker T. Washington at the turn of the century. According to Glazer,[17] Booker T. Washington

> saw that the Negro had been denuded by slavery of the qualities necessary for building an independent and satisfying life. Primarily what concerned him . . . was the devaluation of work produced by slavery, for he felt that independent and productive work was the basis of racial respect. But Washington also assumed that the Negroes, as they gained in education and income, would be enfranchised and would be able to play a major role in politics and in the shaping of their own fate. He fought desperately against the movement to disenfranchise Negroes in the South in the 1890's. When this movement succeeded, and Jim Crow began to fasten its bonds on the Negro people, he was left with half a program. The other half became the program of protest.

Glazer then goes on to state that "we now have a situation which corresponds . . . to the one Booker T. Washington first saw as his major task, the building up of the economic and social foundations of the Negro community."

So long as the Negro could see no reasonable prospect for advancement beyond the most menial jobs, he was behaving more or less rationally in assigning a low value to education, saving, and the other fruitful avenues to advancement. Limited opportunities for employment in the professional fields forced Negroes to concentrate on those areas where there was a Negro market for their services—preaching, teaching, and social work. Because of

17. Book review by Nathan Glazer in *Commentary* (October 1964), pp. 77–79.

their concentration in these low-paid fields the average Negro college graduate, even today, can expect to earn less over a lifetime than the white who does not go beyond the eighth grade. In view of facts such as these, who could argue with the young school dropout who might feel what James Baldwin has expressed so well in the following words: "It is not to be wondered at that if . . . studying is going to prepare him to be a porter or an elevator boy —or his teacher—well, then, to hell with it."

But we now have a chance to change all of this. Whether in fact we will depends upon two things: the extent to which our society opens up and takes the Negro in as a full-fledged participating member; and the extent to which the Negro is prepared to move in should the opportunities present themselves. Only time will tell whether we can succeed in getting both of these forces to move in the right direction at the right time.

A POSSIBLE SOLUTION

The preceding discussion suggests that there are important similarities and differences in the causes of poverty for Negroes and other groups. Unemployment and low wages account for much of the poverty for Negroes just as they do for whites. On the other hand, Negro poverty is more closely linked to regional factors, family structure, and discrimination than it is for most other groups. Although the attack on Negro poverty might take the form of special efforts geared specifically to Negro problems, it may be more fruitful to consider more general solutions. We shall now consider one such solution to the problem of poverty, as that term is now defined, and some of the complications of this kind of a solution for society as a whole and for the Negro in particular. In all that follows it is assumed that current efforts to improve the services to the poor in education, housing, medical care, and other significant aspects of life will be continued. Attention is focused here only on income maintenance.

It can be demonstrated that if reasonable rates of economic growth are maintained for another decade, the poverty gap— that is, the amount needed to bring all families above the poverty line as it is now defined—will be so small that it will be foolish not "to take arms against [this small] sea of troubles, and by opposing, end them." The combined increase in national income and reduction in the number of poor families will obviate the need to fight the battle as an island-hopping expedition in which the enemy is destroyed a little bit at a time, at the rate of about one per cent per year. Rather, a point will be reached—and it will come before 1975—when it will be possible by means of a negative income tax and a public works program to abolish economic poverty. We will be able to afford to guarantee each family an income equivalent to $3,000 in 1962 purchasing power. Some families will get more if they are larger than average and others will get less if they have fewer mouths to feed; but all will get what we now consider to be enough to maintain a minimum standard of living.

The program might work something like this. Each family would have to file an income tax return. Those with incomes under $3,000 (the amount would vary by size of family) would be given the option of going to work on a public works project or participating in a training program, for which they would receive payment at the rate of $3,000 per year. Exceptions would be made for the aged, disabled, and several other groups that would re-reive payment without working or training. On this basis, it can be assumed that a very large proportion of the chronically poor might elect to be entirely supported by the government; but relatively few families above the poverty line would make this choice, since they would be sacrificing income, but would have to continue to work or go to school.

Under these assumptions it can be estimated that if such a program had been in existence in 1963 it would have involved the transfer of about $21 billion—about 3 per cent of the gross national product—from the wealthiest 80 per cent of the families to the poorest 20 per cent. The numbers are derived as follows: In 1963, about 9 million families (19 per cent of the total) had incomes under $3,000. If these families had received their entire support from the government, the cost would have been about $27 billion; however, they received about $6 billion in that year, in the form of transfer payments. The net additional cost, there-fore, would have been about $21 billion. There are, of course, other costs and benefits that enter into the equation, but let us postpone consideration of those items for the moment.

The application of the same proposal in 1975 would cost only about $13 billion (in 1962 purchasing power), or about one per cent of the gross national product. This calculation is based on an assumed rate of growth of 4 per cent per year in average family income. On this basis, only 5.7 million families would have incomes under $3,000 (in 1962 purchasing power) in 1975. If they derived all their income from the government, the cost would be about $17 billion. This total, however, would include about $4 billion paid out under existing programs. The net additional cost, therefore, would be about $13 billion or roughly one per cent of the GNP in that year.

The costs and benefits that have been excluded in the above calculations do not change the picture materially. The major costs incurred would be the administrative costs of the program and the reduction in output caused by the withdrawal of several million workers from the labor force, roughly calculated at about $5 billion. One can only guess at the administrative costs. If it is assumed that 10 per cent of the outlays under this program would go to administration, this element of cost can be roughly figured to be about $2 billion. Therefore, the cost of the program—over and above the transfer payments previously described—would be about $7 billion.

The major benefits from the program would include the value of the public works projects; the present value of increases in personal productivity resulting from increased education and training; and the reduction in crime, delinquency, and other forms of antisocial behavior. Each of these items is extremely difficult to value in monetary terms, but there is every reason to believe that they might easily offset the $7 billion cost described above. For example, if the output of public works projects is valued at only half the amount paid for them by the government, the benefits from this work alone would be about $4 billion.

Many have dreamed about ultimate victory in the fight against poverty. Around the turn of the century, David Lloyd George requested funds from the British Parliament to wage "warfare against poverty." His confidence in the outcome is reflected in his belief that within his own lifetime he would see "a great step towards that good time when poverty . . . will be as remote to the people of this country as the wolves which once infested its forests." In 1928, Herbert Hoover also saw victory in sight against this most ancient of man's enemies. He stated in an address, "We shall soon with the help of God be in sight of the day when poverty will be banished in this nation." Despite the predictions of such able and farsighted men as Lloyd George, Herbert Hoover, and many others, poverty still remains. It is a different kind of poverty from the one they had in mind; but even by the standards of 1900, poverty remains a problem in America. Now, once again, there is talk about ultimate victory—this time within a decade. Can this be just a pipe dream after all? In what way are the present prospects for success better than those of the past? At least three major differences can be detected:

1. At the turn of the century most people were poor even by the low contemporary standards; by today's standards all but a very small part of that population would be considered poverty-stricken. Conditions had improved by the prosperous 1920s; but even then over half the families had incomes below the poverty line as it is defined today. With victory so far away, it is difficult to see how anyone then could have been very confident about the outcome.

2. Productivity has been growing rapidly in recent years. There is good reason to believe that this trend will continue and that it will provide us with far higher incomes than we have had in the past. Part of the increase will undoubtedly be devoted to the eradication of poverty. The prospects for growth are far, far greater than the average citizen realizes. Here is how the matter has been summed up by the Council of Economic Advisers:

> If average productivity gains until the year 2000 no more than match those of the last seventeen years, output per man-hour will be three times as great as today. If working hours and labor force participation rates were to remain unchanged, average family income would approximate $18,000 in today's prices.

With this kind of leverage, the allocation of a small additional fraction of our income to the eradication of poverty becomes a real possibility. The Harvard economist John K. Galbraith stated the case very well for more government spending to combat poverty and other social ills when he asked a congressional committee recently what advantage there is "in having a few more dollars to spend if the air is too dirty to breathe, the water too polluted to drink, the commuters are losing the struggle to get in and out of our cities, the streets are filthy and the schools so bad that the young, perhaps wisely, stay away, and hoodlums roll citizens for some of the dollars they saved in taxes."

3. We appear to have mastered that old bugaboo of capitalism —cataclysmic depressions. It is now over a quarter of a century since there has been a major depression in the United States and, judging from the frenzied activity displayed by the government at every minor turn in the business cycle, we have reason to hope that great depressions, like bubonic plagues, are things of the past. This freedom from fear of want for society as a whole has permitted us to devote our creative energies to the elimination of want for the poorest segments of society. Hopefully, this kind of focus will continue in the future.

If the above calculations are correct, the great day may be approaching when it will be possible for all Americans to have their basic physical needs met at currently acceptable standards without taking a pauper's oath and without losing dignity and self-respect. Even if allowance is made for moderate increases in the poverty line, its ultimate defeat is only a matter of time—ten years or twenty at the most. For one who helped plan the first study of income distribution ever made by the Census Bureau only twenty years ago, even a generation does not seem like a fearfully long time.

Once economic poverty is defeated, it will be interesting to see what new intolerable evils will arise to take its place. It is impossible to foresee all the problems that would arise if "full-belly" security were provided for all, but there is one major question that occurs immediately: What would happen to people if their material well-being were systematically provided for? Experience dictates that *some* aid to distressed persons is essential and that it does more good than harm. It is possible, however, that *too much* aid does more harm than good. But do the guarantees specified here provide too much? There is, of course, no answer to this question nor are we likely to find one. It is, however, basic and well worth thinking about. Before we embark on any such plan it would be essential to ascertain, if we can, whether economic security, when provided entirely by someone else, produces other frustrations. Does it raise the probability of bringing about the "good ant society" rather than the development of the individual society? Perhaps there are serious costs that have escaped our calculus.

Although poverty, as now defined, might be eliminated by the plan described—or some variant of it—there would still be a distribution of families by income levels and some families will have to be at the bottom of that distribution. Who will they be? This is a most important question, since it has been amply demonstrated that the *relative* aspects of income distribution are perhaps as important as *absolute* income levels. The great majority of mankind alive today might look with envy at the level of living enjoyed by the American Negro, even in the South, but this provides little comfort to the Negro when he compares his own position with that of the whites around him.

It was assumed at the outset that the services provided to the poor would continue to improve, thereby facilitating the opportunities for the children of the bottom economic strata to move up to higher levels. Is the provision of such services, however, a sufficient guarantee that within the foreseeable future—say twenty years—the forces tending to stratify society along economic lines would in fact be overcome? I think not, for the reasons previously cited. There is bound to be a gap between the provision of services and their efficient utilization. Attitudes toward the postponement of gratification of immediate wants, investment of time and effort in education, and other necessary attributes for upward mobility are colored by historical and cultural backgrounds. In the case of the Negro the attitudes are not highly developed at present and it may take some time, even under the best of conditions, for them to change. Moreover, the life style of Negro families will also impede upward mobility. Negro family life might become more stable in the future; but it will take more than a higher income floor to produce this change. The high concentration of Negroes in the South will also keep them in the bottom income groups, unless this region is brought up to the national average.

Finally, and perhaps most important of all, there is the uncertainty of our ability to alter the forces of bigotry and intolerance that are deeply rooted in our culture. For all these reasons it seems likely that the Negro will continue to dominate the bottom income groups. Even though their basic needs will be met at fairly high standards and they will technically be above the poverty line, they are likely to remain a large dissident element within our population for a long time to come.

6: Poverty in Appalachia

by Donald A. Crane and Benjamin Chinitz

It is particularly fitting that a study of poverty in America should include a chapter focusing specifically on the Appalachian region. The region has long been identified with conditions of arrested economic development and the whole complex of depressed-area characteristics, and concern about its ills has recently been brought to a head in terms of federal legislation (the Appalachian Regional Development Act of 1965).

Two aspects of the question of Appalachian poverty will be considered here. One is a quantitative appraisal, based on selected indices of regional income, employment, economic structure, and related characteristics. The aim will be to assess to what extent and in what ways Appalachia should be viewed as an area of economic distress. Consideration of the various manifestations of relative regional poverty will lead us to an examination of the rationale for the principal kinds of therapy contemplated under present policies and legislation. We will not, however, attempt to go into the specifics of particular projects, programs, or parts of the Appalachian Region.

THE REGION

First of all, what is the area, this "Appalachia" that we are talking about? All of us have at least a general notion of it as a five or six hundred-mile stretch of territory encompassing the mountain country from Pennsylvania to northern Georgia and

Alabama. We are aware that this is an area of very early settlement, peopled largely by white Anglo-Saxons who have retained many of their old folkways; that, apart from its few manufacturing centers, its economic life has been based heavily on coal mining, forestry, and subsistence farming; that these activities have for some decades provided increasingly inadequate opportunities for earning decent livelihoods; that most of the region is rather static and isolated from the mainstream of economic development; that large numbers of people have migrated out of Appalachia to seek a better living elsewhere; and that the prevailing levels of income, education, and community facilities are substandard.

Setting precise boundaries to such an area, which covers parts of as many as ten different states, is of course to some extent arbitrary. The boundaries of Appalachia are with good reason not precisely or permanently laid out even in the Appalachian Redevelopment Act of 1965, which comes closest to giving the region official status as a unit.

It is worthwhile to look briefly at a few landmarks in the rather long history of attempts to delineate an Appalachian Region for purposes of analysis or policy recommendation. For example, a study by John C. Campbell for the Russell Sage Foundation, published in 1921,[1] defined the area primarily on the basis of physiographic criteria, except that the northern boundary was arbitrarily set at the Mason-Dixon Line. Campbell's Appalachian Region included Birmingham on the south, northern Georgia, a corner of South Carolina including Spartanburg, all of east Tennessee and Kentucky, the entire state of West Virginia, as far east as Lynchburg in Virginia, and the four western counties of Maryland.

A study of the southern Appalachians completed by the U.S. Department of Agriculture in 1935 focused on a somewhat smaller area, comprising the mountain portions of the six states of Virginia, West Virginia, Kentucky, North Carolina, Tennessee, and Georgia.[2]

1. John C. Campbell, *The Southern Highlander and His Homestead* (New York: Russell Sage Foundation, 1921).
2. U.S. Department of Agriculture, *Economic and Social Problems of the Southern Appalachians,* Miscellaneous Publication No. 205 (Washington, D.C.: Government Printing Office, 1935).

A study of the "Southern Appalachian Coal Plateaus" as a problem area, made in 1935 by Frederick Tryon and Bushrod Allen,
defined the region in terms of its mineral resources base.[3] This
included the area west of the Allegheny front, and excluded
Georgia, North Carolina, and most of Virginia, leaving an area
about half the size of that used by the Department of Agriculture
study.

A much more recent brief economic survey, published in 1960,
covered portions of eleven states, from New York to Alabama. The
area was delineated purposely to include the broad outline of the
Appalachian mountain belt, the major coal-mining areas, and the
region of "hard core" unemployment and low incomes, and to
exclude major peripheral metropolitan areas.[4]

The Appalachian Region reported upon by the President's Appalachian Regional Commission in 1964 was designated by the
Conference of Appalachian Governors. Each governor was responsible for specifying what contiguous counties in his own state were
to be included. This procedure resulted in a somewhat larger Appalachia than the earlier versions and seems to have taken into account a variety of previously used criteria such as physiography,
resources base, and economic and social characteristics of the population.[5] The Commission's region includes a major share of the
counties in this section of the United States that were designated
as eligible for ARA aid. Statistics cited here for "Appalachia"
refer, except as otherwise noted, to the region as demarcated late
in 1963 by the Conference and the Commission.

It should not be assumed that the precise boundaries of this
region have been frozen or should be. During the legislative
activities attending the passage of the 1965 Act, the boundaries
underwent a number of minor changes. There may be further

3. Carter Goodrich et al., *Migration and Economic Opportunity* (Philadelphia: University of Pennsylvania Press, 1936), ch. 11, "Southern Appalachian
Coal Plateaus."

4. *Maryland Department of Economic Development: The Appalachian
Region, Annapolis, May 1960* (Reprinted by Conference of Appalachian Governors, Atlanta, Ga., April 1961), p. 3.

5. *Appalachia: A Report by the President's Appalachian Regional Commission, 1964* (Washington, D.C.: Government Printing Office, 1964), Appendix
A, pp. 66–69.

changes as the programs develop. In fact, the Appalachian Regional Development Act specifically opens the door to the possible
addition of certain counties in New York.

INDICES OF POVERTY

Income levels and distribution

Poverty in Appalachia means, first of all, low prevailing levels
of income by American standards (Table 6.1 summarizes this comparison). According to the 1960 Census, the average per capita
income in Appalachia was about 25 per cent below that in the rest
of the country. This gap reflects in part the fact that Appalachia
has a smaller fraction of its population living in metropolitan
areas. Characteristically, metropolitan income levels are much
higher than nonmetropolitan: 41 per cent higher in Appalachia,
and 36 per cent higher in the rest of the country.

TABLE 6.1. METROPOLITAN AND NONMETROPOLITAN PER CAPITA
INCOME IN APPALACHIA, APPALACHIAN STATES,
AND REMAINDER OF UNITED STATES, 1959

	TOTAL	IN METROPOLITAN AREAS	OUTSIDE METROPOLITAN AREAS
Appalachia	$1,423	$1,724	$1,219
Portions of ten Appalachian states outside Appalachia	1,731	1,993	1,245
United States outside Appalachia	1,889	2,130	1,565

Source: Center for Regional Economic Studies, University of Pittsburgh, *The
Appalachian Region Data Book* (July 1964). Calculated from data of *U.S. Census
of Population, 1960*.

But this less metropolitan character of the region's population
explains statistically only about a fifth of the 25 per cent difference
in average income levels between region and nation. In other
words, if Appalachia had the same metropolitan and the same
nonmetropolitan per capita incomes as the rest of the country,

the overall Appalachian per capita income would still be about 20 per cent below the average for the rest of the country. Dwellers in metropolitan areas in Appalachia receive only 81 per cent as much per head as their metropolitan counterparts elsewhere in the country, and the nonmetropolitan population of Appalachia has an average income only 78 per cent as high as the nonmetropolitan population of the rest of the United States.

If we look at the income levels of those parts of the Appalachian states that lie outside of the region proper, we find, not surprisingly, an average intermediate between that of the region and the rest of the country. These non-Appalachian portions of the states are 8.4 per cent below the income average of the rest of the country, and 22 per cent above the average for the region. Considering metropolitan populations only, these remainders of the states are quite close to the national average income. By contrast, the nonmetropolitan income average for the non-Appalachian parts of these states is quite close to the nonmetropolitan income average in Appalachia itself.

Although average income per capita is a handy measure of poverty, public concern is more specifically directed to the bottom layer of incomes. The incidence of poverty by areas can be measured in terms of what fraction of the people have incomes below some specified standard. On this basis too, Appalachia's relative poverty is apparent. As Table 6.2 shows, 30.7 per cent of the region's families in 1959 had less than $3,000 annual income, compared with 20.5 per cent in the rest of the United States. Moreover, the Appalachian portion of each state (except for Pennsylvania) had considerably more than 20.5 per cent of its families in the below-$3,000 bracket. The percentages ranged from 19.5 in Pennsylvania and 24.3 in Maryland to 57.3 in Kentucky.

Here again, differences between metropolitan and nonmetropolitan areas account for a significant though not a major part of the difference between Appalachia and the rest of the country. Thus the proportion of metropolitan families with incomes below $3,000 is 20.9 per cent in Appalachia compared with 15.1 per cent in the rest of the United States, and the proportion of nonmetropolitan families in that income bracket is 37.5 per cent in Appalachia compared with 27.8 per cent in the rest of the country. This relationship between incidence of poverty and nonmetropolitan status also helps of course to explain why the proportion of very low-income families is so much higher in the more rural parts of Appalachia, such as eastern Kentucky, than it is in the more urbanized parts of the region, such as western Pennsylvania.

If we look at the non-Appalachian parts of the Appalachian states as a group, we find the same relationship here as we did with per capita income levels. The metropolitan areas of those non-Appalachian portions of states are close to the national metropolitan norm in terms of proportion of families in the below-$3,000 bracket. But the nonmetropolitan areas closely match the nonmetropolitan areas of Appalachia proper in their proportions of below-$3,000 families.

Appalachia's relative poverty and the long-standing character of that condition are reflected in the cash resources of its residents. In 1960 the average resident of Appalachia owned a total of $514 in deposits in savings accounts at banks and at savings and loan associations—only about 58 per cent of the average for the rest of the United States. Every state in Appalachia was below the average for the rest of the country in time deposits per capita.

TABLE 6.2. PERCENTAGE OF FAMILIES WITH INCOME BELOW $3,000
AND WITH INCOME $10,000 OR OVER IN 1959,
APPALACHIA AND OTHER AREAS

	PERCENTAGE WITH INCOME BELOW $3,000			PERCENTAGE WITH INCOME $10,000 OR OVER		
	Total area	*Metropolitan*	*Non-metropolitan*	*Total area*	*Metropolitan*	*Non-metropolitan*
Appalachia	30.7	20.9	37.5	8.7	12.4	6.1
Portions of ten Appalachian states outside Appalachia	23.3	16.0	37.5	14.0	17.6	7.0
United States outside Appalachia	20.5	15.1	27.8	15.6	19.3	10.8

Source: Center for Regional Economic Studies, University of Pittsburgh, *The Appalachian Region Data Book* (July 1964). Calculated from data of *U.S. Census of Population, 1960*.

Quality of housing

No measure of poverty in monetary terms is fully satisfactory, since needs and purchasing power of money vary between areas. This is particularly true in the comparison of metropolitan with rural real incomes and levels of living. Consequently, it behooves us to examine some other indicators of welfare in Appalachia compared with the rest of the country.

One of these is housing. The 1960 Census classified all dwelling units according to age, presence or absence of plumbing and other facilities, and degree of deterioration or dilapidation. In the United States outside Appalachia in 1960, 75.2 per cent of all dwelling units were reported to be in sound condition and equipped with all major plumbing facilities (hot and cold running water inside of structure, and a flush toilet and bathtub, or shower, inside of structure for exclusive use of the occupants). In Appalachia, only 60.8 per cent of the housing met this standard.

Here again, only part of the regional difference reflects Appalachia's more rural character. The percentage of sound and adequately plumbed housing in metropolitan areas is 72.7 per cent in Appalachia, compared with 81.6 per cent in the rest of the country. Outside metropolitan areas, the percentage was only 52.6 in Appalachia, compared with 66.0 in the rest of the United States.

In Table 6.3, we have a somewhat more detailed comparison of housing condition by areas. The figures shown are not directly comparable with those cited above, for two reasons. First, they refer to a somewhat smaller Appalachian region, which omits all the Ohio counties and a number of counties in other Appalachian states. Second, the figures classify housing according to structural condition only, with no reference to presence or absence of plumbing facilities.

Whichever set of standards we use, however, the familiar pattern emerges. In rural areas, the housing is in worse condition than in urban or metropolitan areas, and Appalachia shows up unfavorably compared to the rest of the country regardless of whether the comparison is overall or between urban areas in Appalachia and elsewhere, or rural farm areas, or rural nonfarm

TABLE 6.3. PERCENTAGE DISTRIBUTION OF HOUSING UNITS
BY CONDITION, 1960

	SOUND	DETERIORATING	DILAPIDATED
Appalachia	73.4	19.1	7.5
Urban	80.8	14.4	4.8
Rural	62.1	28.6	9.4
Rural nonfarm	66.6	22.9	10.5
Portions of Appalachian states			
outside of Appalachia	77.5	15.5	7.0
Urban	83.6	12.0	4.4
Rural farm	60.5	27.6	11.9
Rural nonfarm	68.0	20.2	11.8
United States, outside Appalachia	88.2	15.0	5.4
Urban	85.7	11.0	3.3
Rural farm	70.5	22.3	7.1
Rural nonfarm	72.6	18.6	8.6

Source: Anthony L. Pavlick and Robert L. Coltrane, *Quality of Rural and Urban Housing in the Appalachian Region,* Agricultural Economics Report No. 52, Economic Research Service, U.S.D.A., April 1964.

areas. It is also worth noting that in respect of these measures also, the non-Appalachian portion of the Appalachian states shows up less favorably than the rest of the United States, but better than the Appalachian portions.

Public assistance outlays

The lower levels of income and welfare in Appalachia are reflected also in public assistance costs. For Appalachia as a whole, these approximate half a billion dollars a year.[6] Per capita assistance expenditures in the region (as of June 1963) were running only slightly higher than in the balance of the United States. They were, however, substantially higher than in the non-Appalachian portions of the Appalachian states. As Table 6.4 shows, the extent of participation in each type of public assistance

6. Estimated on the basis of rates of expenditure in June 1963. The estimate is exclusive of programs that operated on a trust fund basis, such as the social security program.

program is greater for Appalachia than for the remainder of the United States—and for most programs, Appalachian participation exceeds by an even wider margin the participation ratios in the non-Appalachian portions of the Appalachian states.

TABLE 6.4. PARTICIPATION IN PUBLIC ASSISTANCE PAYMENTS, JUNE 1963

	APPALACHIA	PORTIONS OF TEN APPALACHIAN STATES OUTSIDE APPALACHIA	UNITED STATES OUTSIDE APPALACHIA
All public assistance			
Per capita expenditures	$2.19	$1.44	$2.12
Percentage of population receiving aid	5.92	3.18	4.08
Aid to Families with Dependent Children			
Percentage of families	3.40	1.77	2.01
Percentage of children	7.01	3.75	4.36
Old Age Assistance			
Percentage of persons 65 and older	14.21	11.35	13.50
Medical Aid to Aged			
Percentage of persons 65 and older	1.14	.44	0.81
Aid to Permanently and Totally Disabled			
Percentage of population	0.34	0.26	0.25
Aid to Blind			
Percentage of population	0.12	0.06	0.05
General Assistance			
Percentage of families	0.84[a]	0.63[a]	1.80

a. Kentucky data not included.

Source: *Appalachia: A Report by the President's Appalachian Regional Commission, 1964* (Washington, D.C.: Government Printing Office, 1964), Appendix C, Table C–20, p. 84.

It seems clear that the rate of public assistance outlays in Appalachia is limited by the extent to which the Appalachian states can and do supply matching and supporting funds for such programs. These states as a group are poorer and more burdened with unemployment and assistance needs than the rest of the country.

At the present time, not one of the Appalachian states has used
its full federal allotment on all programs or reached its federal
statutory maximum on expenditures where such maximums exist.[7]
Some of the public assistance programs presently underutilized
are Old Age Assistance, Aid to Families with Dependent Children,
and Vocational Rehabilitation.

It is also worth noting that in each major public assistance
program the amount of benefits *per individual assisted* runs
substantially lower in Appalachia than elsewhere. This is reflected
in Table 6.5, which shows the region's share in the national total

TABLE 6.5. APPALACHIA'S SHARE OF U.S. TOTAL RECIPIENTS AND
EXPENDITURES IN PUBLIC ASSISTANCE PROGRAMS, JUNE 1963*

| | PERCENTAGES OF U.S. TOTAL | |
	Expenditures	*Recipients*
All public assistance programs listed below	8.81	11.94
Aid to Families with Dependent Children	11.03	
(Percentage of families)		13.66
(Percentage of children)		13.29
Old Age Assistance	7.54	9.25
Medical Assistance to the Aged	5.62	11.92
Aid to the Permanently and Totally Disabled	8.47	11.28
Aid to the Blind	16.04	19.24

*For comparison, Appalachia's percentage of the total U.S. population in
1960 was 8.1.

Source: *Appalachia: A Report by the President's Appalachian Regional
Commission, 1964* (Washington, D.C.: Government Printing Office, 1964), Appendix C, Table C–20, p. 84.

of recipients and expenditures under each such program. The
region in 1960 had 8.1 per cent of the total population of the
United States. In June 1963, Appalachia had 11.9 per cent of all
public assistance recipients; but they received only 8.8 per cent
of the total assistance given. A similar disproportion shows up in
each program individually, more extreme in some cases than in
others. For example, in the program for medical assistance to the

7. President's Appalachian Regional Commission, "Report of the Subteam
on Welfare" (unpublished), Washington, D.C., September 1963, p. 14.

aged, the average payment per person assisted in Appalachia was
less than half what it was in the rest of the United States.

Social and economic conditions associated with poverty

Throughout the nation wherever poverty is found, we find also
most if not all of a set of certain poverty-linked characteristics of
people and environments. Population characteristics strongly associated with poverty are low educational attainment; nonparticipation in the labor force; age over 65; and skin color. As among
areas, we also find poverty associated with rural areas and Southern
regions. When a population group, community, or region has
many of these poverty-linked attributes at the same time, its like-
lihood of poverty is particularly great.[8]

The relatively unurbanized character of Appalachia has already
been noted. In the non-Appalachian part of the United States,
71.9 per cent of the population lives in urban places. In Appalachia as a whole the proportion is only 47.5 per cent. In only one
state (Pennsylvania) is the Appalachian portion as much as 63
per cent urban, and at the other end of the scale, Appalachian
Kentucky is only 17.9 per cent urban and 82.1 per cent rural.
In every Appalachian state, the part outside the region is substantially more urbanized than the Appalachian part; and in
Pennsylvania, Ohio, and Maryland the non-Appalachian part of
the state is actually more urbanized than the non-Appalachian
part of the United States.

It is important to note that fewer than one in five of Appalachia's rural residents lives on a farm. In the rest of the United
States, more than a quarter of the rural population is on farms.
To a greater extent than in other regions, rural poverty in Appalachia involves livelihood, or the lack of it, in occupations
other than farming—especially in forestry and mining. In the
Appalachian portions of three states—Pennsylvania, Maryland,
and West Virginia—farm residents account for an even smaller
part of the total population than the 7.3 per cent they account
for in the population of the non-Appalachian part of the United
States.

8. See the more detailed discussion in *Economic Report of the President,
1964* (Washington, D.C.: Government Printing Office, 1964), pp. 55–84.

Another characteristic quite consistently related to income and poverty levels is education. Nationally, the heads of 64 per cent of all "poor" families (below $3,000 annual income) have had no more than eight years of formal education.[9] The incidence of poverty decreases as the educational achievement—measured by highest school grade completed—increases. Of all families whose heads have less than eight years of completed schooling, the incidence of poverty is 35 per cent. This percentage drops to 8 for families whose heads have completed more than twelve years of schooling.[10]

In Appalachia, the prevailing educational level of the adult population is well below that of the remainder of the United States, and also below that of the non-Appalachian parts of the Appalachian states. Thus, the proportion of persons 25 and older who have completed less than five grades of school is 11.6 per cent in Appalachia as against 8 per cent elsewhere in the United States. And only 5.2 per cent of the region's people 25 and older have completed four years of college, compared with 7.9 per cent in the rest of the country.

Persistence of this differential is suggested by the fact that Appalachia lags behind the rest of the country in respect to the proportions of its teenagers enrolled in school. For those 16 and 17 years old, the percentage not in school in 1960 was 19.0 per cent in non-Appalachian United States, 23.3 per cent in Appalachia as a whole, and 33.1 per cent in the Appalachian part of Kentucky.

Another basic aspect of regional poverty is the relatively high incidence of unemployment. In 1960, the rate of unemployment in Appalachia was 7.1 per cent of the labor force, far above the rate of 5.0 per cent that prevailed in the rest of the country. In each of the Appalachian states, the unemployment rate was higher in the Appalachian portion of the state than in the remainder of the state. About 30 per cent of the labor force of the ten Appalachian states lived within the region, but the region accounted for more than 39 per cent of the total unemployment of the ten states. It is significant that this difference applies consistently both

9. *Economic Report of the President, 1964,* op. cit., Table 10, p. 80.
10. Ibid., Table 14, p. 83.

to the new entrants to the labor force and to the "experienced labor force."

Inadequacy in number and variety of employment opportunities to match the labor supply is normally reflected not only in high unemployment rates but at the same time in subnormal rates of participation in the labor force. Where jobs are clearly non-existent, people give up actively searching for them; moreover, some of the same factors that limit employment opportunities (such as poor mobility or education) also discourage the search for work. It is not surprising then, that Appalachia has a chronically subnormal fraction of its people of working ages in the labor force. The percentage of civilians aged 14 and older who were in the labor force at the 1960 Census was 49.6 in Appalachia as against 55.9 in the rest of the United States. This difference means that if the region had had the national average labor force participation rate and if the additional members of its labor force had been included in the unemployed, Appalachia's unemployment in 1960 would have jumped from 380,000 to 695,000—an increase of more than 80 per cent. Like an iceberg, Appalachia's deficit of employment opportunity is to a large extent hidden under the surface.[11]

The pervasiveness of this deficiency of labor force participation is impressive. The Appalachian participation rates for both men and women in each of the ten states are below the corresponding national rate. And—likewise without exception—these participation rates are well below the corresponding rates in the non-Appalachian portions of the respective states.

We may pause here to highlight the extent to which the two variables just discussed—education and labor force participation—are associated with relative poverty. A statistical regression analysis conducted in the course of our recent work is indicative here. In that analysis, the dependent variable was the median family income level for each county in Appalachia. The county-

---

11. A much fuller analysis of Appalachia's labor force and occupational and wage structure will be included in a staff report in preparation by Herbert A. Chesler, of the Center for Regional Economic Studies, entitled "Migration and Economic Growth with Special Reference to the Appalachian States, 1950–1960."

to-county differences in median income were correlated with ten different "explanatory" variables, which measured for each county the percentage of urban population, the unemployment rate, the percentage of employment in white-collar occupations, the percentage of school enrollment, and others.[12] A combination of just two of these ten variables—namely, the median educational level of adults in 1950 and the rate of labor force participation in 1960—accounted statistically for 70 per cent of the entire county-to-county variance in family income levels. In other words, the coefficient of multiple correlation using those two independent variables was 0.84.

This finding suggests the importance of education as a determinant of earnings levels. The high degree of correlation of family income with labor force participation is likewise impressive but less concretely suggestive in terms of the kinds of policies likely to raise income levels. Essentially, it refers us back to the observation that Appalachia needs, in order to have more adequate incomes, a more adequate number and variety of job opportunities, which could be expected in itself to lead to higher rates of labor force participation.

The mix of occupations

A number of the symptoms of Appalachia's relative poverty are associated with—and, in statistical terms, can be partly "explained" by—the distinctive "mix" of occupations that characterizes the region. Some kinds of employment are overrepresented in Appalachia, compared to the rest of the country, and others are underrepresented. On the whole, the industries and occupations in which Appalachia has more than its proportionate share of the national total are those which are characterized by some combination of slow growth or decline in employment opportunity, high unemployment rates, and low earning rates.

In terms of broad groupings along industry lines, it is clear that the region's heavy dependence on activities with nationally

12. The other independent variables used were the percentages employed in agriculture, mining, manufacturing, and all other sectors.

TABLE 6.6. OCCUPATIONAL BREAKDOWN OF EXPERIENCED CIVILIAN LABOR FORCE IN APPALACHIA AND
THE REMAINDER OF THE UNITED STATES, WITH MEASURES OF INCOME AND UNEMPLOYMENT
FOR OCCUPATIONAL GROUPS

	PERCENTAGE OF EXPERIENCED CIVILIAN LABOR FORCE		DATA FOR UNITED STATES AS A WHOLE, 1959–60		
	Appalachia	Rest of U.S.	Median annual earnings of family heads (relative to median for all reported occupations = 100.0)	Unemployment rate for experienced civilian labor force (per cent)	Percentage of families with incomes below $3,000
All reported occupations	100.0	100.0	100.0	4.8	12
Professional and technical workers	9.6	11.5	138.6	1.4	3
Managers, officials, and proprietors, excl. farm	6.9	8.6	137.3	1.5	9
Sales workers	7.0	7.5	113.6	3.4	7
Clerical workers	11.1	15.2	101.7	3.2	5
Craftsmen and foremen	15.3	14.2	106.3	5.4	11
Operatives	25.8	19.4	91.5	7.4	22
Service workers, excl. private household	7.9	9.0	79.1	5.6	23
Laborers, excl. farm and mine	7.5	5.3	73.2	12.0	45
Farmers and farm managers	4.1	3.9	50.1	0.8	45
Farm laborers and foremen	2.1	2.4	39.2	7.4	56

Source: Calculated from data in *U.S. Census of Population, 1960.*

declining employment (chiefly agriculture, coal mining, forestry, and railroads) would spell some distress in the region even if it were keeping up with national trends in each industry taken separately.

In terms of occupations, Table 6.6 provides an illuminating summary. Ten broad groups of occupations are shown, arranged roughly in descending order of the levels of income they provide. There is a tendency for the higher-income, white-collar occupations to slow less unemployment and a smaller proportion of families in the poverty category (less than $3,000 annual income) as well. It is significant that, with few exceptions, Appalachia is overrepresented in the occupational groups with lower income, higher unemployment, and higher poverty ratios; and under-represented in the occupational groups with higher income, lower unemployment, and lower poverty ratios. A somewhat encouraging exception is Appalachia's slight overrepresentation in the highest-skilled blue-collar group, listed as "craftsmen and foremen," which is a little above the all-occupation average in income, but also a little above the average unemployment rate in the country as a whole. On the whole, though, the region's constellation of occupations (and, by implication, skills and experience), as shown in Table 6.6, is an unfavorable one, accounting in some measure for the region's poor overall standing in income and employment opportunity.

This factor of mix alone, of course, goes only part way, which becomes clear if we examine the average levels of earnings in each occupation group separately, comparing Appalachia to the rest of the country. In Table 6.7 we have this comparison, for the Appalachian portion of each of the ten Appalachian states and for each of six major occupation groups, making 60 comparisons in all. In only one of the 60 does the level of earnings in any of the ten states come up to the level for the corresponding occupation in the United States outside Appalachia. Appalachian-state earnings levels were anywhere from 4 to 38 per cent below the rest of the country in the professional-managerial group, with even larger spreads in some other categories. For example, in service occupations, Appalachian earnings in specific states ran from 3.6 per cent below the outside-Appalachia average (in Pennsylvania) to 53.8 per cent below (in Georgia).

TABLE 6.7. AVERAGE EARNINGS IN APPALACHIA RELATIVE TO U.S. AVERAGE, BY STATE AND MAJOR OCCUPATION GROUPS, 1959

STATE (APPALACHIAN PORTION)	PROFESSIONAL, MANAGERIAL, AND TECHNICAL	CLERICAL AND SALES	CRAFTSMEN AND FOREMEN	OPERATIVES	SERVICE WORKERS	LABORERS
Alabama	.958	.860	.889	.781	.613	.689
Georgia	.780	.647	.670	.578	.462	.518
Kentucky	.621	.586	.606	.603	.487	.547
Maryland	.916	.806	.834	.815	.756	.850
North Carolina	.779	.637	.660	.649	.508	.570
Ohio	.793	.792	.820	.882	.815	.915
Pennsylvania	.903	.866	.896	.929	.964	1.083
Tennessee	.864	.739	.765	.704	.586	.659
Virginia	.734	.621	.643	.552	.466	.523
West Virginia	.885	.912	.944	.975	.769	.863

Sources: Bureau of the Census, *U.S. Census of Population, 1960*, Final Report, PC(1)–1C (Washington, D.C.: Government Printing Office, 1961), Table 140.

    Bureau of the Census, *U.S. Census of Population, 1960*, Final Report PC(2)–7B (Washington, D.C.: Government Printing Office, 1961), Tables 1 and 4.

1950–60 CHANGES

We have surveyed briefly many dimensions of Appalachia's current situation and have uncovered a number of different but related facets of poverty. But a static picture does not tell the whole story. Appalachia's position in the national economy is changing and, in some respects, changing quite rapidly. We need to look at the most significant changes, especially those which may indicate the extent to which the region's chronic problem of inadequate employment and income for its population is either improving or getting worse.

In terms of income levels, the picture for the last complete decade, 1950–60, is encouraging. Income levels, in money and real terms, rose substantially in Appalachia and in the rest of the country, and the percentage of increase was significantly greater in Appalachia. Some headway was made in closing the wide gap in income levels between region and nation. In 1950, only 21 per cent of Appalachia's population lived in counties where the median income was above the national average—in 1960, that percentage had risen to nearly 26.

The record on employment, however, is less encouraging. In every major industry group, employment in Appalachia lost ground relative to the rest of the country. The losses were especially large in mining (59 per cent) and agriculture (52 per cent). The regional loss of 643,000 jobs in those two categories more than canceled out the gains in other sectors, with the result that the number of jobs of all sorts in Appalachia actually declined 1 per cent during the decade, while employment in the rest of the country was increasing by 16 per cent.

In terms of growth of job opportunity, then, the region fell further behind the nation in the 1950s. This was reflected also in the change of unemployment rates. In 1950, when the national average rate was 4.8 per cent, that of the region was only slightly higher (5.0 per cent), and in six of the ten Appalachian states, there was a rate lower than the national rate of unemployment. By 1960, when the unemployment rate outside Appalachia was 5.0 per cent, Appalachia showed higher rates in eight of its ten states, and the average for the whole region was 7.1 per cent, or more than 40 per cent over the rate for the rest of the country.

In labor force participation as well, the gap between region
and nation somewhat widened in the 1950s. For women, the participation rates rose both regionally and nationally, and the gap
narrowed a little—but this was more than offset in numbers by
the fact that the Appalachian participation rate for men fell
substantially more than the national male rate did, thus widening
the previous gap.

Reference has already been made to the fact that the region
suffered particularly heavy relative losses in employment in mining and agriculture. These and other changes in specific industry
groups had the effect of making the region's industrial mix of
employment converge considerably toward the national pattern.
This is brought out in Table 6.8, where the regional and national
percentage breakdowns in 1950 and 1960 are compared. The columns headed "Difference" show the narrowing of differentials
between 1950 and 1960. These structural changes can be interpreted hopefully, since they indicate that Appalachia was making
progress toward more specialization in manufacturing and service
industries, as against the older and stagnating specialties of mining
and agriculture, whose decline has been accounting for so much
of the region's distress.

Failure of employment opportunity in Appalachia to grow in
the 1950s would of course not automatically have led to increased

TABLE 6.8. PERCENTAGE DISTRIBUTION OF EMPLOYMENT
BY MAJOR INDUSTRY GROUPS, FOR APPALACHIA AND REST OF U.S.,
1950 AND 1960

	1950			1960		
	APPALACHIA	REST OF U.S.	DIFFERENCE	APPALACHIA	REST OF U.S.	DIFFERENCE
Manufacturing	27.8	25.8	+2.0	32.2	26.7	+5.5
Mining	9.2	0.9	+8.3	3.8	0.8	+3.0
Agriculture	14.1	12.3	+1.8	6.8	6.7	+0.1
Construction	5.4	6.2	−0.8	5.8	5.9	−0.1
Services	43.5	54.7	−11.2	51.3	59.9	−8.6
	100.0	100.0		100.0	100.0	

Source: Calculated from data in *U.S. Census of Population, 1950* and *1960*.

rates of unemployment. Unemployment did in fact increase sharply in that decade, because the population and the labor force continued to increase even though the demand for their labor did not. There was a large tide of outward migration from the region, but the net outflow was not quite enough to offset the natural increase (excess of births over deaths).

The increase of population for Appalachia as a whole was indeed minimal—only 1.1 per cent in ten years—and of course in many parts of the region there were decreases, for example in West Virginia and in Kentucky, while elsewhere the population grew more substantially. During the 1950s the population of the United States outside Appalachia increased by more than 20 per cent.

A striking phenomenon appears when we look at the regional population change in terms of urban and rural population. Compared to the rest of the country, Appalachia lagged far behind in *urban* population growth (9 per cent compared to 31 per cent) for the decade; the region also showed a much more drastic decline in *farm* population than the rest of the country did (56 per cent compared to 39 per cent). What is surprising is that in *rural nonfarm* population, Appalachia's increase of 29 per cent in the decade was virtually the same as that in the rest of the country.

The difference between rates of population growth in Appalachia and the rest of the country has historically been based primarily on (1) much higher birth rates in Appalachia than elsewhere and (2) a heavy net migration outflow from Appalachia. The further effect of differences in death rates between the region and the rest of the country has been relatively unimportant.

When we analyze the population change of the 1950s, the importance of regional migration stands out. During that decade, migrants out of Appalachia outnumbered migrants into the region by about two millions, which is 13 per cent of the region's 1950 population. The natural increase was about 14 per cent of the 1950 population; so only 1 per cent remained as net regional population growth for the decade.

The incidence of net out-migration was quite uneven, amounting in Appalachian Kentucky to as much as 35 per cent of the 1950 population; in West Virginia, to 22 per cent, and in Appalachian Virginia, to 18 per cent. At the other extreme, it was only 8 per cent and 3 per cent in the Appalachian parts of Maryland and Ohio, respectively, and 9 and 10 per cent in Appalachian Georgia and Alabama.

The net outflow slackened considerably during the decade, it appears: 70 per cent of the total for the decade occurred during the first five years. This slackening does not seem to have reflected improvement of employment opportunity in Appalachia, but rather a worsening of such opportunity (that is, rising unemployment rates) in the rest of the country. As already noted, unemployment rates rose rather sharply in the nation as a whole but only moderately in Appalachia.

Another impressive shift is disclosed when birth rates are compared. Historically, the more rural and lower-income parts of the nation have shown much higher birth rates and rates of natural increase than the wealthier and more urbanized areas; and Appalachia has been no exception during most of its history. But a gradual narrowing of these differences has been in evidence for a long time—and in the 1950s, Appalachia moved from a position above the national average of birth rates to a little below the national average. Actually, the Appalachian birth rate has pursued a generally falling trend, while the national rate turned upward after World War II and leveled off only in the last few years.

Comparisons of crude birth rates are of course affected by differences in the age distribution, but it does not appear that any such difference between Appalachia and the rest of the United States can account significantly for the striking change in the relative birth rates. By and large it is reasonable to say that the region's birth rates and fertility rates are now quite close to the national average. This means that differences in population growth rates will now reflect almost entirely the direction and extent of migration.

THE ATTACK ON APPALACHIAN POVERTY

Since 1930 the main thrust of public policy directed toward the stimulation of economic growth has not traditionally had a spatial dimension. The concern has been primarily to maintain an appropriate level of national aggregate demand and to facilitate the expansion of national productive capacity through public investment and by inducements to private investment. This "traditional role" of government in enlarging the capacity of the national economy is well summarized in the 1962 Report of the Council of Economic Advisers (p. 108):

> First, in those areas of economic activity traditionally allotted to some level of government, public expenditures must provide services which contribute to the growth of potential output and which satisfy the needs that accompany increasing income and wealth. Second, public policy—notably in the fields of taxation, education, training, welfare, and the control of money and credit—inevitably stimulates or retards the growth potential of the private economy, even if no such result is consciously intended.

The Council further suggested that coordination of policy on all government levels is required to facilitate the necessary investment. But the mechanism for planning and coordinating these expenditures has not been fully developed.

In recent years our national policy has come to reflect the need to stimulate economic growth in particular regions of the country. The Area Redevelopment Act of 1961 was the first major step in this direction. It provides funds and other inducements to encourage investment in distressed areas.

In contrast to the Area Redevelopment Administration program, which offers aid on a county-by-county basis, the recently enacted Appalachian program postulates a "regional" approach. Thus the pendulum has swung from a national to a local, and now to a regional, perspective.

This current emphasis in our policy is reflected in the *Economic Report of the President, 1965* (pp. 140–41):

> First, the scale of assistance must be sufficient to make a significant impact on the economic structure of an area. . . .
> Second, the regions to be aided should be large enough to include a resource base for self-sustained growth and to support the full range of community services and public utilities. . . .

Third, new programs must place major emphasis on investment in those community facilities that are commonly deficient in depressed areas. . . .

Fourth, if there is to be assurance that Federal aid to a region is to lead to recovery, the region must develop a plan for its progress.

Development programs on the subnational level can be characterized in three groups: (1) those that are generally oriented toward the environment (upgrading facilities and developing natural resources), (2) those that are oriented to developing human resources, and (3) those that are oriented more directly toward influencing private economic activity. Programs which improve the environment are mainly capital expenditures on facilities related to access, such as roads and airports; hospitals; sewage plants; libraries; and land improvement and other natural resources conservation. Programs to upgrade human resources include the various public assistance programs, manpower retraining and vocational education programs, and such aids to education as student loan programs. Programs which support private economic activity can range from the provision of technical assistance to a business to the lending or granting of funds for construction and equipping of business facilities, including site preparation, building construction, and purchase of equipment.

The Appalachian Regional Development Act of 1965

The Appalachian Regional Development Act emphasizes programs designed to improve the physical environment of the region. This is to be accomplished by increasing the funds available to the region in existing federal investment programs and by enlarging the scope of such programs by making the stimulation of economic development the main criterion for evaluating them. A summary of the programs in the Act is shown in Table 6.9, with information on the authorized funding and duration of authorization. Additional authorizations are necessary for all programs, except the development highway and regional health center construction programs, if they are to remain operative until 1971, when the present Act terminates.

TABLE 6.9. PROGRAMS IN THE
APPALACHIAN REGIONAL DEVELOPMENT ACT

SECTION	PROGRAM	AUTHORIZATION	
		Funds (millions of dollars)	*Duration (months)*
101	Creation of Commission	2.2	27
201	Development and access highways	840.0	72
202a	Construction of regional health centers	41.0	72
202b	Operation and administration of regional health centers	28.0	27
203	Land stabilization, conservation, and erosion control	17.0	27
204	Timber development organizations	5.0	27
205	Mining area restoration	36.5	27
206	Water resources survey	5.0	27
211	Construction of vocational education facilities	16.0	27
212	Construction of sewage treatment facilities	6.0	27
214	Supplements to federal grant-in-aid construction and equipment programs	90.0	27
302	Financing of Local Development Districts, and research	5.5	27

The first round of authorizations is heavily biased toward highway construction, for two reasons, first, because this was indeed felt to be the most critical deficiency of the region's physical environment and, second, to assure an adequate foundation for other investments.

None of the research surrounding the work of the Commission —including our own—demonstrated conclusively that this level of highway investment is justified in terms of "developmental" payoff. Nor does anyone believe that this investment alone is sufficient to cure Appalachia's economic ills. But it is widely regarded as a *sine qua non* of growth. Without good access, no other programs can succeed. The proposed network will reduce travel costs and travel time both within the region and between the region and the rest of the country.

Other parts of the program are designed to improve what's found at the end of the road, so to speak. They are mainly intended to repair the ravages of the past—the social costs of earlier private exploitation of the region's natural resources—and, to a limited extent, to improve the region's human resources. Underemphasis of this last does not imply an underevaluation of the benefits of such investments. It implies, instead, the recognition that such needs are met by other programs, such as manpower retraining and the newer antipoverty programs.

To complement the investment program, the Act establishes the Appalachian Regional Commission, a new mechanism for improving the execution of all federal programs in the region and for encouraging more effective state and local action. The Commission is composed of a representative from each of the states and one from the federal government. The federal representative, appointed by the President, is the Federal Co-chairman of the Commission. It is his responsibility to coordinate the Commission's activities with the federal agencies so that the programs and plans the Commission develops are consistent with existing federal legislation, or so that necessary changes in legislation can be identified and subsequent recommendations made to federal agencies and to the President. It is the responsibility of the state representatives on the Commission to submit plans and projects within their states to the Commission. These plans and projects will be shaped into a regional development plan by the Commission and its staff.

The Act provides for several important deviations in the process of program and project development from those normally employed in federal programs. First, the decisions on the developing and ranking of projects within a state will be made by state groups. Thus, the projects submitted to the Commission will have had their development justification and ranking compared to other projects examined by groups within the state. Second, the Act provides the latitude for changing the criteria for justifying a federal-aid project. The criteria provided in the Act to promote economic development include:[13]

1. the relationship of the project or class of projects to overall regional development including its location in an area determined by the state to have a significant potential for growth;

2. the population and area to be served by the project or class

13. Appalachian Regional Development Act of 1965, Public Law 89–4, S.3.

of projects including the relative per capita income and the
unemployment rates in the area;

3. the relative financial resources available to the state or
   political subdivisions or instrumentalities thereof which
   seek to undertake the project;
4. the importance of the project or class of projects in relation to other projects or classes of projects which may be
   in competition for the same funds;
5. the prospects that the project for which assistance is sought
   will improve, on a continuing rather than a temporary
   basis, the opportunities for employment, the average level
   of income, or the economic and social development of the
   area served by the project.

Finally, let us note a very important feature of development
strategy involving the priorities for different subareas within the
region. The policy enunciated in the Act is to focus aid not necessarily where local distress is most acute but rather where there is
a clear and significant *potential for future growth* and where the
expected return on public investment will be the greatest. The
investment, then, in any of the facilities will be based on criteria
of need only insofar as that need is an indicator of constraint to
the development of an area. The development roads will be built
to improve access, not to relieve congestion, unless existing congestion in one area is a greater constraint to development than
poor access in another area.

In contrast to the Area Redevelopment Administration program, which sought to induce private investment in depressed areas
by direct subsidy, the Appalachian program seeks to raise the
profitability of private investment in the region by upgrading
the quality of the region's resources and social overhead. Nobody
pretends that we know how to maximize the return to these investments. As of now we cannot be sure what combination of
physical investments in what specific locations will yield the greatest return. But the establishment of the Commission as a coordinating mechanism will facilitate vigorous pursuit of better answers
than we now have to these questions.

7: Poverty and Resource Utilization

by Joseph L. Fisher

Clearly, poverty and natural resource utilization are closely related. Where natural resources are abundant and wisely used, poverty is less likely to be found. Good farmland, plentiful and cheap electric power, rich mineral resources, and attractive recreational areas are associated with prosperous communities. Exhausted and eroded soil, severely cut-over forest areas, worked-out mines, and ill-used water resources are linked to poor communities and to a long chain of social and economic problems.

Of course more than poor natural resources is involved in poverty and more than rich natural resources in prosperity. Natural resources remain only potentials until enterprise, capital, skilled labor, and appropriate institutions and organizations are brought to bear on them. When natural resource utilization—or misutilization—gives rise to poverty, the corrective actions will invariably require human or institutional intervention. Education and job training will have to be improved, cheaper credit will have to be provided, new forms of management and organization will have to be found, larger investment in social overhead, such as highways and water development, will be needed, and the level of motivation for both enterprise and labor will have to be raised.

Sometimes the scale of action can be at the community or local government level. In other instances state or multi-state programs will be required, while with increasing frequency national government sponsorship will be looked to. Most frequently of all, concerted action will have to proceed simultaneously at several levels of government. For example, the soil conservation program which has been pursued vigorously and continuously for some thirty years is a federally sponsored program, but it operates through local soil conservation districts established under state laws. Programs of water conservation and development are proceeding in bewildering complexity largely under federal auspices but with many shades and gradations of local participation. Forestry programs include direct federal responsibility for the national forests, private industry responsibility for the great industrial forests, and a mixture of government programs with private action for smaller forest holdings on farms and elsewhere.

But over this wide panorama of resource programs and activities, all of them having as their objective the improvement and effective utilization of the resources and the betterment of the life of the people who depend on them, one can see at virtually every point that low-grade resources and poor utilization are closely associated with poverty. Therefore, it is not surprising that both poverty and poor resource utilization are frequently found in the same geographic, economic, and social setting.

THE POVERTY–RESOURCE RELATIONSHIP

Fortunately the general resource picture for the United States is favorable. The economy has been prosperous and the trend of economic activity has been rising since before World War II. To a considerable extent in recent years the nation's economic problems have become those of affluence.

Similarly the trend of resource utilization has been favorable. Yields per acre in agriculture have increased spectacularly during the past three decades. Productivity in the resource industries, measured in output per man hour, has also increased over a long period of time, somewhat more rapidly than in manufacturing. The labor force in resource industries, though no larger than it was a hundred years ago, now produces enough agricultural products, forest products, minerals, and fuels to supply a population five or six times larger, living at considerably higher levels. At the same time, real costs and prices of resource products and services have not increased significantly during the past fifty or even a hundred years, indicating that resources have not become scarcer relative to other things. And, beyond this, the outlook up to the end of this century at least is favorable, with little indication of any general resource shortage in the United States.

Along about 1930 the United States became a net importer of resource commodities. During the past few years the country has been importing nearly 20 per cent of its crude oil and more than 25 per cent of its iron ore, plus higher percentages of copper, lead, zinc, nickel, and many other metals. It continues to export large amounts of wheat, cotton, coal, and other basic commodities. Foreign trade in resources remains important to the United States economy on both the import and export sides. Projections of future resource availability should take account of foreign sources of supply as well as foreign markets. As long as foreign trade continues to grow and this country is able to import needed minerals and other raw materials, the outlook for resource availability will remain favorable here.

The question of the adequacy of resources to meet the needs of the United States economy to the year 2000 was the subject of a careful study carried out under the auspices of Resources for the Future, Inc. That study concluded:[1]

> The possibilities of using lower grades of raw material, of substituting plentiful materials for scarce ones, of getting more use out of given amounts, of importing some things from other countries, and of making multiple use of land and water resources seem to be sufficient guarantee against across-the-board shortage.
>
> There is, however, great likelihood of severe problems of shortage (or, as in the case of agriculture during the next decade or two, of surplus) from time to time in particular regions or segments of the economy, for particular raw

1. Hans H. Landsberg, Leonard L. Fischman, and Joseph L. Fisher, *Resources in America's Future: Patterns of Requirements and Availabilities, 1960–2000* (Baltimore: The Johns Hopkins Press, for Resources for the Future, Inc., 1963), pp. 4–5.

materials. Deficiencies either of quantity or quality in the environmental resources of land and water undoubtedly will also occur in some instances. Well designed policies and timely actions can frequently prevent or reduce these difficulties.

From this it may be inferred that impending shortage of natural resources and raw materials will not in any general or overall way be a significant cause of poverty in the future. But in specific instances—in particular places or in particular resource industries —poverty may continue to stem from a deteriorated natural resource situation. For example, the poverty and other economic and social problems associated with such declining resource industries as coal, subsistence agriculture, cut-over forestry, worked-out metal mines, depleted fisheries, and the like account for a large portion of the poverty problem in this country. Other instances of economic and social distress have been closely related to resource situations; for example, difficulties during recent decades in the textile industry in the northeastern part of the country were closely tied to the development of synthetic fabrics and the increase in locational advantages of the Southeast compared to the Northeast. The role of technological change has also been of great importance along with shifts in the pattern of demand for resources themselves.

The anatomy of poverty in the United States is becoming better understood as more discriminating research is undertaken and as experience is gained with programs designed to alleviate particular kinds of poverty. The poverty line of $3,000 of income a year for a family has been used as a definition of poverty, although increasingly it is recognized that other factors such as family size, the persistence of low income, and the amount of wealth and property holdings have a significant bearing on the matter. It has been found that the incidence of poverty is especially great among families headed by older persons and females, among nonwhite families, and among farmers. In addition, poverty is associated with low level of education, poor physical or mental health, lack of labor skills, dependence on welfare programs, adjustment difficulties among migrants, family instability, and low motivation. Inadequate and unequal civil rights and voting power are also factors of significance. Poverty is more than insufficient dollars, calories, or housing. It is a sense of hopelessness and failure, a psychological condition in which people are literally "poor in spirit." When the psychology of poverty takes hold in a family, poverty tends to become chronic and escape from it immeasurably more difficult.

EXAMPLES OF THE RELATIONSHIP

In addition the roots of poverty frequently go deep into the natural resource situation and outlook. Particularly, the geography of poverty is closely associated with natural resources deterioration, with technological change in the way resources are used, and with changes in demands for products and services reflected in an economic worsening of the resource base.

When several types and locations of poverty overlap, the problem tends to become chronic and most difficult to solve. For example, an Appalachian coal-mining area with a disproportionate number of older people, with poor schools, with high birth rates, and with few immediately available alternatives for employment is likely to present a severe case of poverty for many of its families. Or an urban center based on a declining resource or industry, with a large Negro population and poor schools, is likely to be another example of chronic difficulty. Or, poverty is likely to be concentrated in rural farm areas in the South with worn-out soil, poor schools, and inadequate motivation to move away or create new economic enterprises in the area.

To the extent that poverty is concentrated in resource areas or in resource industries the lines of solution are likely to involve resource policies and programs. Usually these will have to be related to other policies and programs bearing directly on education, health, migration, industrial development, social welfare, and regional planning. Sometimes the correctives can be found in national policy and action; frequently national efforts will have to be tailored to local conditions and strongly supplemented by local action.

Each person from his own background has had experience with poverty, at least as an observer. Some reflection on this will indicate how widespread poverty still is in this country, although more affluent Americans are aware of it only occasionally, so completely is most of it kept out of sight. My own experience is not unique and perhaps may be suggestive of some of the types and locations of poverty that have a close connection with natural resources. I draw the following examples from personal experience.

Closely connected with the natural resources of the area is the poverty problem in eastern Maine, which has been on the government's list of distressed rural areas more or less continuously for many years. This is an area with no dominant industry. By turns during the course of a year a typical member of the labor force there is a farmer, factory worker, lumberman, fisherman, and service worker. In addition, he probably works for the state on highways or something else for a short time each year. All of these together hardly yield a living. He develops only modest skill at any one type of employment although he is passably adept at doing almost anything. To a considerable extent his difficulties derive from the natural resources of his area. The farmland is rocky and poor; furthermore, the market for hay, which was once the principal crop, has dwindled since the advent of the automobile. The coastal fisheries have declined, partly because of overfishing. The once valuable forest lands have been cut over and are being restocked slowly to lower-grade species. Except for seasonal berry, poultry, or fish processing, other kinds of manufacturing have been slow to establish themselves. An increasing source of employment for the two summer months has been in the tourist service industry.

The problems of this area are fairly clear, but what to do about them is not. The principal growth industry in sight is that of providing for outdoor recreation. Here the possibilities are reasonably good with adequate planning and investment, but the short season is a severely limiting condition. Always on the horizon is the development of tidal power at Passamaquoddy Bay. Unfortunately the economics here are not favorable at present, but it does constitute a bright, though distant and uncertain, hope for the future. Migration from the area has been considerable during recent decades; many of the towns now have only half the population they had at the turn of the century. Many families are living well below the poverty line, which is reflected in poor work performance, inadequate diets, and resistance to migration. Short of some unexpected stroke of good fortune, there appears to be no way out of the dilemma except through more careful planning for resource development with discriminating emphasis upon the few lines which seem to offer hope of additional employment and incomes.

A second example is southeastern Alaska. Here the decline of the salmon fishery, probably due in large part to mismanagement and overfishing, has created severe problems especially for the native Indians who, from time immemorial, have depended upon fishing. The rather nice resource and institutional balance that the Indian population had worked out was seriously disturbed by the coming of the whites, and Indian poverty became intensified through the whites' introduction of various diseases. The expectation level of the native people has subsequently been raised, creating further frustration and difficulty. Efforts to introduce the Indians to other forms of employment, usually requiring training, frequently proved abortive. As a result of all these factors, a substantial number of Indian families and some white families continue a rather miserable existence well below the poverty line. Social as well as economic discrimination is part of the problem.

Programs have been launched to deal with this problem and have found some success, although the native people have by no means been brought fully into the American social, economic, and educational systems. The correction of poverty in this case will require better programs for resources conservation and development. The salmon, halibut, and other fisheries need to be restored and conserved. The considerable forest resources, almost completely within the national forest system and under government control, are being developed according to the best known principles of conservation, but the establishment of additional forest enterprises is needed for employment and incomes. Tourism, so far only lightly tapped, offers considerable promise for the future although here also the length of season is short. The situation in southeastern Alaska is paralleled by poverty and incomplete economic development in other parts of the country with large Indian populations dependent upon one or a few natural resources that have not been developed in accordance with efficient conservation and management practices.

A third example is furnished by the numerous mining towns scattered through the Western states, once thriving and full of life, but now virtually deserted. Unfortunately the period of deterioration may extend over many years to the detriment of those persons who try to live on in them and eke out a living. Occasionally such a place can be converted to some other use, as for example Central City, Colorado, which has become a major tourist attraction, but more typically these towns grind slowly down to nothing. The solution frequently will be a set of policies by which the inhabitants are encouraged to move out once the mines close down. The better established the towns have become, the more difficult it is to get people to abandon them.

Towns based on forestry sometimes have run a similar course, although total abandonment is seldom the outcome. Quite a few towns in the northern Great Lakes states passed their heyday prior to World War I and then declined. The nearby forests were cut over rather completely, with little thought of sustained yield or permanent employment. The contraction process proved difficult and painful. Jobs disappeared, the younger and more imaginative people left, and sources of local public revenue dried up. State and federal government programs were launched to analyze the situation, retrain those who had lost their jobs, and establish new industries, as well as to meet immediate needs for food and welfare. My own experiences in this cut-over area in the later 1930s in connection with the surveys of the National Resources Planning Board brought home to me the intractable nature of the shake-down and readjustment process in an area that has lost the best of its resource base for employment and incomes.

A similar story could be told for coal-mining centers after the nearby coal seams have played out, or for agricultural towns and areas where soil fertility has been allowed to deteriorate. In certain Appalachian communities poverty has become especially stubborn because the decline in coal has been accompanied by a decline in farm productivity and a cutting-over of nearby timber land.

Another kind of example is furnished by the southern New England textile city of Pawtucket, Rhode Island. In this case unemployment and poverty do not stem directly from natural resource conditions in Rhode Island, but indirectly from a variety of economic and resource factors there and elsewhere. Pawtucket, a city of 70,000 or 80,000 people, depended heavily on textile mills for employment and economic life until the 1920s. Beginning then and continuing ever since the textile operations have been closing down or even moving from this city, principally to the southeastern states. Spinning, weaving, finishing, and dyeing elements in the industry were all affected.

The textile industry in America had been started in Pawtucket in the late eighteenth century by Samuel Slater. For a century and a quarter this had been a favorable location, with adequate small-scale water power to drive the mills, a humid climate, a plentiful labor supply drawn from the surrounding area, which had become urbanized at an early date, and reasonably cheap transport of cotton from the South. Slowly these advantages eroded as markets shifted south and west and as the unique advantages of water power diminished. Furthermore labor costs tended to rise to a point where the cheaper labor in the Southern states became a decisive factor. Nearness to raw material had always favored the South. In addition, the very advantages of early industrialization turned into disadvantages as the old multi-story brick mills located along the river, and frequently in the heart of the city, were replaced elsewhere by modern one-story mills located outside towns where there could be ample space for employee parking and for the handling of shipments in and out. The interest of enterprisers and owners had tended to decline in the older area, although in many instances management was alert to the advantages of shifting location to the Southern states.

Accompanying the decline in textile manufacturing was the rise in unemployment, underemployment, and the incidence of poverty. Social distress has been widespread in the Providence-Pawtucket area as well as in other New England communities in recent years. New industries need to be attracted to these communities, and industries which are based on local resources are likely to be particularly helpful and dependable. Such industries would be suitable replacements for the textile industry which has migrated to areas closer to its resource base in the South.

A final example of poverty with an indirect connection to natural resources is to be found in many of the large metropolitan areas of the Northeast, stretching northward from Washington and Baltimore on the eastern seaboard and St. Louis and Cincinnati in the Midwest. In Washington, D.C., for example, there has been since the war a major inflow of Negroes from the South. About half the population, and three-quarters of the children enrolled in public schools, are Negro. Fortunately, unemployment is not excessively high, because of numerous opportunities for Negroes in government and in service activities, even though as a whole their educational and training levels may be low. Other cities are not so fortunate in having an adequate number of jobs for the new in-migrants. Even in Washington, however, many families live in poverty, perhaps because of underemployment or because they are very large.

What has happened here is that rural poverty, from southside Virginia, or from other Southern states, has been transferred to the metropolitan area. To the extent that solutions could not be found in the resource-based rural areas and small towns to the South, solutions now will have to be found within the large urban centers. To some extent it may be possible to indoctrinate and train persons in the smaller towns and villages before they leave for the urban areas so that they will not fall into the despondency and frustration of continued poverty.

In the suburbs surrounding Washington and other Northern cities is to be found a new kind of poverty, associated with formerly rural families who have left their homes for the cities, and after finding life unsatisfactory there, have moved to the suburbs. Generally this environment proves equally unsatisfactory, and the problems that are created are difficult both for the poor and the authorities who wish to help them.

Other suburban poor are among the old-timers who lived there before the recent growth and who have been by-passed economically and socially. These poor families find themselves surrounded by high-income and well-educated people who are largely unaware that poor people live in their pleasant communities. The children of the suburban poor are frequently lost in the college-oriented schools, while the parents have difficulty finding any social group within which to obtain security and encouragement. In many suburbs extreme poverty exists precariously in the very midst of affluence and comfort. This type of poverty is less directly related to resource phenomena than others thus far described, although some of these poor once made their living in farming.

IMPLICATIONS FOR PUBLIC POLICY

Often a high incidence of poverty is closely related, either directly or indirectly, to a deteriorated natural resource condition, usually associated with particular geographic areas. In some instances poverty results from mismanagement or poor utilization of a natural resource and is correctable with re-education, more skillful management, and changed perceptions of how the resource may be handled. Frequently public policies will be necessary to set improvements in motion; these typically will involve investments in land improvement programs, reforestation, water resource development, or resource-using industries. Increasingly in many of the depressed areas, the development of outdoor recreation facilities can play a part in ameliorating the situation. According to available statistics, outdoor recreation as an "industry" has been growing at around 10 per cent a year, as indicated by the increase in number of visitor-days at various kinds of parks, forests, and other recreation places.

In other instances improved programs of soil, water, and forest conservation, coupled with the establishment of appropriate small local industries to process the available raw materials, can point the way toward economic betterment. Increased out-migration, though difficult from social and political viewpoints, is not inconsistent with resource and industrial improvement within the area; indeed considerable out-migration to offset natural population increase and to lower population density somewhat may be a necessary condition of betterment.

Poverty is many-faceted with regard to its causes, its consequences, and its cures. Nearly all the chronically distressed rural areas listed by the Department of Commerce have an obviously close relation to the local natural resource base of agriculture, forestry, mining, fisheries, and others. Of the distressed urban areas also, a significant number appear to have a rather close tie with natural resources, as for example coal-producing areas. In others the connection, though still present, is more indirect, as in the case of metal processing and textile manufacturing areas.

Just as deteriorated natural resources are by no means the only cause of poverty in this country, resource development programs cannot be relied upon to cure all poverty. But such programs if they are well conceived and timely can help in reducing poverty, and frequently they will be indispensable. Most of the elements in the present antipoverty campaign have been tried before— the job corps, special training programs, more basic educational efforts, among others. What is new and of great significance, it seems to me, is that the phenomenon of poverty in America is now being viewed in its full scope and complexity in an effort to find all of its significant causes, and thus corrective programs can be designed which will be interrelated and will not overlook any major aspects of the problem. The nation is trying to make a comprehensive approach to the poverty problem; that is what is new and exciting.

Natural resource programs in agriculture, water development, forestry, and all the rest should be gone over with a fine-tooth comb to identify clearly those elements which properly should be related to the cluster of activities called the antipoverty program. In addition, all of the antipoverty activities should be reviewed in terms of their effects on natural resources. These two strands— the resource programs and the antipoverty programs—frequently can be brought together in a meaningful and positive way in area development programs, as for example in Appalachia. In the current program for this major depressed and poverty-stricken region, significant sums will be devoted to water development, forestry, and outdoor recreation. Existing programs already are seeking to give special attention to agricultural improvement. But the bulk of the Appalachia program is for highway construction, the rationale behind this being that better highways will open up the region for resource development. Farmers would be able to get their produce out to the towns more easily. Better truck access to timber lands would be assured. Tourists and vacationers would find it easier to get to the more remote mountains and valleys. Local resource-based industries could draw workers from a wider area and could ship products out more cheaply. The chief risk in this program may lie in keeping the various elements in balance so that, for example, highway construction will not proceed too far in advance of improvements in local agriculture and forestry or in the development of parks and tourist facilities.

Natural resources conservation, the development of resource-based industries, the opening up of remote resources through highway construction, and social and educational improvements can be considered advantageously in terms of a system of resources and economic development for a given geographic area. In such a system these major elements are thought of as deriving from the population and labor force in the area plus the natural resources and locational features to which investments and other programs may then be applied so as to increase employment, raise incomes, and reduce poverty. It does not seem far-fetched that the main features of an area resource and economic development system can be brought together in models into which data can be inserted and analyzed, and from which preferred courses of action can be derived. Even if total systems of this sort cannot be made workable, it might prove feasible to deal with subsystems—for example one which would bring together a set of more closely related variables such as forest resources, outdoor recreation potentialities, and access facilities. Or, as another example, data could be brought together relating to water resources, hydroelectric capacity, coal-based electric capacity, and aluminum and other electrometallurgical industries.

What I have attempted to do here is to indicate the close relation between natural resource conditions and prospects on the one hand and unemployment, social distress, and poverty on the other. The connections between the two sets of conditions, though obvious to many in a general way, are not nearly as well understood in depth as would be desirable to insure success in extracting from resource development programs everything that can be useful in overcoming poverty and, vice versa, to insure that poverty programs will have a constructive bearing on natural resource development. Establishment of new jobs and the reduction of poverty generally will have to be based both on knowledge of resource potentials and on appropriate training, education, and migration programs.

Part 4: Approaches to the Elimination
of Poverty

8: Public Approaches to Minimize Poverty

by Theodore W. Schultz

Once upon a time in the good old days before computers and the flood of statistics and theoretical models, there were economists who would appeal to Common Sense to buttress their analysis. It would be ever so convenient if there were a Common Sense approach to poverty that would be clear, cogent, and useful, but the plain fact of the matter is that poverty is very complicated both socially and economically. Try to convince your fellow man that your definition of poverty is real and relevant and you will see what I mean! Living at subsistences measured in food and shelter is not a meaningful definition. Nor can poverty be defined simply in terms of being below a particular level of income, because some families with relatively little income nevertheless own substantial amounts of wealth. Neither income, nor wealth, nor consumption is a dependable measure. Even when all three are used in combination, the resulting measure will not tell us why and the extent to which our society redefines poverty so as to raise the so-called poverty line over time. Common Sense is indeed a rare gift but it is not sufficient for this task.

Poverty is a complex socioeconomic state that characterizes particular families in a particular society. There can be no doubt that a part of any meaningful concept of poverty is socially determined, because it depends in substantial part upon our class and family structure. Nor is it independent of our social attitudes, for example, with respect to discrimination. The simple fact that people in general in our society hold that poverty is undesirable is a consequence of our social values. But a part of our concept of poverty is also economic, as is clear when we consider the possibilities of reducing the incidence of poverty. The type of economic growth we have had during recent decades reduces poverty; no doubt our types of taxation and public expenditures have also reduced it. It is obvious that poverty can be reduced at some price. What is not so obvious is that there are important aspects of poverty that are akin to economic instability, or to a depression, when there is less than full employment, in the sense that it can be reduced in ways that would leave no one worse off while improving the economic lot of some who would otherwise be in poverty.

THE DISUTILITY OF POVERTY

Thus, I propose to treat poverty as a socioeconomic state in which a part of our families live. I shall take it to be true that the values of our society are such that people generally would prefer to have fewer rather than more families in this state of poverty. From these social values one can straightaway infer the disutility of poverty. What this means is that our preferences are such that a reduction in poverty enhances our satisfactions. The question then arises: What is the price of obtaining such additional satisfactions? How much has to be given up by those who are not in poverty to reduce or eliminate the existing poverty? Since there are a number of ways of reducing or eliminating poverty and since some of them are more costly than others, knowledge about the costs and efficiency of the alternatives is both relevant and important in this area of social choice.

The economics of poverty therefore rests on the preferences and the capability of a people to satisfy these preferences. The application of these two basic concepts may seem elementary and easy; but as we shall see, these concepts are beset with difficulties and there is much confusion in bringing them to bear on the problems of poverty.

Building on preferences

Here we face a flock of hard questions. How do we specify these preferences? How are they revealed? Should they be changed? Does economic analysis tell us how to alter them? The core of economics takes preferences as they are; they are, as I have already noted, a consequence of the cultural values of a people. Thus, whether we view economics as a kit of tools or as a body of knowledge, it is not designed to change people's preferences. The values and taste of a people may be deemed inferior by some social standard but a cultural reform to improve such preferences goes beyond economics. Once we see clearly that economics takes preferences as they are, a lot of confusion is dispelled with regard to the economics of poverty and the limitations of the contributions of economic analysis.

But this clarification by no means makes it easy to identify the relevant preferences. How do people reveal their preferences with respect to poverty? We turn to their behavior. We can observe private charity—e.g. gifts to private agencies that minister to the poor, and gifts to colleges and universities that are in part invested in students, who thereby enhance their subsequent earnings. We observe local, municipal, state, and federal governmental bodies responding to their respective electorates by authorizing programs and appropriating funds to alleviate poverty. But for all that it is very hard to specify and measure the revealed preferences from such behavior.

The utility-of-poverty doctrine

There undoubtedly are countries that have pursued policies over many decades which would support the view that their governments were not averse to poverty for the rank and file of people. There is a century in English history during which the poverty of the lower classes was thought to be desirable; for the then prevailing public view was that such poverty rendered good results. Between 1660 and 1775 the dominant nationalism of England produced an intricate system of foreign and domestic policy that sought to rationalize by all manner of arguments the utility of poverty. Edgar S. Furniss in his prize-winning Hart,

Schaffner, and Marx essay devotes a long chapter to "The Doctrine of the Utility of Poverty."[1] The beliefs of illustrious individuals of that period will seem novel to us. Thomas Mun's view was that "penury and want do make a people wise and industrious." Arthur Young asserted that "every one but an idiot knows that the lower classes must be kept poor or they will never be industrious." John Law argued that "laborers were to blame for recurring high prices, because of their 'insufferable' habits of idleness contracted when food was cheap." William Petty joined in this chorus.

Even David Hume was not immune. He supported his belief by stating that in "years of scarcity, if it be not extreme, the poor labor more and really live better than in years of great plenty when they indulge themselves in idleness and riot."[2] Nor did Hume spare farmers. His defamation of them is terse: "A habit of indolence naturally prevails. A greater part of the land lies uncultivated. What is cultivated yields not its utmost for lack of skill and assiduity in the farmers." Hume calls them not only indolent but also squanderers. It follows logically from these beliefs that the real wages of the laboring classes must be held low. One of the ways of doing this, so it was argued, is to increase the price of necessities. When corn becomes plentiful, measures should be taken to subsidize its export. There should be taxes on consumption. Access of the poor to amusements, including strolling players, should be curtailed. The consumption of tea on the part of the poor was viewed as an evil.[3] Charity was thought to be the nursery of idleness. A larger population would keep laborers poor, and the logic of this was to encourage immigration and to be more lenient in naturalization policies. George Berkeley, Bishop of Cloyne, proposed to reward parents of large families and to tax families that had no children to attain this objective.

1. Edgar S. Furniss, *The Position of the Laborer in a System of Nationalism* (Boston: Houghton Mifflin, 1920). The quotations that follow are from Ch. 6.

2. See my *Economic Crises in World Agriculture* (Ann Arbor: University of Michigan Press, 1965), pp. 26 and 27.

3. There was solicitude over the increase in the consumption of tea by the poor; tea-drinking was deemed to be "wasteful of time and destructive of industry among the class of people whose duty was to labor continuously." Arthur Young put it thus: "The employment of women and children in drinking tea; . . . an extremity that may surely be called luxury in excess!"

Poverty-prone people

Another variant of the doctrine of the utility of poverty rests on the belief that there are subcultures in our society composed of people who prefer to be poor. Kenneth Boulding states that "a certain amount of the poverty of the hillbilly or of the sub-sistence farmer, and even of the slumdweller and of the bum involves the rejection of the psychological cost of getting rich and a rejection of the middle-class way of life rather than the inability to find opportunity."[4] Harry Johnson struck the same note in a recent comment.[5]

It is noteworthy that neither Boulding nor Johnson placed professors in this subculture, despite the long-standing myth that professors prefer to be poor. They escaped this particular myth because of what they know about their colleagues! It is undoubtedly true that there are classes of people who are proverty-prone for all manner of reasons other than the state of their preferences. Nor would anyone deny that particular occupations are preferred over others and that some people, for example some farm families, acquire a preference for the work and the way of living to which they have become accustomed. But surely such preferences are not inconsistent with the disutility of poverty.[6]

APPROACHES TO MINIMIZE POVERTY

For us to develop a society free of poverty should be fairly easy. By world standards we obviously enjoy very high incomes. New sources of income have been forthcoming not only to support a huge defense establishment, a lot of foreign aid, and a rapidly growing population but to raise personal consumption expendi-

4. Kenneth E. Boulding, "Reflections on Poverty," *The Social Welfare Forum* (New York: Columbia University Press, 1961).

5. *Amer. Econ. Rev., 55*, No. 2 (May 1965), 543–45.

6. There are of course many people who prefer to remain poor rather than accept doles or gifts, although much depends on the manner in which such income transfers are legitimatized. But a meaningful opportunity for them to earn additional income avoids this psychological cost. The implication of Boulding's argument that it would be necessary to impose a "middle-class way of life" in order to reduce or eliminate poverty is unwarranted; to attempt to do so would be intolerable.

ture on a per capita basis and in real terms about two-fifths since World War II. The economy has produced all this additional income despite the slack in employment during recent years and despite the depression of particular regions, industries, and occupations. Compared to India, where masses of people are in dire poverty, our poverty is minuscule. It is clearly in the realm of economic possibilities for us to be free of poverty.

The choice to have such a society is ours to make. We may of course prefer not to avail ourselves of this choice whatever the social or political reasons may be. The conventional thing to do is to believe in a natural law which will cause poverty to disappear. What remains in the affluent society is pockets of people who because of their preferences or circumstances have not been cleansed by progress.

Proceeding then on the proposition that poverty has for us as a society a disutility, we have at hand an array of approaches to alleviate it or to remove the causes of part of it. I shall restrict my comments to public approaches: first to minimum wages and farm price supports; then to progressive taxation; next to economic growth and employment; and lastly to public investment in poor people.

Raising wages and prices by legislation

This approach, which continues to have a wide appeal politically, involves raising the low wages of unskilled workers and the low prices received by farmers by means of minimum-wage laws and high farm price supports. It rests on the belief that this line of legislative action is a direct and effective way of reducing poverty and that it increases the income streams where it really matters. Labor unions and some farm groups are committed to this approach. However, economists have repeatedly shown that it not only impedes allocative efficiency but as a rule worsens the personal distribution of income among laborers and among farmers. J. E. Meade, in some recent lectures,[7] stresses the marked disadvantages of minimum real wages, whether for a limited class of workers, or for workers in all occupations, or by limiting the

7. J. E. Meade, *Efficiency, Equality and the Ownership of Property* (London: George Allen and Unwin, 1964).

amount of work so that the overall resulting unemployment is shared. Each of these approaches is very inefficient.

As presently administered in the United States, farm price supports predominantly benefit farm families who are well above the poverty line; high price supports impede efficient resource allocation and also confound the income-wealth paradox in agriculture.[8] Consider why "farm families" are so rich in wealth and so poor in income. The facts are (1) the net worth of the assets owned by farm operator families is on the average twice as large as that of nonfarm families ($44,000 and $21,700 respectively[9]) and yet (2) the proportion of farm families who are below the poverty line of less than $3,000 income is two and a half times that of nonfarm families (43 and 18 per cent respectively). The value of wealth, which consists mainly of farmland, is subsidized; the value of farm work is depressed by acreage allotments and other measures to contract production. Thus, these programs are strongly biased in favor of farm wealth (income from property) and against income from farm work. The financial benefits in general and the government payments to farmers in particular go predominantly to the more well-to-do farmers, those at the top of the farm ladder, as the estimates in Table 8.1 show. The overall effects of the

TABLE 8.1. GOVERNMENT PAYMENTS TO FARMERS IN 1963

	DISTRIBUTION OF FARMS	GOVERNMENT PAYMENTS		
Farms with sales of	*(per cent)*	*Total (million dollars)*	*Per farm (dollars)*	*Distribution of total (per cent)*
$20,000 and over	10.7	918	2,391	54.5
$10,000 to $19,999	16.6	398	670	23.6
$5,000 to $9,999	17.0	213	350	12.6
$2,500 to $4,999	13.0	80	173	4.7
Less than $2,500	42.7	77	51	4.6
Total	100	1,686	472	100

8. See my "Economic Basis for a New Agricultural Policy Consensus," in *Proceedings of the Fifth Annual Farm Policy Review Conference, Washington, D.C., January 25–27, 1965* (Ames: Iowa State University, in press).

9. *Federal Reserve Bull.*, March 1964.

high farm price supports and associated programs upon the size distribution of personal income among farm families are clearly regressive. Could it be that there is here a "war *for* poverty?"

Progressive taxation

We have come to rely heavily on progressive taxes for revenue and to reduce the economic inequalities between the rich and the poor.[10] Progressive taxation undoubtedly has considerable positive effect in this direction, but it is not free of legislative faults; the tax law is beset with loopholes—for example, special depletion allowances for oil and other minerals and the "swindle sheet" which allows particular personal expenditures to be deducted as business expenses. Much more serious, however, is the fact that the income from business which is not paid out in dividends escapes personal income taxation. To compensate we settle for a poor second best, namely special large taxes on corporations.

In extending the logic of progressive taxation to alleviate poverty, my colleague Milton Friedman has proposed a *negative income tax.*[11] Under this proposal, when the taxable income of an individual or family falls below a figure set by public policy, the taxpayer "would pay a negative tax, i.e., receive a subsidy." There is indeed merit in this approach in alleviating some classes of poverty in our society for reasons cogently presented by Friedman in his book.

10. The classic treatment of this subject is by the late Henry C. Simon, *Personal Income Taxation* (Chicago: University of Chicago Press, 1938).

11. Milton Friedman, *Capitalism and Freedom* (Chicago: University of Chicago Press, 1962), Ch. 12. On pp. 191–92, Friedman states: "First, if the objective is to alleviate poverty, we should have a program directed at helping the poor. There is every reason to help the poor man who happens to be a farmer, not because he is a farmer but because he is poor. The program, that is, should be designed to help people as people not as members of particular occupational groups or age groups or wage-rate groups or labor organizations or industries. This is a defect of farm programs, general old-age benefits, minimum-wage laws, pro-union legislation, tariffs, licensing provisions of crafts or professions, and so on in seemingly endless profusion. Second, so far as possible the program should, while operating through the market, not distort the market or impede its functioning. This is a defect of price supports, minimum-wage laws, tariffs, and the like. The arrangement that recommends itself on purely mechanical grounds is a negative income tax."

Reforms are also long overdue in the domain of federal estate and gift taxation. Douglas Dillon, on retiring as Secretary of the Treasury, called attention to the untaxed wealth that is acquired through capital gains. Profesor Meade, in the lectures to which I have referred, makes a strong case for radical reforms in death duties and taxes on gifts *inter vivos*. He gives Sweden a good mark on this score: "In Sweden there is (i) a progressive tax on capital gains, (ii) a progressive annual tax on total personal wealth, (iii) a progressive tax on gifts *inter vivos,* and (iv) a progressive tax on individual bequests."[12] The case here does not rest on grounds that income from property is rising relative to total income, or that the personal distribution of wealth is becoming more unequal, or that the incomes of families who are presently in poverty will be lifted appreciably in a decade or two. It rests on the serious defects in the tax treatment of inherited wealth and on the longer-run implications of these defects upon the personal distribution of wealth and income. It will suffice to mention only one of these defects: earnings of business enterprises that are not distributed as dividends escape taxation as current personal income and as capital gains simply by transferring private wealth thus acquired through inheritance.

Growth and employment

Although they are yoked together by theory and policy, it is useful to distinguish between the rate of economic growth and the rate of unemployment in studying poverty. A searching dialogue is underway in economics to clarify the effects of each upon poverty. I am indebted here to my colleague Harry G. Johnson, whose chapter, "Unemployment and Poverty," deals with a related problem. I shall restrict my comments to three issues: (1) the observed decline in poverty associated with economic growth, (2) the incidences of poverty attributed to unemployment, and (3) the extent of so-called "structural poverty."

As I have pointed out elsewhere,[13] growth in our economy is

12. Friedman, op. cit., Preface.
13. See my "Investing in Poor People: An Economist's View," op. cit., pp. 510–20.

very pervasive; among other things, it leads to increases in income per family, which in turn leads to a rise in the poverty line because of our social preferences. Even though our concept of poverty measured in terms of real income changes over time, economic growth has reduced substantially the proportion of families that fall below this rising poverty line. For example, since 1935, real income per family has doubled, and we have raised the poverty line about 55 per cent (from $1,950 to $3,000 in 1959 prices), yet the proportion of families below this rising line has fallen from about one-third to one-fifth of all families.[14] To gain perspective historically, let me divide the period since the industrial revolution into two parts: first, economic growth with no appreciable rise in per family income; and second, a fairly recent development, economic growth with increases in per family income. Classical theory continues to be relevant in investigating poverty in an economy in which there is growth but no rise in per family income,[15] but our economy is obviously not of this type. Unfortunately there is no theoretical scaffold in economics that integrates the functional and personal income streams for an economy of our type. I shall advance the hypothesis later that earnings of laborers have been rising as a consequence of the growth of investment in human beings and that this development has been the primary factor in reducing poverty during recent decades.

Lowell E. Gallaway's estimates[16] relating growth and unemployment to poverty bear directly on the first two issues I introduced above. Using the definition of poverty which places families with less than $3,000 of income below the current poverty line, he shows that if the 1947–56 growth rate and 4 per cent unemployment had been maintained from 1956 to 1963, poverty would have declined by almost 2 percentage points more than it actually did

14. I draw here on Eugene Smolensky, "The Past and Present Poor," mimeographed paper, University of Chicago. Also, see Ruth Mack's estimates of (1) a contemporary definition of subsistence and (2) a 1960 definition of subsistence cited in n. 3 of my paper in *Amer. Econ. Rev.*, op. cit., p. 512.

15. The magnificent dynamics of Malthus, Ricardo, James Mill, McCulloch, and Senior—the leading classical economists—consists of a model in which earnings per laborer do not rise.

16. Lowell E. Gallaway, "The Foundations of the 'War on Poverty,'" *Amer. Econ. Rev.*, 55 (March 1965), 122–31.

(to 16.6, compared to the actual of 18.5 per cent). When he applies the 1947–56 growth rate and 4 per cent unemployment, his projected poverty for 1970 declines to 12.6 per cent, but to only 14.2 per cent when he applies the 1957–63 growth rate and 6 per cent unemployment. The estimates of Gallaway and of the Council of Economic Advisers of the percentage of families in the poverty class are compared in Table 8.2.

TABLE 8.2. PERCENTAGE OF FAMILIES IN THE POVERTY CLASS

| | GALLAWAY'S ESTIMATES | | COUNCIL OF ECONOMIC ADVISERS' ESTIMATES | |
	1947–56 growth rate and 4% unemployment	*1957–63 growth rate and 6% unemployment*	*1947–56 rate of elimination*	*1957–62 rate of elimination*
1947 (actual)	31.7		31.7	
1956 (actual)	22.2		22.2	
1963 (actual)		18.5		18.5
1963 (projected)	16.6			
1970 (projected)	12.6	14.2		
1980 (projected)	6.4	8.7	10.0	13.0

The difference between Gallaway's and the Council's projected decline in poverty may be taken as a measure of differing views of the magnitude of structural poverty. I would not, however, take either of these two implicit concepts of structural poverty seriously, because in making these estimates no attempt has been made to specify, identify, and measure the components that cause structural poverty. A simple projection of the observed decline in poverty during recent decades associated with economic growth conceals the components that matter. What we want to know here are the particular new sources of income that have accounted for the observed decline in poverty. Once this is known, we can proceed to determine whether further investments in such sources would reduce poverty and by how much. The poverty that would still persist might be called structural, but a large part of it might also be amenable to treatment by other and additional forms of investment.

Investment in poor people

I now turn to the last of the four public approaches to minimize poverty to be considered here. It is especially relevant in coping with what is commonly concealed under so-called structural poverty. I shall show that much of the poverty of many Negro families and of the poor families in agriculture and in the South is a consequence of long-standing chronic disequilibria rooted in inadequate investment in particular classes of people, who are therefore poor.

Let me begin by calling attention to important shifts in the sources of income that have characterized our type of economic progress. Income streams can be given quantitative dimensions per unit of time—i.e. a one-dollar-per-year income stream. Except for income transfers, to obtain possession of an income stream it is necessary to acquire the source of income in that stream. These sources are valuable, and each has a price which may be low or high. The underlying assumptions are quite conventional. The sources of income streams are acquired at particular prices, which change over time; people respond to changes in these prices subject to the restraints of the capital market, their preferences and capacity to save, the effects of taxes and subsidies and of discrimination with respect to employment and investment in human sources. We can then postulate a dynamic process and derive the following complementary hypotheses that pertain to the process of growth in our economy:[17]

1. The price of the sources of income streams that represent the acquired human capabilities of value in economic endeavor declined during this period relative to the price of other income streams.
2. In responding to this change in the relative prices of these two sources of income, the rate of investment in human sources rose during this period relative to that in material sources.
3. The increase in the investment in human sources of income relative to the investment in nonhuman sources has

17. I follow closely here my paper "Investing in Poor People: An Economist's View," op. cit.

increased income of persons relative to property income, and the more equal distribution of investment in men has tended to equalize earnings among human agents.

These are testable hypotheses, and they appear to win support from a number of new studies. The private rates of financial return to those who complete more years of schooling support the first. My attempt to test the second, admittedly rough, indicates that, for the period between 1929 and 1957, investment in the stock of reproducible tangible wealth increased at an annual rate of about 2 per cent, while investment in education of the labor force rose at a rate of 4 per cent, and investment in on-the-job training of males in the labor force, at over 5 per cent. The marked increase in the proportion of the labor force that has attended high school and college is one of the developments in support of the third hypothesis.[18]

Over the long run both the demand for and supply of sources of income streams are subject to change, some of which are cumulative and become large over time. Among the factors that alter the demand, three are of major importance.

1. The aggregate demand for goods and services. The level of this demand was obviously far from sufficient during the massive unemployment of the early 1930s, although more nearly adequate during the high employment of the mid-1950s. Since then there has been much slack; idle plants and idle men reduce the demand for the sources of income. Clearly poor people have much at stake in a government policy that will maintain full employment.

2. Advances in knowledge, commonly concealed under "technological change." New knowledge that is useful in economic endeavor requires either new forms of material capital or new skills

18. During a normal business cycle the supply—the sources of these income streams—does not change substantially. The demand, however, shifts back and forth considerably during recessions and booms and, as a consequence, the income from corporate and some other forms of property fluctuates more over the cycle than national income. The fluctuations in income from wages and salaries are largest for unskilled labor, for workers who are least specific in their training in terms of the labor requirements of employers, and for workers who have the least seniority, with the result that the inequality of the personal distribution of income decreases in years of prosperity and increases in years of depression.

on the part of labor or, what is true in general, both are required. This factor, so it appears, has increased the demand for high skills relative to low skills.

3. Changes in restrictions "on the opportunity for individuals to participate in the productive process to the full extent of their potential."[19] What matters here is hiring discrimination against Negroes, against the aged who still are willing and able to do productive work but who are required to quit working or work only part-time to be eligible for retirement and survivor payments, and against women in the labor force.

The long-run changes in the supply of the sources of income streams may be explored either in terms of adjustments to shifts in the demand, or in terms of factors that are relatively independent of shifts in demand. The adjustment process in which the demand and supply interact is at the core of the economic behavior underlying the formulation of hypothesis 2 above. The major "independent" factors affecting the supply are: research and development activities and dissemination of the resulting useful knowledge from these activities; the mobility (immobility) of particular sources, predominantly labor, in leaving declining industries and occupations; the amount and distribution of public investment in schooling and, closely related, the discrimination against Negroes, rural farm children, and others with respect to schooling.

Thus, the analytical task at hand is to account for the observed decline in poverty or, alternatively, to account for the poverty that remains. Although the latter has the appeal of being more direct, it may be less efficient, because the first task is undoubtedly a prerequisite to the second. I shall therefore continue to concentrate on the first task.

Income from property

By all accounts the functional share of income from property has been declining. The stock of tangible reproducible wealth has not increased at as high a rate as the acquired abilities of workers. Differences in the private rates of return have favored investment

19. I follow closely here Harry G. Johnson's "Unemployment and Poverty," Chapter 9.

in human capital. True, the relative decline in income from material wealth would undoubtedly have been somewhat less during the recent past had the tax on corporate income remained at the pre-war level. Meanwhile, what has been happening to the personal distribution of wealth holdings? It is hard to believe that the decline in poverty has been brought about by the fact that poor people have been acquiring a substantially larger share of material wealth. The stock of wealth represented by houses may be an exception in the sense that a house has been an attractive investment for many low-income families while the economy has been adjusting to the favorable tax treatment of home-ownership. But houses owned by families with less than $3,000 of income in 1962 had a mean value of only $3,750. Any plausible increase in the net worth of low-income consumers since the mid-1930s could account for only a very small part of the decline in poverty.

Income from labor

Meanwhile, labor's functional share of national income has been rising. The demand for workers with high skills has been increasing at a higher rate than the demand for low skills. The incentive to increase skills has been strong, and the supply of skills has been responding; for people have been investing much more than formerly to increase their skills. But why has the demand for skills been shifting upward in this manner? In my judgment, it is mainly a consequence of the dynamic process in which the development of skills and growing knowledge have been gradually raising per capita income and changing the pattern of goods and services demanded so as to call for a more rapid rate of increase in the need for high skills relative to the need for low skills. Another factor in this process has undoubtedly been the increase in the demand for producer durables and services by the military establishment.

Implications

The first and most general implication is that the observed large decline in poverty is primarily a consequence of increases in income from labor and not in income from property. The real earnings of workers have been rising because the demand for high skills has been increasing relative to that for low skills and because workers have been acquiring the more valuable skills.

Another implication is that a substantial part of the remaining poverty is a consequence of a number of disequilibria. Although workers have been responding to the changes in the market for skills, the economy in this respect has been in substantial disequilibrium at many points. The reasons why this is so are fairly obvious: namely, unemployment, the adverse incidences of economic growth in some sectors, inadequate knowledge, and a lack of opportunity to invest in acquiring the more valuable skills because of discrimination and the restraints on the capital market in providing funds for this purpose. Let me call attention to three of these imbalances.

1. The market for the skills required in agriculture has been long depressed. Although the labor force devoted to farming has declined by half since 1940, the market for these skills is still in serious disequilibrium. Older members of this labor force have had no real alternative but to settle for the depressed, salvage value of the skills they possess. In many farm areas the quality of elementary and secondary schooling has been and continues to be far below par, and thus the oncoming generation in these areas is ill-prepared to take advantage of the strong market in other parts of the economy for high skills. It should also be repeated here that the vast expenditures by the federal government on behalf of agriculture have not been used to raise the level of these skills; on the contrary, they have been used in ways that enhance the income from some classes of property and that worsen the personal distribution of income among farm families. Thus it should not come as a surprise that, although farm families are presently a very small fraction of all U.S. families, they account for much of the observed poverty, and in addition many of the families in urban areas who are below the poverty line have recently come from farms.

2. The market for the skills of Negroes has also been long depressed, and the poverty component here is large. This market has been intertwined with that of agriculture and, both on our farms and in our cities, there has been and continues to be much job discrimination. More important still is the low level of skills of Negroes, which is mainly a consequence of the history of dis-

crimination against Negroes in schooling. Not only have Negroes obtained fewer years of schooling but the schooling has been of very low quality; it was especially so for the older Negroes in the labor force.

3. The South is burdened with much more poverty than other regions, basically for three reasons: (1) it is more dependent upon agriculture than the rest of the United States (it accounted for over 45 per cent of all U.S. farms at the time the 1959 census of agriculture was taken); (2) the labor force in the South is more largely Negro than in the North and West and, in terms of marketable skills, the Negroes in the South are even worse off than the Negroes in other regions; and (3) relatively more of the whites in the labor force in the South have low skills than whites in other regions. In short, the South has been lagging seriously behind in providing people the opportunities to invest in acquiring the high skills for which the demand has been increasing at so rapid a rate, predominantly because of social, political, and economic discrimination that continues to work against poor people.

A level of aggregate demand that would make it possible to attain a rate of economic growth which would provide full employment ranks high as an approach for reducing poverty over time. But more than this is clearly warranted. An important complementary public approach calls for investment in poor people. Our so-called structural poverty is to a large extent a result of such investment opportunities in human beings having been thwarted by social, political, and economic discrimination adverse to poor people.

9: Unemployment and Poverty

by Harry G. Johnson

In asserting a relationship between unemployment and poverty, I do not mean merely to refer to the well-known fact that individual cases or groups of cases of poverty are frequently attributable to the unemployment or only partial employment of the individual or the family head. Rather, I mean to refer to a relationship between the level of unemployment in the economy—the percentage of the labor force unemployed—and the prevalence of poverty. The level of unemployment normally characteristic of the economy has, in addition to its direct influence on the number who are poor, a variety of indirect influences on the prevalence of poverty, such that unemployment is a much more important cause of poverty than may appear at first sight.

In consequence of this, the maintenance of a low level of unemployment is an essential precondition of success in the war on poverty, in two major respects: first, to activate to the full the natural processes by which a free enterprise economy tends gradually to eliminate poverty; second, to ensure that many of the detailed programs of the war on poverty will be successful, in the dual sense of the poor being motivated to take advantage of them and of the programs actually succeeding in raising people above the poverty line. To maintain a low unemployment percentage, however, it is necessary for the government to establish and maintain a high level of demand in the economy; and this may give rise to two related problems: price inflation and a worsening of the balance of payments—problems which call for recognition and discussion.

For the present purposes, I define poverty in the usual sense, as existing when the resources of families or individuals are inadequate to provide a socially acceptable standard of living. Both the specification of what standard of living should be regarded as socially acceptable (the poverty standard) and the measurement of the resources available to people for comparison with that standard, in order to evaluate the size and shape of the poverty problem, bristle with difficulties; but these difficulties have been discussed elsewhere in this volume. Defined in this way—as inadequacy of financial resources or "income"—poverty inevitably has a multiplicity of causes, or, to put the same point another way, the poor have no unique common characteristics that distinguish them from the nonpoor other than their poverty itself. This fact, in turn, generates a strong tendency for those concerned with poverty to adopt a categorical approach, and to think in terms of a long list of remedial programs aimed at mitigating or eliminating particular subspecies of poverty. While this is a necessary part of the attack on poverty, preoccupation with the categories of poverty can obscure or prevent understanding of the broader economics of the poverty problem and of the economic strategy required for the war on poverty. I should like to begin, therefore, by sketching out an analytical framework which I have found useful in my own thinking on the poverty problem.[1]

In a free enterprise economy, production, distribution, and consumption are organized for the most part by the self-interested decisions of two types of economic units. Production is organized by the profit-seeking decisions of business firms, and consumption by the satisfaction-seeking decisions of households or individuals. The households or individuals obtain their incomes from the use, or sale to firms, of the services of labor and capital they command.

1. See my *The Social Policy of an Opulent Society* (Ottawa: The Canadian Welfare Council, 1961), reprinted as Ch. 16 in my *The Canadian Quandary* (Toronto: McGraw-Hill Co. of Canada, 1963); and "Poverty and Unemployment" (mimeographed, University of Chicago, October 1964).

The level of economic welfare enjoyed by any individual depends on the quantities and values of the services of the labor and capital commanded by himself, or the household (family) to which he belongs, and on the number of individuals who share in the income obtained by using or selling these services. Poverty—a level of economic welfare inferior to a socially acceptable minimum standard—is therefore the resultant of an interaction between the income yielded by the resources of labor and capital commanded by the consuming unit and the number of individuals dependent on the income of the unit. It is, however, both conceptually possible and analytically useful to distinguish between the two broad causes of or factors determining poverty: low income of the consuming unit arising from the low values or small quantities of the productive services the consuming unit can provide to the economy, and low income per individual arising from the presence of an exceptionally large number of individuals in the consuming unit—in brief, low earning power and large family size. Approaches to the poverty problem may focus on either of these factors.

CAUSES OF POVERTY

The importance of family size as a determining factor in poverty was overlooked in the analysis of poverty presented in the 1964 *Annual Report* of the Council of Economic Advisers, which used a crude definition of poverty in terms of a family income of $3,000 regardless of family size and thus (among other things) grossly overstated the extent of poverty among young adults and people over 65. Subsequent criticism of the *Report's* analysis[2] and a more comprehensive analysis of the incidence of poverty by Mollie Orshansky[3] have reinstated the large family as a potent factor in poverty. Large family size operates primarily to reduce the share

2. Rose D. Friedman, *Poverty: Definition and Perspective* (Washington, D.C.: American Enterprise Institute, February 1965).

3. Mollie Orshansky, "Counting the Poor: Another Look at the Poverty Profile," *Social Security Bull.*, January 1965, pp. 3–29. I am grateful to Eveline Burns for reminding me of the importance of family size as a factor in poverty, which I had overlooked in an earlier formulation ("Poverty and Unemployment," op. cit.), and for calling my attention to Orshansky's recent work on the analysis of poverty.

of the family income available to meet each individual member's needs; but it also can operate in various ways to reduce the total family income, notably by preventing the mother from working.

The association of large family size with poverty, it may be remarked, is a consequence of reliance on the free enterprise system of economic organization, on the one hand, and of the combination of personal freedom and institutionally cultivated ignorance that governs family formation and family size under our social arrangements, on the other. A competitive free enterprise system will not (and cannot afford to) pay more for a productive service obtained from one source than it pays to another source, simply because the welfare of more individuals depends on that source. But if knowledge of the means of family limitation were universal and resort to them socially sanctioned and encouraged, variations of family size would reflect rational choices stemming from differences in people's preferences as between higher consumption per head and more heads in the family, and, apart from families headed by incompetent adults, there would be no genuine problem of poverty associated with variations in family size. It is the combination of a rational economic system and a largely irrational system of family size determination that underlies this part of the poverty problem.

Correspondingly, there are two alternative approaches to solving the problem of poverty caused by family size excessive in relation to means. One is to de-rationalize the economic system (or, perhaps more accurately, to rationalize it in terms of social rather than economic objectives) by arranging in one way or another to pay families incomes proportioned to the number of their members —in other words, to pay for the production of people as well as of goods and services. This is the method of family allowances or the negative income tax. The other is to rationalize the determination of family size to make it accord with earning capacity. This is the intent of the current movement to disseminate birth control information among the poor; logically the approach could extend to legalized abortion, and even beyond that to compulsory sterilization or euthanasia in certain circumstances to be legally defined.

The other broad factor determining poverty is low earning power, or more specifically the inability to sell productive services sufficient in quantity and/or value to support the socially accept-able minimum standard of living.[4] Such inability may be sepa-rated into three broad types: (1) poverty caused by the failure of the economy to provide enough jobs for those able and willing to work, and capable of earning an adequate income if allowed to work; (2) poverty caused by the inability of individuals to contribute enough service to the productive process to earn an income above the poverty line; (3) poverty caused by the existence of restrictions of greater or lesser severity on the opportunity for individuals to participate in the productive process to the full extent of their potential. The first of these is a question of de-mand for, the second a question of supply of, productive services; the third can be classed indifferently as a question either of supply or of demand, depending on whether one takes the view of those imposing or those burdened by the restrictions.

Poverty of the first type, resulting from unemployment or under-employment, is ultimately the consequence of a failure of govern-ment policy to keep the level of demand for goods and services high enough to provide as many jobs as are wanted. This was a major cause of poverty in the 1930s, and it has become a significant cause of poverty in the past eight years. In the 1930s, the failure of policy was a consequence of government ignorance of how to manage the economy; more recently, it has been a consequence not of ignorance but of giving priority to other objectives of eco-nomic policy, first the prevention of inflation and then the remedy-ing of the balance-of-payments deficit. Poverty of this type is cur-able by fiscal and monetary policy, aimed at keeping aggregate demand at an adequate level; if this remedy is ruled out by other policy objectives, a strong argument can be made that those on whom the pursuit of these objectives imposes the costs of un-employment should be adequately compensated, either by decent unemployment benefits or, possibly, by training designed to equip them for reabsorption in the labor force in ways that will not generate inflationary pressure or have adverse effects on the balance of payments. As I shall argue later, however, there are good reasons for doubting that compensation could or would really be provided

4. This and the following paragraphs draw on my earlier paper, "Poverty and Unemployment," op. cit.

777777777777777777

on an adequate scale, and even stronger reasons for preferring the pursuit of full employment, even at a cost in terms of inflation and the balance of payments.

Poverty of the second type can be described as essentially due to immobility of the labor force, if immobility is conceived of broadly to include inability to acquire the skills necessary to earn a decent wage as a result either of innate deficiencies or deficiencies of family background, inability to participate full-time in the labor force for physical, psychological, or family reasons, inability to move from contracting to expanding industries or occupations, and inability to move geographically. Poverty of this kind calls for government policies of assisting mobility, through the provision of education facilities, employment services, and assistance to migration, all of which can be looked on as investments in increasing earning power or, in the now fashionable economics jargon, investments in the creation of human capital.

This approach motivates the Economic Opportunity Act. To the economist, it involves two dangers. The first arises from the fact that politics is about places rather than people; this is an inevitable consequence of the fact the political representation is based on geography. The political process consequently has a strong bias toward attempting, not to make people better off by the most efficient means, which frequently demands radical changes of location and occupation, but toward attempting to make them better off in their existing locations and in their accustomed activities; the result is frequently to perpetuate the poverty problem into future generations rather than to solve it.[5] The second danger arises from the fact that investments in human capital, like other investments, may have too low and risky a pay-off to be worth society's while, either because the immobility in question is irremediable (e.g. mental and motivational deficiency) or because the investment is extremely expensive in relation to the improvement in well-being it produces. It may be much cheaper for society to pay a poor person an adequate income than to train or retrain, equip or re-equip, or relocate him. Our society has a marked aversion to eliminating poverty by the simple ex-

5. On this and other problems of democracy, see my "The Economics and Politics of Opulence," *Univ. of Toronto Quart.*, *34*, June 1965, and "The Political Economy of Opulence," Ch. 15 in *The Canadian Quandary*, op. cit.

pedient of paying cash; but it is prepared to make an exception for the casualties of military service, and it might well accord similar consideration to the casualties of economic progress.

Poverty of the third type is essentially due to discrimination, and it is more widespread than might appear at first sight. The notion that discrimination is responsible for the greater incidence of poverty among nonwhites is a familiar one, and has been thoroughly documented in recent years.[6] But discrimination is also involved in the case of the aged poor, whom our society frequently forces to retire from remunerative work before their productive capacity and willingness to work are exhausted, and whom we are prepared to assist with public money only on condition that they do not work, or work only part-time for low wages. In a more subtle way, discrimination against the aged is involved in one of the causes of aged poverty, the erosion of the real value of people's savings by inflation. In allowing unions and corporations to raise wages and prices, we sacrifice the interests of past participants in the productive process to those of present participants.

Furthermore, discrimination is at the root of the high incidence of poverty among households headed by women; for our society discriminates against the participation of women in the more remunerative occupations in countless ways: through giving women inferior educational opportunities, through restricting the job opportunities open to them and denying them promotion on equal terms with men, and through insisting that women with young children should remain home to look after them, which both prevents women from acquiring the employment experience necessary to command good jobs should they eventually have to support themselves, and prevents them from working, or from working full-time, if they find themselves in the position of heading families with young children. Finally, I suspect that discrimination is partly responsible for the association of poverty with low levels of educational attainment in another, unacknowledged way: a requirement of educational qualifications may frequently be less a matter of the necessity of the education than a simple means of narrowing down the applicants that have to be considered to a manageable number.

6. See, for example, Allan B. Batchelder, "Decline in the Relative Income of Negro Men," *Quart. J. Econ., 78,* no. 4 (November 1964), 525–48.

As in the case of poverty caused by immobility, there are two ways to tackle poverty caused by discrimination. One is to direct policy at the elimination of discrimination—policies of this kind would involve preventing people who wish to discriminate against the nonwhite, the aged, the female, and the uneducated from doing so; bribing them not to do so by the expenditure of public funds; and investing in the development of the talents of the categories of humanity discriminated against, so as to enable them to pass over the poverty line either by becoming acceptable to the discriminators or by earning a sufficient income despite discrimination. The alternative is to recognize that the existence of discrimination is economically disadvantageous to those who are discriminated against and to compensate them for it. Thus, if we want older people to retire from the labor market, either because others want their jobs or because it is considered that work will be injurious to them, we should make it worth their while to retire, rather than push them out into poverty. Similarly, if the competition of women in the labor market is feared, or if it is believed that society will gain more from the exercise of their child-rearing talents than from their economic activities, society should pay women enough to make them content with the role assigned to them, instead of condemning them to poverty by preventing them from working. The cases of the aged and the female worker, of course, raise a genuine problem of balancing social and economic considerations; a policy of bribing the nonwhite or the uneducated to remain economically inferior would make little sense, even though in some ways our society does precisely that.

INFLUENCE OF UNEMPLOYMENT ON POVERTY

So much for the general framework of analysis, which in brief attributes poverty to family size and to low earning power caused by unemployment or underemployment, immobility (defined in a very broad sense), and discrimination (also defined in a very broad sense). Our concern here is with the influence of unemployment on poverty.

There can be no doubt that unemployment and underemployment—that is, being out of work or being able to obtain work only part-time—are a significant part of the explanation of poverty. Unfortunately, it is extremely difficult to establish quantitatively how significant it is. The difficulty is partly due to the fact that statistical research on the poverty problem has been largely concerned with enumeration and the analysis of incidence, rather than with the still more difficult task of explanation in terms of causal factors. There has also been a marked tendency in official analyses of the poverty problem—quite natural under the circumstances—to stress other factors in poverty than unemployment, factors that are amenable to attack through specific government programs, and to emphasize the prevalence of poverty among the full-time employed. But there are inherent difficulties in isolating the influence of unemployment, particularly of the aggregate level of unemployment, on the prevalence of poverty.

It is well-established that the incidence of poverty is substantially higher for families with heads not in the labor force than for families with heads in the labor force, and for those whose heads are unemployed than for those whose heads are employed. To put it the other way around, a substantially higher proportion of the heads of poor families than of nonpoor families are not in the labor force, and a substantially higher proportion of the heads of poor families who are in the labor force are unemployed than is true of nonpoor families; likewise, the proportion of heads of poor families enjoying full-time work is significantly smaller than for nonpoor families.[7] There is therefore a presumption that a reduction in the amount of unemployment, achieved by government policies increasing the general demand for labor, would decrease poverty, not only by drawing the unemployed into employment and providing fuller-time work for the only partially employed but also by drawing some of the poor into the labor force. (It is a well-confirmed fact that participation in the labor force is a function of the unemployment percentage.)

However, nonparticipation in the labor force by the poor is particularly likely to be the result of inability to participate rather than of deliberate economic choice. Moreover, as already mentioned, full-time employment frequently yields an income insufficient to surmount poverty, and there might be reason to expect that those of the poor drawn into employment by a higher

7. See Orshansky, op. cit., pp. 17–21.

demand for labor would be particularly likely to go into lower-paid employment. On the other hand, in connection with the emphasis that has been placed on low-income occupations as an important factor in poverty, it should be noticed that there is some tendency toward a direct relationship between the unemployment rate and the proportion of the labor force engaged in the lower-income occupations, so that a decrease in unemployment would tend to move people into higher-paying occupations. Thus it is uncertain how far an increase in demand for labor and a consequent reduction in unemployment would operate directly to reduce poverty.

The only concrete evidence on this particular question of which I am aware is contained in a recent article by Lowell E. Gallaway.[8] Gallaway presents a statistical analysis of the relation between the poverty percentage, as calculated by the Council of Economic Advisers, and two economic variables: median family income, taken to represent economic progress, and the unemployment rate. While the increase in median family income over the period 1947–63 explains most of the reduction in the poverty rate during that period, the rate of unemployment has a significant influence on the poverty rate—an increase in the annual average unemployment rate of one percentage point increasing the poverty percentage by a half of one per cent of itself.

Unfortunately, as already noted, the Council's method of measuring poverty is seriously defective, and the defects are such that the influence of unemployment on poverty is more likely to be overstated than understated by Gallaway's calculation. Nevertheless, to the extent that the Council's figures can be taken as reasonable approximations to the magnitude of the percentage in poverty, in view of their faulty method for analyzing the composition of the poor,[9] the calculation does indicate that a decrease in the unemployment rate would have a significant, though by no means decisive, effect in reducing the prevalence of poverty.

8. L. E. Gallaway, "The Foundations of the 'War on Poverty,'" *Amer. Econ. Rev.*, *55*, no. 1 (March 1965), 122–31.

9. Orshansky, op. cit., p. 11, points out that although the total numbers of the poor are approximately the same (actually, about 4 per cent less) whether one uses the Council's definition or her more refined standard, the change in definition makes a great difference to the statistical composition of the poor.

The argument expounded so far, however, is concerned only with the direct and short-run relation between unemployment and poverty. There are cogent reasons, supported by evidence of a broader and more qualitative kind, for believing that the state of demand for labor has an important indirect and longer-run influence on the prevalence of poverty, and specifically that maintenance of a high level of demand for labor and a low unemployment rate would in the course of time greatly reduce the percentage of the population in poverty. There are two aspects to this proposition: one concerns the effects of maintaining a low average rate of unemployment, the other concerns the effects of avoiding fluctuations in the rate of unemployment.

To take the latter aspect first, both general economic reasoning and some detailed evidence indicate that fluctuations in the unemployment rate, associated with the business cycle, leave a residue of poverty that could be avoided by maintaining economic stability. The reason is that periods of unemployment have a permanent effect on the earning power of the unemployed, an effect that is not compensated for by periods of high demand for labor. Specifically, there are two major groups of victims of cyclically heavy unemployment: the youthful entrants to the labor force, whose failure to find work permanently impairs their future earnings because they miss the opportunity to obtain the on-the-job training necessary to fit them for higher-paying employment later in their careers; and the older workers, who find it difficult to become re-employed, or re-employed in as well-paying jobs, in the subsequent period of cyclically high employment. For both groups, cyclical unemployment not only increases the current incidence of poverty but increases the likely future incidence of poverty. The existence and importance of this effect is well documented in a recent study of changes in the income situation of the different age groups since 1947 by Dorothy S. Brady and F. Gerard Adams. These authors report:[10]

> The new generations of young men are experiencing a relative decline in their incomes which for those under 25 seems

10. Dorothy S. Brady and F. Gerard Adams, "Changes in the Income Situation of the Different Age Groups" (mimeographed paper, University of Pennsylvania, May 1964), p. 46.

about to become an absolute reduction in level. Each of the
recurring recessions, every three or four years, had reduced
the incomes of the youngest and the oldest men relative to
those between 35 and 55 and recoveries did not offset the
losses in their comparative income status. The secular changes
in the structure of skills appear to intensify the impact of a
recession by leaving a part of the youngest and the oldest age
cohorts in a permanently lower income position.

The effects of cyclical fluctuations in unemployment on earning
capacity and therefore on poverty are indicative of the relationship
between the average percentage of unemployment characteristic
of the economy and the prevalence of poverty and the rate at
which general economic progress tends to reduce it. The point here
is that the state of demand relative to supply in the labor market
determines the extent to which the economic system generates
incentives for the improvement of individual earning power and
thus for raising individuals out of poverty. When the demand for
labor is high, there are abundant incentives to employers to invest
in improving the skills of their labor force and for employees to
invest in improving themselves. When, on the contrary, the demand for labor is slack, these incentives are reduced or disappear:
employers can obtain skilled labor in the market without having
to invest in training, while the decreased probability of obtaining
employment reduces the prospective return to investment by the
individual worker in self-improvement.

A tight labor market is in fact a powerful solvent of poverty
attributable to immobility and discrimination. A high demand for
labor provides incentives not only for the upgrading of unskilled
labor but for the migration of labor to better-paid occupations
and to higher-income geographical locations. An example of the
latter was the massive movement of people off the farms into
urban employment and away from the South during World
War II; another is the current massive movement of labor in
Europe as a result of abundant employment opportunities in the
Common Market countries, a movement from the lower-income
Mediterranean countries—Italy, Greece, Turkey—to the high-
income northern countries, especially Germany. Equally, a high
demand for labor tends to weaken or eliminate barriers to the

employment of individuals owing to discrimination based on sex, color, age, or lack of adequate education: undesirable labor is better than no labor. Again, wartime experience provides a striking example: the pressure of wartime demand for labor virtually eliminated anti-Semitism as an economic force and opened up an extensive range of new and better-paid employment opportunities for women and colored people.

Conversely, however, a slack labor market reduces the incentives to overcome immobility, and accentuates the practice of discrimination. The incentives to change occupation, to educate oneself, or to move geographically, are obviously smaller when the risk of being unemployed afterwards is higher. Also, when jobs are scarce and applicants are plentiful, so that jobs have to be rationed, it is inevitable that the rationing will be done according to social standards of preference—or, more bluntly, by discrimination. Color, sex, age, inexperience, and inferior educational attainment are obvious characteristics that can serve as a means of automatically excluding individuals from the competition for scarce jobs.

Moreover, in times of job scarcity those favored by discrimination will be led by collective self-interest to insist on its enforcement, to reduce their own exposure to the risk of unemployment. It is no accident that unemployment falls more heavily on Negro than on white males, and more heavily on the young than on married men with families. A striking illustration of the connection between the level of unemployment and discrimination is provided by Allen Batchelder's finding that whereas in the tight labor market of the 1940s the income position of Negro men improved relative to that of white men, in the slack labor market of the 1950s the relative income position of Negro men deteriorated in each of the four major regions of the country, and Negro men became more dependent on the earnings of Negro women.[11]

The maintenance of economic stability, a tight labor market and a low level of unemployment would therefore make a substantial contribution to the reduction of poverty, both directly through the employment provided and indirectly through economic incentives to overcome immobility and discrimination. It

11. Batchelder, op. cit.

could not, of course, succeed in eliminating poverty, since there are important sources of poverty, such as excessive family size and physical or mental incapacity, that the provision of job opportunities cannot touch. Nor could it entirely remove the need for specific programs of education, retraining, and relocation, since for many of the problems at which these programs are directed, the competitive market economy, even when operating at sustained high capacity, is incapable of providing sufficiently effective or rapid solutions.[12] (This is not to say, of course, that the programs themselves will necessarily be more effective or expeditious; as already mentioned, cash transfers to the poor might in many cases be the most economical and efficient solution.)

But the maintenance of high-level economic stability is essential to the success of these specific programs, in two major ways, since most of them depend on attracting the poor to participate in government-supported programs intended to establish them in positions in the economic system in which they can earn an income above the poverty level. Success in overcoming the poverty of those who participate in the programs depends on their being able to market their newly acquired skills, which requires that employment opportunities with a demand for those skills be available. Success in recruiting the poor to participate depends on the success of the programs in raising the income-earning capacity of the participants, and this again depends on there being employment opportunities with a demand for the skills acquired. In addition, there may be some truth in the notion that public opinion will be more willing to sanction the war on poverty, and tolerate the expense of it, if the economy is buoyant and the average citizen is steadily becoming more affluent.

EFFECTS OF POLICY TO REDUCE UNEMPLOYMENT

From an economic point of view, therefore, a policy of maintaining high-level stability and a low unemployment rate is crucial to success in the war on poverty. The means of implementing such a policy are well known and rapidly becoming accepted by public

12. For evidence on this point, see W. H. Locke Anderson, "Trickling Down: The Relationship between Economic Growth and the Extent of Poverty among American Families," *Quart. J. Econ.*, *78*, no. 4 (November 1964), 511–24.

opinion; essentially they involve using fiscal policy—tax cuts and government expenditures—together with monetary policy—low interest rates and a sufficiently rapid expansion of the money supply—to make the level of total demand in the economy high enough to yield the desired unemployment rate, and to keep it expanding rapidly enough to keep the unemployment rate down and the pressure on the labor market up.

These methods, which have been applied by the federal government during the past few years, have been successful in reducing the unemployment rate substantially; they have also contributed to the recent reduction of the poverty percentage. But, in my judgment, they have not been carried nearly as far as they should be, if one looks at policy from the viewpoint of the war on poverty. The unemployment rate should be much lower, and the pressure on the labor market much stronger, in order to overcome the factors of immobility and discrimination and to reduce their contribution to the existence of poverty.

The use of fiscal and monetary policy to raise demand and employment has been inhibited by concern over two likely interrelated consequences of greater economic buoyancy: inflation and an adverse effect on the balance of payments. While a full discussion of the policy issues raised by these problems is beyond the scope of this paper, it is necessary to say something about them.

So far as the inflationary consequences of a higher level of demand and a lower rate of unemployment are concerned, I would argue that it would be in the social interest to endure an appreciable but not high rate of inflation—say, up to something like a 4 per cent per annum increase in the consumer price index —in order to reduce the percentage of unemployment. This may seem like a substantial inflation to some, but it is not, since an appreciable proportion of the general price increase measured by the Consumer Price Index is a spurious increase, resulting from the failure of the official price index to take account of the improvement in the quality of goods, which tends to lower the cost of living, correctly measured, by one to 2 per cent per annum.

The logic of the argument is that the cost of unemployment to the country is a real loss of output, in addition to the other losses in the way of avoidable poverty that I have already discussed. The cost of inflation, however, at least a relatively mild inflation, is not a loss of output—rather, there should be a gain in output —but the social consequences of the redistribution of income in the inflationary process. The redistribution affects only a small proportion of the population, especially when interest rates and other contractual payments are adjusted to the expectation of inflation; and while inflation would tend in some ways to increase poverty, since some of the losers—notably aged people living on retirement income and the recipients of social security and assistance payments, which tend to lag behind prices—are among the poor, it should be possible to arrange compensation for their losses, for example by pegging these income payments to the cost of living. Thus a balancing of the social gain and loss from reducing unemployment at the cost of inflation ought to come out at some positive rate of inflation.

Essentially, this policy problem involves a choice about the distribution of national income. The argument for maintaining an unemployment rate no lower than is consistent with the absence of inflation is an argument for reducing the incomes of the sellers of labor in order to furnish those who remain employed with the convenience of a stable value of money. The argument for bearing some rate of inflation is an argument for increasing the earnings of the labor force and for stimulating the economic system to implement the reduction of poverty, by its own natural and automatic processes, at the expense for everyone of the inconvenience of a depreciating value of money, and for some of income losses that could be compensated for. In addition, it must be recognized that the argument for policies of raising aggregate demand sufficiently to induce some degree of inflation is an argument for some probable redistribution of income from organized labor and those employed by government and nonprofit institutions to unorganized labor—a form of redistribution that I would consider socially desirable. It seems to me that we have reached the crucial point in the recovery from the last recession at which these issues must be faced. If one examines the unemployment figures in detail, it appears that unemployment has been reduced to very low levels indeed for married men with families—that is, men who are an established part of the labor force—but that it remains high for young people seeking to enter the labor force. To reduce unemployment further would require generating enough demand to draw these young people into employment, and the process would probably bring about significant price increases; on the other hand, the result of refusing to accept the inflation involved would be a serious aggravation of the poverty problem in the years ahead. To my mind, it would be well worth while to accept the inflationary consequences in order to mitigate the poverty problem.

On domestic grounds alone, then, the inflation that would be likely to result from the adoption of a vigorous full-employment policy raises problems of a manageable sort and should be tolerated as the price that has to be paid in return for the benefits in reducing poverty that would follow from such a policy. Unfortunately, however, the chronic balance-of-payments deficit position of the United States prevents policy from being determined solely by domestic considerations. In fact, the slackness that has been allowed to prevail in the U.S. economy during the past eight years is ultimately attributable to the balance-of-payments problem. Both the expansion of demand necessary to reduce unemployment substantially below present levels and the rise in prices likely to result from it would have adverse effects on the balance of payments, which would not be welcomed by the policy-makers who would have to cope with them.

The balance-of-payments problem is therefore the ultimate obstacle to the pursuit of an adequate full-employment policy. This is doubly unfortunate, because full employment would not only contribute to the solution of the poverty problem in the United States, but would, by raising our demand for imports of raw materials and primary products, contribute to the solution of the problem of the poverty of the less developed countries, which is an important objective of United States foreign economic policy.

ULTIMATE OBSTACLE TO FULL EMPLOYMENT

The reason why the balance-of-payments problem is the ultimate obstacle to an adequate full-employment policy, in spite of the fact that the international transactions of the United States are smaller in relation to the country's total economic activity than are those of any other advanced Western industrial nation, is inherent in the structure of the present system of international monetary organization. That system is a system of fixed exchange rates; but the member countries have been attempting to maintain fixed exchange rates among themselves on the basis of an inadequate supply of international monetary reserves, and have increasingly come to use the U.S. dollar as a substitute for the primary reserve of the system, gold. Use of the dollar as an international reserve money means that the United States policy-makers must be governed by the necessity of maintaining foreign confidence in the dollar, which means essentially confidence in the orthodoxy of American economic policy; and this imposes the necessity of giving priority to the elimination of the balance-of-payments deficit. In order to free the United States policy-makers from this obligation and permit the adoption of a thorough-going full-employment policy, it would be necessary to change the international monetary system.

There are two alternatives: to negotiate a substantial increase in the available international monetary reserves, to enable the United States to finance a continuing deficit; or to alter the exchange rate—the value of the dollar in terms of other currencies—so as to make the United States competitive enough in the world market to be able to balance its international accounts consistent with domestic full employment. The other leading countries have made it clear in recent months that they are strongly opposed to financing further United States deficits, and they have begun to insist that such deficits must be paid for in gold rather than dollars. Perhaps the time has come to consider changing the international value of the dollar. If, instead, the United States seeks to remedy its balance-of-payments deficit by reverting to its past policy of lower aggregate demand, more unemployment, and a slacker economy, the war on poverty may turn out to have been a mere diversionary tactic, instead of a strategy for achieving the great society.

10: Strategies in the War on Poverty

by Otto Eckstein

Not in many years has the problem of poverty attracted as much intellectual attention as it has in the last two years. President Johnson's launching of the war on poverty was a turning point in social legislation in this country. After decades of slow—but still significant—progress, the Economic Opportunity Act has been quickly followed by the Education Act, the Appalachia program, the Economic Development Act, and Medicare. The country has, at last succeeded in translating its conscience into action once more.

In the chapter on poverty in the 1964 *Economic Report of the President,* the Council of Economic Advisers first set down the $3,000 income limit, which has been widely used since then to appraise our progress in eliminating poverty. In the 1965 *Economic Report,* the Council reported additional modifications in defining the poverty line, and was able, on the basis of recent work, to provide some quantification of the clearly relevant factors of persistence of poverty, family size, and the wealth position of households. These sophistications do not affect the numerical totals of people living in poverty compared to the earlier $3,000 income limit, but they do serve to change the composition of the group considered to be living in poverty. The inclusion of a wealth criterion eliminates some retired families. Correction for family size greatly increases the number of children living in poverty; many large families actually are in the poverty class even though their incomes may exceed $3,000.

But this ground has been covered in our *Report,* and it is not necessary to go over it again. Nor do I wish to add to the discussion of the definition of poverty as an absolute as opposed to a relative concept. I have no doubt that our society will view poverty as a little bit of both. What is considered an adequate standard of living will rise as the consumption patterns of the society change with rising incomes, but basic subsistence will always remain an absolute component in our criteria.

Instead, I shall devote my remarks to four other matters: First, our changing goals, in a rather narrow, technical sense; second, some new materials on the consumption patterns of the poor as compared to the average family in our society; third, a new econometric analysis of the incidence of poverty; and finally, the major policy approaches in relation to this analysis.

CHANGING GOALS OF INCOME REDISTRIBUTION

A few years ago economists' lists of the standard economic objectives would not have found room for the alleviation of poverty per se. The list would have included efficiency, full employment, economic growth, international payments equilibrium, and, of course, the achievement of an equitable distribution of income. Economists thought of income distribution either in functional terms—the proper distribution between wages and property incomes—or the distribution of income by size—the shares of total income accruing to the various income brackets. Study of the functional distribution of income has a long history, and indeed is at the heart of the classical theories of Ricardo and Marx. We still find a lively interest in the functional distribution of income when we come to such matters as wage-price guideposts. Relative size became the dominant formulation of the objective of income distribution in the 1930s; its main practical result was the emphasis on progressive taxation of personal income.

But in the postwar period, as incomes and economic well-being rose sharply for the vast majority of Americans, neither of these two formulations provided much of a focus for the country's ever-present idealism. Functional redistribution—raising the share of national income going to wages—lost some of its appeal as the wages of highly organized workers entered the $3–$5 an hour range and the typical manufacturing wage provided a solid middle-class standard of living. Size redistribution—and with it the attractiveness of extremes of progressive taxation—ceased to be a popular cause when the large majority of our population reached income levels where redistribution from the top quintile to the next three quintiles did not serve any clear-cut ends of social justice. As the depression-free performance of the economy reduced the frictions in our society, and as the progressive income and estate taxes had their effect over the years, popular feeling against the very top income brackets became much attenuated. In the light of these developments, it is not surprising that the relative size distribution of our national income, as measured by the Department of Commerce, was left virtually undisturbed over the entire postwar period.

Formulation of the goals of reducing and ultimately eliminating poverty has given the redistribution objective new life and meaning. There had never been a serious question in anyone's mind that there were plenty of poor people in this country. And indeed the growth of our vast system of direct income maintenance payments for old age, disability, unemployment, and other causes is clear testimony to our willingness to redistribute income to help alleviate poverty.

The new "war" is a major departure. It seeks to remove the causes of poverty, chiefly through investment in human resources, and it sets clear-cut quantitative goals for measuring our progress toward eliminating poverty.

It has four basic strategies. First, every individual should have the opportunity to develop his potential fully. He should have access to as much education and training of good quality as he is able to absorb profitably. Second, every individual should be aware of the opportunities open to him and of the rewards that will come from his own efforts. Third, every individual should have all employment opportunities for which he is qualified open to him on an equal basis. Finally, and perhaps most controversially, every individual should be exposed to the values shared by the vast majority of our population—the desire for achievement and the full use of his potential.

These strategies will not eliminate poverty by themselves. Because many poor families include no one capable of being in the labor force, there will be continued need for a broad system of income maintenance. In addition, there must be adequate job creation to assure full use of our human potential, through good economic expansion fostered by stimulating fiscal and monetary policies. And to cope with regional concentrations of poverty we need programs of area and regional development, coupled with retraining and relocation of workers.

Nor should we expect victory overnight. The human problems now being tackled in earnest have developed over many decades. The cultural bases of poverty are deeply embedded. Special education programs for teenagers generally come after the youngsters' values and attitudes are broadly formed. Programs for young children will not fully overcome the inadequacies of their home environment.

But even the first steps are important, and the Neighborhood Youth Corps, the Job Corps, and other programs have been set up just at the time when increased numbers of teenagers reach the labor market. As growing numbers of youngsters search for their first job, many of them will find a useful place in these programs.

Because the quantitative definition of poverty permits us to see the magnitude of the problem and to chart our progress, the Council of Economic Advisers proposed the figure $3,000 as the demarcation point. Setting a limit also provides a framework for analyzing the causes of poverty—and even reminds us that four-fifths of our families are at higher income levels.

We are all aware of the limitations of the current measures. The classic theoretical problems of index number construction and of interpersonal comparisons confront us in attempting to draw comparisons among families of different types. For many statistical purposes we will have to continue to use the $3,000 poverty line because so much of the statistical material is available in this form. It should be stressed that this poverty line is less than half of the 1963 median family income of $6,249. It is a long way from raising everyone to the middle class standards of living enjoyed

by the country as a whole and is no more than an attempt to
set a socially acceptable floor to which we would like to raise all
families.

CONSUMPTION AND POVERTY

A comparison of the expenditures on current consumption by
urban families living in poverty and families living in the median
income range of $6,000–$7,499 reveals the differences in the standard of living of the two groups (see Table 10.1). For families

TABLE 10.1. CURRENT CONSUMPTION EXPENDITURES OF
URBAN FAMILIES AND SINGLE CONSUMERS, 1960–61

	INCOME CLASS	
	Under $3,000	*$6,000–$7,499*
Money income after taxes	$1,882	$6,710
Current consumption expenditures	2,142	6,229
Food	618	1,508
Housing	777	1,816
Medical care	175	405
Recreation	53	260
Education	11	59
Automobile transportation	111	867

Source: Bureau of Labor Statistics, *Consumer Expenditures and Income*
(Washington, D.C.: Government Printing Office, 1964), Report No. 237–238.

living in poverty, current consumption expenditures are greater
than money income after taxes. As these consumption statistics
indicate, poor families spend less both on necessities and on items
that might be considered luxuries. Food expenditures are very
much smaller, and even payments for necessities such as medical
care are cut by over 50 per cent.

CAUSES OF POVERTY

By now everyone is familiar with descriptions of the groups
that comprise the 19 per cent of our families who live in poverty.

These statistics indicate that families headed by females, persons over 65, and Negroes suffer particularly severely from poverty. In all three of these categories nearly half the families are below the poverty line (see Table 10.2). Only 10 per cent of white non-farm families headed by males under age 65 are in poverty.

TABLE 10.2. DISTRIBUTION OF POVERTY IN 1960

TYPE OF FAMILY	INCIDENCE OF POVERTY*	PER CENT OF ALL FAMILIES IN POVERTY
The aged (head 65 and over)	48.4	30.6
Nonwhite (head under 65)	44.8	17.5
White females (head under 65)	43.3	11.0
White farmers (male head under 65)	39.5	10.0
White nonfarmers (male head under 65)	9.7	31.0
Total	21.4	100.0

*The incidence of poverty is the percentage of all families with a given characteristic who are poor.

Source: *U.S. Census of Population, 1960, United States Summary* (Washington, D.C.: Government Printing Office, 1963).

Descriptive classifications, however, do not give any indication of the relative importance of the different factors that contribute to poverty. Do 51.6 per cent of the families in Mississippi live in poverty because there is discrimination against Negroes, because educational levels are low, or because Mississippi is a less developed area of our country? All three of these factors play a role in the incidence of poverty, but their quantitative importance is difficult to determine from a description of the state.

One method of isolating the relative importance of the several factors is through use of an econometric model. Using this method, Lester Thurow, of the CEA staff, has analyzed the variation in the incidence of poverty among the 50 states and the District of Columbia. In 1960, when the national incidence of poverty was 21.4 per cent, the incidence among states varied from a low of 9.8 per cent in Connecticut to a high of 51.6 per cent in Mississippi.

The model explains the incidence of poverty in these 51 areas in 1960 in terms of (1) percentage of families living on farms, (2) percentage of families headed by a nonwhite, (3) percentage of families with no one in the labor force, (4) education of the family head, (5) percentage of the population working full-time, (6) industrial structure of the state, and (7) a dummy variable necessary to correct for the particular effect of the nonwhite population of Alaska and Hawaii.

The model is specified by the following equation:

$$P = a + b\,F + c\,N + d\,L + e\,E - f\,W - g\,I - h\,D + u\,,$$

where   P = percentage of families in poverty (income less than $3,000)

        F = percentage of families living on farms

        N = percentage of families headed by a nonwhite

        L = percentage of families with no one in the labor force

        E = percentage of family heads with 0 to 7 years of school completed

        W = percentage of population 14 and above who worked 50–52 weeks per year

        I   = an index of the industrial structure of the state[1]

        D = dummy variable for Alaska and Hawaii

        u = error term

A regression using this model needs to be weighted by the population of each state since the dependent variables and most of the independent variables are in percentage terms. Since a large state provides more of the total number of families living in poverty, it should have a larger weight in the regression.

---

1. The index, which measures the prevalence of high-wage industries in the state, is defined as follows:

$$I = \sum_{i=1}^{n} X_i W_i\,,$$

when X_i = percentage of labor force in industry i, and

        W_i = the ratio of the median income of industry i divided by the overall median income in the U.S.

A weighted regression gives the following results:

$$P = 96.5125 + .2978\,F + .1133\,N + .5410\,L + .4345\,E$$
$$(23.1516) \quad (.0978) \quad (.0544) \quad (.1677) \quad (.0480)$$
$$** \qquad\qquad ** \qquad\qquad * \qquad\qquad ** \qquad\qquad **$$

$$- .5368\,W - .7600\,I - 10.3777\,D$$
$$(.1117) \qquad (.1978) \qquad (4.8210)$$
$$** \qquad\qquad ** \qquad\qquad **$$

$\quad$ * = significant at 5% level $\qquad$ d.f. = 43
$\quad$ ** = significant at 1% level $\qquad$ S_e = 2.3
$\qquad\qquad\qquad\qquad\qquad\qquad\qquad\qquad$ R^2 = .98

The regression indicates that most of the variation in the incidence of poverty among the states can be accounted for by these variables. All but one of the variables is significant at the 1 per cent level and it is significant at the 5 per cent level.

Substituting other explanatory variables provides some interesting insights into the causes of poverty. Instead of the percentage of families with no one in the labor force, the percentage of families headed by females and the percentage headed by persons over 65 were used, but they proved to be poor substitutes, of lesser statistical significance. The number of families with no one in the labor force is also affected by other factors, including, for example, the availability of job opportunities.

When the median number of years of education was substituted for the percentage of family heads with 0 to 7 years of school completed, it proved to be a much less effective variable. Poverty appears to be more closely related to conditions at the bottom of the educational structure than to the median level of education.

State unemployment rates substituted for the measure of full-time work proved to be statistically insignificant, with coefficients close to zero. This can be explained by the fact that because many of those living in poverty are employed but work in part-time or seasonal jobs. The percentage of persons who worked 50 to 52 weeks per year is a measure that takes into account both the number of part-time workers and the full-time unemployment rates.

POLICIES TO REDUCE THE INCIDENCE OF POVERTY

Policies that act to reduce poverty fall under five general headings: (1) income maintenance programs, (2) investment in human resources, (3) promotion of general economic expansion, (4) programs of area and regional development, and (5) promotion of equality of opportunity. The econometric model outlined above permits us to relate these programs to the reduction of poverty, as some of the inferences of the analysis will show.

Human investment, general economic expansion, area programs, and the promotion of equality of opportunity are all important in our nation's drive to eliminate poverty among Negroes. As the regression indicates, the percentage of nonwhites in the population is an important variable in explaining poverty on a state-by-state basis. The significance of this variable points to past and present discrimination as an important cause of our national problem of poverty. If there were an end to job discrimination and if general economic expansion improved Negro job opportunities, the equation indicates that poverty in the U.S. would have been reduced by 1.1 percentage points to 20.3 per cent in 1960.

General economic expansion alone will not eliminate the gap between white and Negro median incomes. A study of postwar experience demonstrates the possibilities and the limitations of using general policies. Table 10.3 traces the path of white and Negro incomes since 1947. The ratio of nonwhite to white incomes rises during periods of low unemployment and expanding job opportunities. From 1947 to 1952, the ratio of nonwhite to white incomes rose from 51.1 to 56.8 per cent, but most of the earlier gains were lost in the period of slow growth and frequent recession. With high unemployment and fewer job opportunities, Negroes found jobs increasingly scarce and increases in their median income fell behind that for whites. From 1952 to 1963, the ratio of nonwhite to white median incomes fell from 56.8 to 52.9 per cent. During every recession in the postwar period, the ratio has dropped very sharply. Negroes have less seniority, on the average, and are particularly adversely affected in times of lay-offs. The rapid expansion of 1964 almost restored the earlier peak levels, and 1965 probably has brought further gains. Thus a rise of

TABLE 10.3. MEDIAN INCOMES IN THE POSTWAR PERIOD, 1947–64

YEAR	WHITE	NONWHITE	RATIO OF NONWHITE TO WHITE MEDIAN INCOMES (PER CENT)
1947	$3,157	$1,614	51.1
1948	3,310	1,768	53.4
1949	3,232	1,650	51.1
1950	3,445	1,869	54.3
1951	3,859	2,032	52.7
1952	4,114	2,338	56.8
1953	4,392	2,461	56.0
1954	4,339	2,410	55.5
1955	4,605	2,549	55.4
1956	4,993	2,628	52.6
1957	5,166	2,764	53.5
1958	5,300	2,711	51.2
1959	5,643	2,917	51.7
1960	5,835	3,233	55.4
1961	5,981	3,191	53.4
1962	6,237	3,330	53.4
1963	6,548	3,465	52.9
1964	6,858	3,839	55.9

Source: U.S. Bureau of the Census, *Current Population Reports,* Series P–60, Annual Series.

national income raises Negro incomes more than proportionately, narrowing the Negro-white income gap.

Income maintenance, human investment, and general economic expansion are the most important means for eliminating poverty owing to the lack of a wage earner. General economic expansion will draw some individuals into the labor force, but there also has to be heavy reliance on income redistribution to reduce poverty. For the old, the sick, and those with other incapacities, poverty can only be eliminated by welfare programs.

The federal-state public assistance program is the largest single protection against want and deprivation for needy families who have no private resources. Financial and medical assistance will be provided in fiscal 1966 to about 8 million of our nation's poorest citizens. The federal-state vocational rehabilitation program is expected to restore an estimated 145,000 individuals to employ-ability. Other federal programs such as unemployment insurance and old-age insurance are major planks in a policy of income maintenance. More than half of these payments go to families above the poverty line, but they are also important sources of income for many families in poverty.

Investment in human resources through education is one of the most effective ways of reducing the future incidence of poverty. If the optimistic educational projections of the Census Bureau prove to be correct,[2] changes in the educational structure alone will lower the incidence of poverty to 18.8 per cent in 1970 and to 16.8 per cent in 1980 on the $3,000 income criterion. These optimistic estimates of the effect of education depend on a suffi-ciently rapid economic expansion to generate jobs for our more highly educated labor force.

The President's program recognizes the need for both a strong school system for the young and a strong training system for in-dividuals who are beyond school age. The new primary and secondary education program is specifically aimed at children from families in poverty. In fiscal year 1966, the federal government is planning to spend $2.7 billion on education, plus $275 million on manpower development and training. By the end of fiscal year 1966, an estimated 700,000 workers will have benefited from the retraining programs.

The percentage of full-time workers is closely related to the economic prosperity of a region. In 1960 there were five states with unemployment of 3.1 per cent or below. The average per-centage of full-time workers in these five states was 9.5 percentage points above the figure in the five states with the highest unem-ployment rates.

Solutions to the low-income problem in farming are not likely to come soon. The decline in the per cent of the population in agriculture has been very rapid in the last 25 years, and this migration from agriculture has not yet run its course. Thus, the

2. See U.S. Bureau of the Census, *Current Population Reports,* Series P–20, No. 91.

incidence of poverty from this source will continue to decline in the coming years. Government must continue to help maintain incomes and aid adjustment in this sector.

The war on poverty, with its great emphasis on attacking the causes of poverty, is a bold, new undertaking. It reflects a renewed concern with the achievement of a fair distribution of income, a concern based not on envy but on compassion. If combined with general economic policies to create job opportunities and with increased equality of job opportunity, the new investments in human resources should yield a handsome and satisfying return to society. However, these programs cannot reach all families in poverty, and there will inevitably continue to be a considerable reliance on programs of income maintenance as well.

11: Ends and Means
in the War on Poverty

by Robert J. Lampman

President Johnson, in his 1964 State of the Union Message, in his Economic Report, and in a special message to the Congress, called for a national war on poverty. The object, he said, was "total victory." The Congress, in adopting the Economic Opportunity Act, declared: "It is . . . the policy of the United States to eliminate the paradox of poverty in the midst of plenty in this Nation by opening to everyone the opportunity for education and training, the opportunity to work, and the opportunity to live in decency and dignity." On signing the Act, the President asserted that "today for the first time in all the history of the human race, a great nation is able to make and is willing to make a commitment to eradicate poverty among its people."

These statements and others point the federal government toward a goal which involves the moving of all American families and unrelated individuals above income lines of $3,000 and $1,500 respectively (in 1962 prices)[1] within some finite period of time.

1. Thus identifying poverty by reference to an income line is an example of the assignment of extensive measures to intensive magnitudes, which is a prerequisite to many operations in the social as well as the physical sciences. From a very detached point of view we can say that the particular extensive measure selected is less important than the fact that *some* measure be selected so that experiment may proceed and predictive control may be developed.

In 1947, 32 per cent of families were below that line, but by 1963 only 19 per cent were; thus the goal from year to year may be seen as keeping up or accelerating the recent rate of decrease, which, if continued, would bring the poverty rate to near zero in twenty years. The latter notion was implied by the President's statement in his Economic Report for 1964 that "we cannot and need not wait for the gradual growth of the economy to lift this fifth of our Nation above the poverty line." It is consistent with the above to think of the goal in terms of narrowing the poverty income gap—the aggregate amount by which the incomes of all the poor fall short of $3,000 per family—which now totals $12 billion, or about 2 per cent of GNP. If this gap could be narrowed by $1 billion per year, the aim of the war on poverty would be reached in 12 years.

Thus stated, the antipoverty goal is a nova in the constellation of purposes which guide our national efforts. Or, to switch metaphorical horses, it is a rather specialized branch of a tree of goals whose roots are embedded in concern with the individual's freedom and security, his opportunities and responsibilities, his right to privacy, and his responsibility to participate. These goals, and government's role in pursuing them, have changed over time in response to shifts in the economic and social environment and with new insights concerning what is feasible in social affairs.

The decision to pursue the year-to-year reduction of poverty would seem to follow naturally enough out of a long train of extensions of citizenship and a gradual conversion from thinking of the poor as a hostile force, to be isolated and contained, over to the vision of them as full members of a democratic society, whose fate is linked with that of the general community and who are, therefore, worth investing in as latent assets to the community.[2] The decision to adopt an antipoverty goal may also be said to flow from earlier decisions concerning such closely related policies as assuring security against income loss, facilitating collective bargaining, and promoting full employment and economic growth.

2. For a valuable study of the evolution of the goal, see Robert H. Bremner, *From the Depths: The Discovery of Poverty in America* (New York: New York University Press, 1956).

The way our goals evolve contributes to their overlapping character. Often one goal has been implicit in earlier ones. Hence, one could argue that declaring economic growth as a goal is merely a new rationalization for policies which had already been justified on other grounds. Similarly, the antipoverty goal offers a new purpose for, or reason for, interest in the goals of full employment, economic growth, and equality of opportunity. Making the elimination of poverty an explicit goal, thus, is to refresh and reinvigorate earlier commitments.

But it is more than a restatement. It carries with it a challenge to some established purposes and policies; it puts a sharper edge to the measurement of the performance of our national economy. It asks not only whether we have high employment, but who is unemployed. It asks not only whether average income is rising, but what is happening to incomes of specific groups. It even asks whether hot and heavy pursuit of the goals of full employment and rapid economic growth is like enriching the diets of all simply because a few are underweight.[3] It asks whether unemployment can be more generously shared by the nonpoor, and whether the poor can participate more directly in measures to promote economic growth. Consideration of the antipoverty goal also involves asking whose incomes are being secured, whose wages and whose prices are being protected, thus raising anew the issue of legitimacy of claims by private parties to government support and protection.

Is poverty a good basis for discriminating among claimants or for limiting government participation in economic affairs? Is it possible that we don't have a farm problem or an old-age problem or an urban problem or a housing problem—but that all these are, in essence, insofar as governmental intervention is needed, one and the same poverty problem? Does one who has a certain income or occupational status and then loses it have more claim than one who never had such status? In other words, should protection of income continuity be viewed as more important for government attention than promotion of income adequacy?

3. This is a rough translation of one of the leading questions raised by John K. Galbraith in his book, *The Affluent Society* (Boston: Houghton Mifflin, 1958). The question's cogency is partly due to the fact that most of today's unemployed are not poor.

What goals or values are we willing to compromise for a gain in the speed of poverty reduction? Will we depart from our traditional emphasis upon self-reliance and individual initiative to recognize positive sanctions for new patterns of dependency along the lines suggested by schemes for a guaranteed minimum income for all? Should we override states' rights and local autonomy in pursuit of a national minimum of benefits and services to the poor?

Perhaps that is enough to indicate that, by setting out an antipoverty goal, President Johnson did more than restate traditional purposes. His declaration carried with it a whole set of potentially disturbing questions about prevailing goals and attitudes. It challenges us to ask whether there are policies and practices in effect which, while originally justified as a means to an end, may now be perpetuated as ends in themselves.

But this confusion of ends and means is a near and present danger in the statement of the antipoverty goal itself. Antipoverty work should be distinguished from a generalized helping and doing good for people. Many people have trouble distinguishing the poverty problem from other problems such as unequal access to the protection of the laws, lack of education, lack of housing, lack of health services, delinquency and crime, limited citizen participation, spiritual and cultural deprivation, lack of fellowship, and geographic isolation. These problems are not exclusive to the poor; if government sets out to help the sick and disturbed, or those who need or want better housing, not only may the greater part of the help go to the nonpoor but it may do precious little to reduce poverty.

In instituting antipoverty programs there is a danger that these programs will be indentified as "good things," that we may never get around to measuring whether the original end is being accomplished and, if so, whether the programs have had anything to do with it. The confusion is only somewhat lessened if we insist that the programs be of benefit to the poor exclusively. Poverty reduction does not mean merely "doing something for the poor" any more than economic growth means "doing something for business." There is value in continually relating means back to the end.

It is important to note how different this goal-oriented thinking is from the theories of government-by-pressure-group that picture government as a service agency whose function it is to respond to the felt needs of its constituents. According to these theories government does not pursue national goals but seeks a workable balance among the wishes of private interests, all of which are seeking government support. Some would even go so far as to argue that statements of national economic goals are merely slogans rationalizing a particular pattern of distribution of government largesse. Hence, they would urge that it is inequitable to insist upon a higher standard of goal-oriented achievement where the poor are involved than where other groups are involved.

CAUSES OF POVERTY SUGGEST MEANS TO THE GOAL

We have thus far asserted that the goal of reducing poverty is a distinctive one. This implies that it may be associated with a unique problem having its own set of remedies or means of solution. Let us, then, array the possible means to the goal by reference to several broad theories of the causes of poverty in late twentieth-century America.

One theory is that poverty arises out of failure to achieve the general goals of our democratic, capitalistic system. Hence the remedy is to make the existing system work better in achieving full employment and economic growth. A second theory is that the cause of poverty is in the failure to adapt the system to the needs of the poor and that the remedy is to be found in new regulations, service programs, and cash payments for the poor. A third theory is that the basic cause of poverty is in the culture, informal social organization, and personal socialization of deprived individuals, and that hence remedies must be sought in ways to remake or change the poor—their motivations as well as their abilities—and adapt them to the needs of the system.

Make existing system work better

Will poverty disappear if we can return to full employment and maintain or increase the rate of economic growth? Can we rely on free market forces and ordinary self-interest to operate within a well-functioning economy to achieve more exits from than retreats into poverty from year to year? Should, then, our emphasis be upon aggregative measures of fiscal and monetary policy and general market measures aimed at encouraging efficiency of production? Or is the structure of the economy and of the poor population such that the poverty problem is relatively untouched by general economic progress? Is it true, as Professor John K. Galbraith wrote in 1958,[4] that "the most certain thing about modern poverty is that it is not efficiently remedied by a general and tolerably well-distributed advance in incomes"? R. A. Gordon recently said:[5]

> Until not so long ago, it could be fairly said that the chief causes of poverty in the United States were low wages and unemployment, accentuated by our unwillingness (before the New Deal) to develop an adequate social insurance and welfare program. This is no longer true, although we would do well to remember that the incidence of poverty is still appallingly high among families whose chief breadwinner is an unskilled laborer, a farmer or farm worker, or a domestic or other unskilled service worker. Today's poverty problem, as it has been frequently put, is largely structural in character. It is the kind of poverty that feeds on itself. It does not automatically disappear as the favored majority becomes steadily more affluent. We are reaching the hard core of the underprivileged and the unfortunate. The time has clearly come for strong measures aimed directly at the specific and particular problems of the poor.

Some have gone further than either Gordon or Galbraith to assert that not only is poverty not reduced by growth but higher growth causes or will cause increases in poverty. Thus the Ad Hoc Committee on the Triple Revolution forecasts steeply rising output per man-hour concurrent with increasing unemployment and asserts that this indicates a need for a guaranteed minimum income system.[6]

4. Ibid., p. 325.

5. "An Economist's View of Poverty," *Poverty in America* (San Francisco: Chandler, 1965), pp. 10–11. In support of his conclusion, Gordon cites the paper by W. H. Locke Anderson in the November 1964 issue of *Quart. J. Econ.* (pp. 511–24), "Trickling Down: The Relationship between Economic Growth and the Extent of Poverty among American Families."

6. *New York Times,* March 23, 1964.

It is my view that any down-grading of the importance of high employment and rapid economic growth both in preventing massive increases in the numbers of poor and in reducing poverty is misguided. Over half of poor family heads are in the labor force, and 70 per cent of poor families have at least one earner. This degree of association of poverty and wage-earning is heightened if we consider number of *persons* rather than *families* in poverty. It is true that the non-labor-force heads have increased as a percentage of all poor-family heads during the postwar years, but the demographic trends responsible for this are not expected to continue. Indeed, the reverse is true, with the greatest swelling of the labor force expected from the younger age groups.

Not only is poverty closely associated with labor force participation on a cross-sectional basis, but the rate of poverty reduction appears to be responsive to the rate of economic growth. The largest yearly reductions in the number of families in poverty occur in those years when average incomes increase the most, although it is possible to interpret the data as indicating a slight decline in the degree of responsiveness over time. Lowell Gallaway disputes even the latter point. He calculates that the percentage of families in poverty in 1963 would have been 16.6 per cent, rather than the 18.5 per cent which prevailed, if 1947–56 growth rates and 4 per cent unemployment had been maintained. He also projects that the poverty families will be between 6.4 and 8.7 per cent of all families in 1980, rather than 10 to 13 per cent as the CEA projects, depending on the rate of growth and unemployment. He concludes, therefore, that there is relatively little case for "substantial anti-poverty programs of a selective character. . . . Rather, greater consideration should be given to the role which economic growth can play in eliminating poverty."[7] It is not clear from Gallaway's statement whether he believes seeking to reduce unemployment below 4 per cent or to further improve the rate of growth would be efficient ways to achieve a faster rate of poverty reduction than his forecast implies. Few would argue that any employment growth that is feasible would by itself eliminate poverty in the near future.

7. "The Foundations of the 'War on Poverty,' " *Amer. Econ. Rev., 55,* No. 1 (March 1965), 122–31.

The argument about the structural nature of contemporary poverty has an aridity to it that is reminiscent of the controversy concerning the allegedly rising significance of structural unemployment after 1957. It poses a hard choice only if the needs for growth dictate that there should be no "substantial anti-poverty programs of a selective character," or vice versa. It should be possible to pursue both lines of policy simultaneously, and it may be that the two lines can reinforce one another. For example, if the growth of aggregate demand requires expenditure for public works, they could be concentrated in areas where the poverty incidence is high; if a tax cut is called for, it could be slanted toward the poor rather than the rich. If investment in education and training and relocation are seen as ways to increase the nation's economic capacity, those investments can be aimed at the poor. The benefits of growth policy could be thus made to trickle up rather than down. This kind of slanting may not be the most efficient route to growth, but it need not be that such special anti-poverty efforts are antithetical to a satisfactory rate of growth. In fact, it may be possible to accelerate the rate of poverty reduction by adapting the system to confront certain causes of poverty.

Adapt the system to the needs of the poor

While some see the slow reduction of poverty amid rising affluence as a consequence of failure of the existing system to operate properly, others see it resulting from failure to modify the system sufficiently to reach the needs of the poor. If it is viewed as the latter, it could be interpreted as ironic, since many adaptations (e.g. social security, collective bargaining, farm and housing subsidies, and progressive taxation) have already been made under antipoverty banners. As Irving Kristol observes, "Poverty, after all, was the problem the welfare state most particularly set out to solve."[8] Some have argued that if we simply modify the rationale and extend the application of existing policies to the remainder of the poor, then a substantial part of the poverty problem can be cut away without waiting for 1980. The adaptations that can be made under this general heading include dealing more directly

8. "The Poverty of Equality," *The New Leader*, March 1, 1965, pp. 15–16.

with specific locations, conditions, and problems encountered by the poor; developing the economies of areas that can be identified as pockets of poverty; legislating and bargaining low wage rates up to above-poverty levels; providing jobs for all able-bodied poor by subsidizing private employers (including self-employed farmers) and by public work or work relief; prohibiting discriminatory barriers to employment on account of color, age, sex, or education; expanding and supplementing presently operating transfer payment programs to block more completely retreats into poverty and to narrow the poverty-income gap.

It is uncertain what the effects of these adaptations are, on balance, in reducing poverty. Thus, it is not clear that taxing growing areas of the economy to make more capital available to declining regions is going to contribute more to poverty reduction in the latter than it subtracts from poverty reduction in the former, or that mobility of capital into a depressed area is less wasteful than mobility of labor out of the area to more prosperous areas. (We should note, however, that the development of community facilities such as roads and schools, by reducing cultural isolation, may actually encourage out-migration.) Similarly, it is not clear that legislating a higher minimum wage does more for those who keep their jobs at the higher rate than it disadvantages those who may be dismissed or may not find jobs because of the higher minimum.

There can be no disputing the facts that many of the poor are in relatively poor regions (almost half the poor are in the South) and many people earn low wages (at least 10 million workers get less than $1.50 per hour), and it is clear that development of those regions and legislating away those low wage rates would help some of those who are poor. But this may be one of those cases in economics in which around the barn is the shortest way home. The unintended side effects may or may not more than offset the direct positive effects. (Such side effects arise in connection with many policies. For another example, consider this hypothetical case: if agricultural price policy were to raise the price of all food by 10 per cent, this would amount to a 3 per cent tax on the incomes of many poor families, thus helping some farmers, many of whom are not poor, at the expense of all other families, some of whom are poor.)

A still more direct way to seek to raise low incomes is by either gradual or rapid increases in income-maintenance payments, which now total $36 billion per year and go to over 30 million people. This class of income—which is 6 per cent of national income—is 40 per cent of the income of the poor population, yet most of it goes to the nonpoor, and at least half the poor do not receive any of it. A possible step in the war on poverty would be to increase the size of benefits going to the aged, the disabled, and dependent children. To take all those in certain beneficiary categories out of poverty overnight would require only that minimum benefits be raised to the poverty-income line.

To indicate how far (or near) we are from that line now, the average social security benefit for a retired couple is now about $1,600. The benefit scale is tied to past earnings in covered employment and is slanted toward the poor, in the sense that low wage earners get a benefit that is a higher percentage of preretirement earnings than do high earners. To get the minimum benefit up to the poverty line, we would have to do great violence to the wage-related benefit formula and to incentives to work after age 62 by making some benefits more than 100 per cent of earnings. In the face of this difficulty, some have urged that the present system be supplemented by a "demogrant" (a payment related to a demographic characteristic of the recipient) for the aged payable out of general revenues and made without any conditions of coverage or eligibility whatsoever.[9] For example, the plan could read that every aged person regardless of employment history, retirement status, or current income could be paid $1,000 per year. This would cost about $18 billion per year (most of which would go to the nonpoor), but would virtually end poverty among the aged, now about one-fourth of the nation's poor and likely to continue to be a substantial part of that category.

The demogrant approach could also be applied to other groups in the population, e.g. the nation's 75 million children or, in its most extreme form, to all families. The latter is, in essence, the "social dividend" or guaranteed minimum income scheme put forward by Lady Rhys Williams. To pay a demogrant of $3,000

9. For a valuable discussion of this and several of the following points, see Eveline M. Burns, "Social Security in Evolution: Towards What?," *1964 Proceedings of the Industrial Relations Research Association.*

per family would amount to about $150 billion per year, which would require that tax revenues be raised by the same amount. The amount of the income transfer and the pattern of the shift from rich to poor, as well as the effect on incentives to work and save, would depend on who was asked to pay more and who less than $3,000 of new taxes.

An arrangement similar to the universal demogrant is to pay every family 100 per cent of the difference between its actual income and, say, $3,000. This would cost, at the minimum, $12 billion (the present poverty-income gap) and, at the maximum, over $27 billion per year (if all presently poor families plus some above the poverty line completely stopped working as a result of the guarantee, there would be a wage loss of at least $15 billion, which should be added to the present size of the poverty gap). The degree to which any of these transfer plans would make a contribution to solution of the poverty problem would depend, of course, on how much the new taxes paid by the poor and loss of present assistance benefits were exceeded by the additional benefits received by them.

A more modest proposal is to pay out only a fraction of the difference between a poor family's actual income and the poverty-level income. This could be integrated with the administration of the federal personal income tax, and benefits could be calculated as a percentage of a family's unused exemptions and deductions. These unused exemptions now total about $20 billion; hence, paying, say, a fourth of them (a negative tax rate of 25 per cent) would cost about $5 billion per year and would fill almost half the poverty-income gap. With the growth of the economy this gap will narrow and the size of the transfer would shrink. Hopefully, not many of the present poor would be induced to reduce their income-earning efforts, so long as the receipt of extra income did not reduce the size of the grant substantially or, in other words, so long as the marginal negative tax rate did not, as it now does in the case of assistance formulas, approach 100 per cent. The $5 billion under consideration would approximately offset taxes other than income taxes paid by the poor. It follows that the same result would ensue if we would simply revise the tax system to relieve the poor of all tax burdens.

An alternative way to raise the incomes of the poor is to find or create jobs for those who do not now have one. Extensive labor market services, including counselling, training, and relocation, can be especially slanted to the needs of the poor among the unemployed. Public work can be fashioned for young people in school (e.g. the Neighborhood Youth Corps is providing part-time work for 150,000 young people in and out of school) or for others who are both poor and unemployed. The extreme form of this proposal is for a government agency to stand ready to buy all labor time offered at the legally established minimum wage, much as it now stands ready to buy all corn or wheat offered at what is set as a parity price. This might prove to be much more costly to taxpayers than simply using the most efficient means to get government work done and paying transfers to the poor. If the work guarantee is less than complete it raises difficult questions of rationing of jobs and of equity among the poor, with some perhaps getting paid less for working than others are paid on a transfer basis.

It would seem to be clear that the system could, if we were willing to pay the price, be so adapted to the needs of the poor that, assuming no great reversal of the overall workings of the system, poverty could be reduced at a rate well above that of recent years. It is interesting to speculate about why we have not done more in adapting the system to the needs of the poor. Is it a fear and mistrust of the poor by the nonpoor majority, or is it more the result of the inability of the poor minority to mount effective protest? Is it, as Nathan Glazer suggests, the result of excessive emphasis upon individualism and localism in the face of racial and ethnic diversity?[10] Have we bogged down in what Richard Titmuss called "the troubled area between equality and the needs of the poor for unequal treatment?" Are we hung forever on the present balance among principles in the income maintenance field and unwilling to relent somewhat in the emphasis upon assuring continuity of income, via the insurance principle of equity, as opposed to assuring adequacy of income? Have we run out of imagination concerning ways to extend the positive sanctions for dependency we now have to new categories, say to children in poor but otherwise normal homes?

10. "A Sociologist's View of Poverty," *Poverty in America*, pp. 12–26.

Or, is the reason why we have not done more to adapt the system founded on the belief that all such plans are foredoomed unless, as a prior condition, the poor are themselves changed.

Changing the poor to fit the system

According to a third theory, the remedies of poverty are to be found only in therapy on a case by case basis, especially adapted education, radical change in the social environment, and small-group, self-help organizations of the poor. The goals, attitudes, and motivations of the poor and the subculture that carries the values alien to the nonpoor culture must be fundamentally changed. The intergenerational circle of poverty breeding poverty must be broken before the escape from poverty that a well-functioning economy offers can be meaningful.

Students of poverty have long noted that the poor are different, alien, even barbarous (as George Bernard Shaw called them), and a few have argued that poverty is character-building. But there has long been debate over the question put by Sir Benjamin Thompson in 1790: "To make vicious and abandoned people happy, it has generally been supposed necessary to make them virtuous. But why not reverse this order? Why not make them first happy, and then virtuous?"[11] Many have concluded with Jeremy Bentham that "the conduct of the poor will depend—not upon the remote and casual influence of the rich, but upon the direct and constant exercise of plastic power."[12] Sidney and Beatrice Webb included, along with prevention, universal provision, and curative treatment, the principle of compulsion among their remedies for poverty.

Some who depart from a cultural view of poverty conclude that the object is to exclude the poor (reduce immigration and discourage internal migration and integration) and seek to reduce their numbers (promote sterilization and birth control among the poor, avoid a family allowance or any other incentives to larger family size among the poor). Others are more optimistic concerning the possibility of transforming the poor; they remain unimpressed by assertions that poor children are notably inferior

11. As cited by Pumphrey, op. cit.
12. *Works* (Edinburgh: W. Tait, 1843), p. 395.

in genetic terms, and pin their hopes on environmental improvement, the transmission of general community values to children, and ultimately on the appeal of opportunities to join the nonpoor majority. They put their emphasis upon breaking down the cultural isolation of the poor by roads, schools, mass media, city planning to intermix poor and nonpoor neighborhoods, and special efforts to reduce infant mortality and natal defects.

The specific remedies in this category include rehabilitative work with physically handicapped and disturbed persons, family counselling and consumer education, urban redevelopment, area development with emphasis on community facilities, special health services that reach out for, rather than merely wait for, cases of medical need, and preschool and extraschool experiences to widen the horizons of culturally deprived youngsters. A method much favored by those who espouse the third theory is the development of local, indigenous leadership and community organizations that can make effective use of outside technical assistance.

Many of these remedies are in effect now and the question is how far and how fast to extend them. Some critics have claimed that most of the contemporary American poor are not isolated and alienated and would respond favorably to better job opportunities or to more transfer payments. I suppose all are agreed that most of the "change the poor" remedies would be more effective if the poor were not so poor and if they had clearer evidence that reform would lead to better employment prospects. But, also, all are agreed that some programs to change the attitudes, motivations, and potential productivity of the poor—and particularly of poor children—can make an independent contribution to a faster rate of poverty reduction, allowing for a time lag of one or two decades. There are outstanding examples of success with programs of this kind, and there assuredly are cases of poverty that appear to be beyond the reach of broad-based economic reform.

Selecting the means to use

This review of the possible methods to use in an antipoverty campaign with reference to broad theories of causation has cast up a range of testable, predictive propositions. They can be formulated thus: if we do this, poverty will be reduced, or the poverty income gap will be narrowed. The policy variables touched upon include monetary-fiscal policies, area redevelopment, minimum wage laws, demogrants and tax revision, public work, immigration and population policies designed to reduce the numbers of the poor, plans to minimize isolation and concentration of the poor, rehabilitation and special health and education efforts, and self-help organizations of the poor. Of course, the choices may be thought of as combinations of several of these variables.

How do we then select from this range the methods to use? The judgment may be made that certain methods are unacceptable or that some should be preferred because certain groups among the poor may have political priority. These are matters for judgment akin to the setting of the goal. Among them are decisions about whether one wants to encourage a few major programs versus a large number of special programs, whether to favor general measures versus those that are specific to the poor (it will be recalled that some of the remedies discussed involve paying out more benefits to the nonpoor than to the poor), whether one wants to deal broadside with all the poor or selectively with certain groups among the poor, perhaps singling out the most "deserving" of the poor, or the cases of the most "grinding" poverty, or those who are not only poor but have some other handicap as well and have the least basis for hope. Some might prefer to emphasize aid to those who have low income and also lack access to public facilities. Some might reject a method because it does or does not involve a high degree of centralization or co-ordination, or because it leaves out participation in planning and execution by certain groups including the affected poor, or because it involves a high degree of compulsion or a heavy tax burden for some. In the political process, certain values may play a significant role in selecting from the array of testable propositions for experiment. Some proposals will have great appeal because they appear to relate closely to certain values, aside from income adequacy, e.g. self-reliance, family solidarity, fair prices or wages, local autonomy or states rights, voluntarism, or community spirit and fellowship.

EFFECTIVENESS OF ALTERNATIVE PROGRAM

All the above political constraints and more may enter into the framework within which antipoverty programs are to be judged.

But a key part of the decision-making process should be a judgment concerning the relative effectiveness of the several possible programs in reducing poverty and in filling the poverty-income gap. In calculating the result, some weighting might be given for the shortness of time required, for the success with hard cases, for the distance people are moved past the poverty line, and for additions to the incomes of the nonpoor. (The latter could be thought of as negative costs.) The results should be related to the costs, and these, too, must be calculated in more than one form, with weights assigned to the different forms. There are programs where all the costs are tax costs, there are others where the primary burden is not in the form of taxes but of extra effort or higher prices paid by private persons, including in some cases the poor. The cost of some programs will include lowering of incentives, which in turn will measurably result in lost national product. When all the benefits and costs are known, a cost-benefit ratio can be calculated, and when this is done for two or more programs, including the status quo, there is then a basis for choosing one program over another, all other considerations being equal.[13] Table 11.1 shows a form for relating the concepts of benefit-cost analysis to any particular antipoverty program.

However, even the narrowly conceived cost-benefit ratios for competing antipoverty methods require facts and information about functional relationships that we do not now have. In many cases the causal linkages from original input to result are intricate. Suppose, for example, funds are appropriated for preschool training. How much does this affect a child's performance in high school and how much does this improve his chance of escaping from poverty? Suppose in the meantime his parents receive a family allowance and he is given a part-time job in the Neighborhood Youth Corps? Does each program reinforce the other? If so, by how much? All these questions are, in principle, answerable but the fact is that we don't know how to answer them now, even though some of the questions are as old as economics.

The sad situation is that we have not been measuring the effectiveness of many "grand experiments" in public policy. In the postwar years we have increased public and private outlays on

13. Logically, the preferences concerning methods and groups to be served could be included in the cost-benefit formulations.

TABLE 11.1. FORM FOR ESTIMATING BENEFIT-COST RATIOS FOR ANY PARTICULAR ANTIPOVERTY PROGRAM

	POOR POPULATION (BY SELECTED SEGMENTS)	NONPOOR POPULATION	TOTAL POPULATION
Benefit (plus or minus)			
Added income			
wages			
transfers			
Less foregone income			
wages			
transfers			
Added potential for future wage income			
Weighted total benefit			
Cost (plus or minus)			
Added taxes			
Addition to prices paid			
Loss of leisure			
Weighted total cost			
Benefit-cost ratio (weighted total benefit divided by weighted total cost)			
Yearly change in number of poor persons per unit of weighted total cost			
Yearly change in size of poverty-income gap per unit of weighted total cost			

both education and health at a rate of 8 per cent per capita per year, and we have increased other outlays on public income maintenance at an even faster rate. I know of no study of the effect these expenditures have had on the rate of poverty reduction. This paucity of empirical research is not unique to the problem here under consideration. George J. Stigler made lack of testing the effectiveness of many basic policies (including some antipoverty policies) the subject of his presidential address at the 1964 meetings of the American Economic Association.[14] Hence, any progress that can be made over the years ahead in developing cost-benefit ratios for alternative antipoverty programs will have significance not only for the war on poverty but for all social science in its application to public policy.

But in the meantime decisions have to be made about ways to speed the rate of poverty reduction. The lack of complete information should not necessarily inhibit decision-makers in this field any more than it does in others. Neither should it be allowed to cancel out the use of the best estimates of costs and benefits that can be made.

The best way to achieve a purpose is to state clearly what the goal is, to list all the possible means to the goal, to select and implement those means which have the greatest benefits (or advantages) net of costs (or disadvantages), keeping it in mind that experience, research and reflection, objective conditions, and democratic processes can lead to changes in the nature of the goal, the list of possible means, and the estimate of benefits and costs associated with the several means.[15] Those who are making policy for the war on poverty, no less than policy-makers in other fields, will find all these elements gloriously entangled. Benefits and costs are calculated with reference to values or goals of various sorts, and the decision of how fast and how far to go with how many means calls for decisions about the priority of the antipoverty goal among all national goals. If the elimination of poverty were the only goal, it would follow that every means that promised to contribute anything to that goal should be employed to the fullest. Finally, the antipoverty goal is justifiable solely as a means to more fundamental ends. Only if its step-by-step achievement makes a net contribution to the potentialities and the dignity of the human condition is it worth pursuing further.

14. "The Economist and the State," *Amer. Econ. Rev., 55,* No. 1 (March 1965), 1–18.

15. The tentative nature of the first steps in the war on poverty was emphasized by President Johnson in his March 16, 1964, message to the Congress. He said, "It [the Economic Opportunity Act] will also give us a chance to test our weapons, to try our energy and ideas and imagination for the many battles yet to come. As conditions change, and as experience illuminates our difficulties, we will be prepared to modify our strategy."

Index

Ability: personal, 4, 15, 216; poor children, 57
Abortion, 185
Academic climate, 57, 59
Achievement, pupil, 54, 56–57
Acreage allotment, 171
Adams, F. Gerard, 192
Ad Hoc Committee on the Triple Revolution, 217
Adult education, 60, 62, 63, 90, 91
Affluence, 84, 151, 154, 159, 170, 195, 217, 219
Age, 15, 22, 83, 192–93; composition of population, 20, 144, 192; related to informal association, 66; working, 21
Aged, the, 5, 24, 42, 102, 104, 154, 209 (see also Family, heads); affected by inflation, 197; benefits to, 172n., 202, 221; composition of poor, 23, 24; discrimination against, 178, 189, 220; income, 193; income, guaranteed, 118; labor, 192; Negro, 107
Aggression, 81, 83. See also Animosities; Hostility
Agricultural: aid, 211 (see also Government, support; Price, supports); areas, 157; employment, 141; income, 171; migration, 210 (see also Farm, movement off); productivity, 151; resource programs, 161, 172n.; skills, 180; surplus, 152; training, 96
Agriculture, 49, 110, 113, 139, 160; government expenditures on, 180; Negroes in, 180; subsistence, 153 (see also Farming)
Aid, 11, 121, 122, 146 (see also Public assistance); agricultural, 211 (see also Government support; Price supports); Appalachian, 149; Area Redevelopment Administration, 126; county, 145; educational, 146; mutual, 51; regional, 145
Aid to Families with Dependent Children, 133
Alabama, 126, 144
Alaska, 155, 156
Alcoholism, 81, 84. See also Drinking
Alleghenies, 126
Allen, Bushrod, 126
Almshouses, 5
American Economic Association, 229
Anderson, W. H. Locke, 42, 195, 217
Anglo-Saxon, 125
Animosities, 77. See also Aggression; Hostility
Anomy, 82, 83, 88, 95
Antipoverty: goals, 202, 213, 214, 215, 216, 229; legislation, 115; policies, 124, 137, 149, 154, 167, 208, 219; programs, 60, 63, 99, 102, 148, 151, 153, 154, 156, 161, 162, 182, 183, 190, 195, 210, 215, 218, 226–27, 229; Appalachia, 124, 200; participation, 195
Anti-Semitism, 194

Antisocial: behavior, 79, 85, 119; goals, 89 (*see also* Delinquency; Deviant group; values, 70

Anxiety, 75, 80, 82, 83

Apathy, 80, 82, 91, 95

Appalachia, 47, 104, 124–49, 154, 161; education, 125, 135; employment, 124; families, 129; farming, 134; housing, 130; income, 126, 128, 129, 131; industries, 137, 141; occupations, 139; rural, 46, 47, 49, 57, 59, 129, 130; unemployment, 135, 141, 143; urban, 129, 130, 134

Appalachian region, 124, 125, 126

Appalachian Regional Commission, 126, 147, 148, 149

Appalachian Regional Development Act, 124, 125, 126, 127, 146, 148, 149

Aptitudes, pupil, 55

Area development, 161, 220

Area Redevelopment Act, 126, 145

Area Redevelopment Administration, 145, 149

Areas, 126, 134; agricultural, 157; depressed, 124, 145, 146, 149, 155, 160, 220; farm, 154, 180; geographic, 160, 162; metropolitan, 126, 158, 159; rural, 130, 134, 154, 155, 159, 160; underdeveloped, 205; urban, 159, 160, 180

Aspirations, 57, 59, 60, 62, 71

Asset holdings, 24, 171; community, 213

Assimilation, of social norms, 71, 84, 92

Assistance. *See* Public assistance

Attitudes, 70, 77, 82, 92, 116, 224, 225; anomic, 95 (*see also* Anomy); youth, 203; prevailing, 215; social, 8, 12, 95, 166; toward authority, 81

Automation, 101, 112

Bakke, E. Wight, 65

Balance of payments, 183, 186, 187, 196, 198, 199, 201

Baldwin, James, 117

Baltimore, 158

Barriers, economic, 69, 114, 193–94, 220

Basic education, 63, 161

Batchelder, Allen, 188, 194

Beech Creek, 49, 66

Benefits: disability, 202, 221; guaranteed income, 119; old age, 172n., 202, 221; payments, 197, 226; public, 133, 134, 215, 221, 222, 227; unemployment, 50, 186, 202; welfare, 178

Benevolence, private, 8. *See also* Charity

Bentham, Jeremy, 224

Berkeley, George, 168

Birmingham, 125

Birth control, 185, 224, 226

Birth rate, 40, 41, 143, 144, 154

Booth, Charles, 13

Boulding, Kenneth, 169

Brady, Dorothy S., 192

Breadwinner, 50, 51, 217

Bremner, Robert H., 12, 13, 14, 15, 16, 213

British Parliament, 119

Broken families, 5, 26, 52, 53, 108, 109

Brown, James Stephen, 49

Burns, Eveline M., 184n., 221

Business cycles, 7, 103, 121, 177n., 192. *See also* Fluctuations, economic

Butte, Montana, 16

California, 26

Campbell, Helen, 8, 10

Campbell, John C., 125

Capacity: emotional, 79; for improvement, 10; intellectual, 79, 195; physical, 6, 75, 195; productive, 145, 188, 219

Capital, 74, 86, 150, 183, 184; Appalachia, 129; availability, 220; expenditures, 146 (*see also* Investment); gains, 20, 173

Capitalism, 121, 216

Carey, Matthew, 14

Carnegie Corporation, 72

Case method, 20

Catholic faith, 86

Caudill, Harry M., 58
Cavan, Ruth Shoule, 49, 50
Census Bureau, 102, 104, 121, 210
Central City, Colorado, 157
Channing, William Ellery, 9
Characteristics of poor, 28, 73–85, 134, 137, 183
Charity, 8, 11, 13, 167, 168
Charleston, West Virginia, 60
Chicago, 55, 107
Chicago Area Projects, 66
Child care, 20, 78
Child rearing, 48, 81, 108
Children: composition of poor, 22, 23; geographic distribution, 40; mal-treatment, 77; middle-class, 54, 55; Negro, 159; poor, 22, 48, 53–54, 57, 60, 76, 104, 168, 201, 210, 225; pro-grams for, 203; Road, 92; rural farm, 178
Church: as formal association, 63; at-tendance, 65; membership, 65; so-cials, 77
Cincinnati, 158–59
Cities, 7, 25, 53, 55 (*see also* Metropoli-tan); Northern, 103, 159; social or-ganizations in, 64
Citizens without Work, 65
City planning, 225
Civil rights, 153
Civil Rights Act, 99, 115
Civil rights movement, 115, 116
Civil War, 6, 7, 11
Class: as membership qualification, 45; lower, 12, 47, 167, 168; patterns, 64; segregation, 54
Classical economists, 174n.
Clothing of the poor, 75, 92, 93
Cloward, Richard A., 57, 71
Clubs, 65, 67, 70
Coal, 152; communities, 46, 59; min-ing, 125, 126, 139, 153, 154, 157, 160. *See also* Mining
Collective bargaining, 213, 219. *See also* Unions
College graduates, 117, 135
College Qualifying Test, 59

Colorado, 157
Commercial setbacks, 7. *See also* Business cycles; Fluctuation, eco-nomic
Common Market, 193
Commons, John R., 3, 8
Communities, 13, 15, 45, 54, 73; afflu-ent, 61, 73, 88, 150; Appalachia, 125, 157; coal, 46, 59; depressed, 61, 73, 75, 76, 77, 84, 92–95, 150; facilities (*see* Facilities); homogeneous, 46, 88; rural, 46
Community: action, 11, 63, 66, 91, 150 (*see also* Group action); activities, 63, 64; approval, 52; assistance, 11; cohesion, 79, 92 (*see also* Group ac-tion); development, 96; integration, 95; life, 7; Negro, 104, 116; rehabili-tation, 72, 90 (*see also* Development, community); responsibility, 5, 6, 8, 10; setting, 45; size, 83; status, 65
Conant, James B., 51, 55, 68
Conference of Appalachian Gover-nors, 126
Congenital defects, 11
Congress, 14, 121, 212, 229n.
Connecticut, 33, 205
Conservation, 146, 153, 156, 161; pro-grams, 160; soil, 151, 160; water, 151
Consumer: education, 225; goods, 7; price index, 196; prices, 109; satis-faction, 19; units, 30, 48, 184
Consumption, 19, 165, 168, 183; ex-penditures, 19, 169–70, 204 (*see also* Expenditures); patterns, 201; per capita, 185
Contact: culture, 84; personal, 63, 91
Cornell Program in Social Psychiatry, 72
Cornerville, 67
Cost-benefit analysis, 227, 229
Costs: antipoverty programs, 119, 227; guaranteed income program, 119; living, 4, 14
Council of Economic Advisers, 18, 19, 32, 104, 106, 120, 175, 184, 191, 200, 203, 205, 218

Craftsmen, 110, 139

Crime, 77, 119, 215

Cultural: assimilation, 84, 93–95; background, 57, 59, 60, 122; base, 203; deprivation, 215, 225; discontinuity, 56, 61, 70; facilities, 58; theory, 216, 224; values, 167

Culture of poverty, 13, 69, 88, 107n., 122

Current Population Survey, 106

Day-care centers, 60

Delinquency, 66, 68–69, 119, 215

Demand: aggregate, 145, 181, 186, 196, 197, 199, 219; expansion, 198; for goods, 154, 177, 179; for imports, 198; for labor, 143, 179–80, 190, 191, 192, 193, 194, 197–98; for resources, 153; for services, 154, 177, 179, 186

Democracy, 11, 70, 103, 187n., 213, 216; characteristics, 20

Demogrant, 221, 222

Demographic considerations, 20, 30, 32–33, 41

Demonstrations, 103, 115. *See also* Protest

Department: of Agriculture, 104, 125, 126; of Commerce, 160, 202; of Health, Education and Welfare, 91, 104, 106

Dependency, 4, 5, 8, 13, 15, 16, 47, 50, 61, 153, 215, 223

Depressed, counties, 60. *See also* Communities, depressed; Areas, depressed

Depression, 7, 9, 16, 49–50, 121, 166, 170 177n., 202. *See also* Business cycles; Commercial setbacks; Fluctuations, economic

Deprivation, cultural, 215, 225

Desertion, 49

Destitution, 6, 8

Detroit, 107

Deutsch, Albert, 5, 16

Deutsch, Martin P., 60, 79

Developing countries. *See* Underdeveloped countries

Development programs, 146, 203, 208; area, 161, 203, 208, 220; community, 96; economic, 7, 95, 124, 146, 147, 148, 149, 156, 162; funds, 146; industrial, 11, 154; regional, 148, 203, 208, 220; resource, 156, 160–61; urban, 225; water, 150, 151, 160, 161

Deviant group behavior, 89, 90

Dillon, Douglas, 173

Disability, 25, 30; benefits, 202, 221

Disabled: by disease, 75; guaranteed income to, 118

Disadvantaged, 8, 75, 85, 87

Discrimination, 25, 47, 87, 94, 114–15, 117, 123, 156, 166, 188, 189, 193, 196, 208, 214, 220; aged, 188, 194; employment, 176, 178, 180–81, 220; female labor, 188, 189, 194, 220; Negro, 99, 178, 180–81, 188, 194, 205

Disease, 75, 156

Disequilibria, 176, 180. *See also* Business cycles; Fluctuations, economic

Distribution, income (*see* Income distribution); wealth, 9, 17, 173, 179

District of Columbia, 100, 115, 159, 205

Disutility, of poverty, 166, 169, 170

Divorce, 51, 53

Doctrine of the Utility of Poverty, 168

Dominion Provincial Mental Health Grants of Canada, 72

Drinking, 10, 13, 64, 75, 77, 78, 94. *See also* Alcoholism

Dropouts, 59, 60, 61–63, 117

Durkee, Peter, 18n.

Dwelling units, 130. *See also* Housing conditions

Earnings, 177; business, 173; labor, 139, 174, 179, 197 (*see also* Wages); level, 137, 139, 174, 197

Econometric: analysis, 210; model, 205, 206, 208

Economic: activity, 146; aspirations, 59; change, 103; collapse, 86 (*see also* Business cycles); development (*see* Development, economic); disorders, 16 (*see also* Business cycles); expansion, 4, 7, 16, 203, 208, 209, 210; gap, 99, 100, 101 (*see also* Poverty-income gap); growth, 22, 71, 117, 120, 144, 145, 151, 166, 170, 173–74, 176, 180, 181, 201, 213, 214, 215, 216, 218; inequality, 47 (*see also* Equality); opportunities (*see* Opportunity, economic); progress, 188, 191, 193, 217; segregation, 57; stability, 166, 195 (*see also* Business cycles)

Economic Development Act, 200

Economic Opportunity Act, 61, 63, 187, 200, 212, 229n.

Economic Reports of the President, 145, 200, 201, 212, 213

Education, 41, 46, 48, 52, 59, 60, 83, 86, 122, 136, 137, 145, 148, 150, 160, 212; Appalachia, 125, 135; attitudes toward, 70, 77, 92, 116; consumer, 225; discipline in, 55, 78; handicapping, 62; improved, 115, 117, 162; investment in, 114, 177, 178, 210, 219; Negro, 114, 159, 181; program, 102, 119, 154, 162, 195, 203, 210, 226; rural, 58; therapy, 224; training in, 96; vocational, 63, 71, 133, 146, 210

Education Act, 200

Educational: achievement, 59, 68; aspirations, 57, 60, 62, 71; attainment, 24, 41, 57, 64, 134, 135, 137, 153, 157, 177, 188, 205, 215, of family head, 24, 135, 206, 207; differential, 135; expenditures (*see* Expenditures, education); facilities, 62, 187; handicaps, 55; motivation, 56, 59, 60; performance, 58; qualifications, 54, 188; quality, 25, 58, 61, 66, 99, 104, 114, 202; system, 156; techniques, 96

Effects of poverty, 73, 89

Elmtown, 63

Emotional: response, 81; ties, 48, 53, 68

Employment, 70, 86, 87, 93, 137, 155, 157, 170, 176, 177; Alaska, 156; Appalachia, 124; declining, 139, 141,

157; educational requirements, 54; farming, 110; fluctuating, 8, 74; full, 16, 166, 177, 181, 187, 198, 199, 201, 214, 216; full-time, 23, 109, 168, 206, 207; government, 115, 159; mining, 141, 142; Negro, 110, 112, 114, 159; opportunity (*see* Opportunity, employment); part-time, 28; practices, 115; seasonal, 74; textiles, 158; white-collar, 110

England, 167

English history, 167; welfare practices, 5

Environment, 15, 203, 213; improvements, 225; limiting, 54, 59, 61, 70, 79, 147; oriented, 146; social, 213, 224

Equality: employment opportunity, 99, 188, 202, 208, 211, 214; occupational, 112, 114; of conditions, 4

Estabrook, A. H., 11

Ethnic: diversity, 223; groups, 47; homogeneity, 67

Eugenic theory, 11

Europe: labor mobility, 193; welfare practice, 11

Euthanasia, 185

Exchange rates, 198–99

Expenditures: clothing, 8; consumption, 19, 169–70, 204; family, 106; food, 104, 106, 204; government, 121, 131, 132–34, 145, 166, 180, 189, 196, 219; health, 227–28; housing, 106; patterns, 48; personal, 172; public works, 219; training, 99

Experience: job, 28, 95, 96, 136, 188, 194; range, 225

Extended family, 49, 52. *See also* Kinship ties; Kinship system; Responsibility, family

Facilities: community, 145, 146, 149, 220, 225; Appalachia, 125; education, 21, 62, 187; public, 226; recreation, 160

Families: Appalachia, 129; broken, 5,

26, 52, 53, 108, 109; expenditures, 106; farm (*see* Farm families); higher-income 48, 54, 202; husband-wife, 108; lower-class, 48, 49n., 53, 69 (*see also* Female-based household; Patriarchal families); middle-class, 53; Negro, 108, 122, 176; nonfarm, 171, 205; nonwhite, 25, 106, 108, 153, 206; per cent in poverty, 19, 32, 174, 175, 204, 213, 218; poor, 20, 26, 33, 155, 156, 179, 190, 203; professional, 69; rural, 159; Southern, 42, 176; total, 212; urban, 204; Washington, D.C., 159; white, 156

Family: age-sex composition, 22; aged, 24, 30, 33, 41, 153, 205, 207; as social organization, 63; conjugal, 49; earners, 30, 207, 218; extended, 49, 52; formation, 185; head, 25, 104; headed by female, 28, 33, 42, 51, 108, 153, 188, 205, 207 (*see also* Female-based household); income (*see* Income, family); limitation, 185; matriarchal, 51, 108 (*see also* Female-based household); nonearner, 23, 32, 33, 190, 206; patriarchal, 48, 53, 69; relationships, 49, 50, 51, 68, 93; solidarity, 50–53, 76, 226; stability, 107, 122, 153; structure, 45, 117, 166 (*see also* Social organization); unemployed head, 182, 190; unit, 24, 47, 52, 54; young, 32, 41

Farm: Appalachia, 134; families, 49, 106, 169, 171, 176, 180, 206; income, 22, 65, 171, 180, 210; land, 150, 155, 168, 171; labor, 100, 180; movement off, 32, 41, 193 (*see also* Migration); problem, 214; residents, 22, 25, 30, 32, 33, 104, 134, 143; subsidy, 219, 220. *See also* Price supports

Farmers, 153, 155, 168, 170, 172n.; Negro, 107, 110, 112

Farming, 86, 154, 159; Appalachia, 134; cooperative, 49; employment, 110; subsistence, 102, 125, 169

Feder, Leah H., 6, 7

Female-based household, 46, 48, 51–54, 68, 69, 70, 108, 188

Female: employment, 46, 48, 51, 52; labor, 194; discrimination against, 178, 188, 189, 194, 220

Fields of employment: growing, 112; low-paid, 117; lucrative, 114; professional, 116

Fisher, Joseph L., 152

Fisheries, 155, 156, 160

Fishman, Leonard L., 152

Fluctuations, economic, 7, 8, 16, 20, 28, 74, 86, 192, 193. *See also* Business cycles; Commercial setbacks

Food: expenditures, 48, 104, 106, 204; prices, 8, 104, 220

Ford, James, and Katherine, 12, 16, 17

Ford Foundation, 72

Forecasts, 114, 174–75, 217. *See also* Predictions; Projections

Foreign: aid, 169; born, 11; markets, 152; policy, 198; trade, 152

Forests, 134, 157

Formal associations, 45, 63–66, 77. *See also* Social organization

Frazier, E. Franklin, 52

Free enterprise system, 182, 183, 185, 195. *See also* Capitalism

Friedman, Milton, 172, 173

Frontier opportunities, 12

Fruitland, New Mexico, 84

Full employment, 16, 166, 177, 181, 187, 198, 199, 201, 214, 216

Full-time employment, 23, 109, 207

Furniss, Edgar S., 167

Galbraith, John K., 120, 214, 217

Gallaway, Lowell E., 42, 174, 175, 191, 218

Gangs, 45, 68, 89

Garment industry, 51, 52, 103

Geographic: isolation, 49; location, 42; mobility, 187, 193

George, David Lloyd, 119, 120

George, Henry, 9

Georgia, 125, 126, 139, 144

Germany, 193

Glazer, Nathan, 101, 116, 223

Goals, 84, 87, 95, 201, 215; antipoverty, 202, 213, 214, 215, 216, 229; democratic, 216; limited, 80, 224; national, 212, 214, 216, 229

Gold reserves, 199

Gordon, R. A., 217

Government: action, 145, 183; aid (*see* Aid); control, 156; employment, 115; expenditures, 121, 180, 189, 196; federal, 115, 150, 154, 157, 167, 210; local, 115, 148, 150–51, 154, 167; programs, 118, 157, 172n., 195, 210 (*see also* Antipoverty programs); role, 145; state, 115, 148, 151, 157, 167; support, 118, 119, 214, 216. *See also* Price supports

Grandparents, 51, 76

Gratification of personal wants, 75

Great Depression, 49

Gross National product, 42, 118, 119, 213

Group: action, 95, 224, 226; dynamics, 66

Growth rate, 174, 175, 218. *See also* Economic: growth

Handicapped, 225, 226

Handicapping characteristics, 20, 24–25, 42, 57. *See also* Age; Disability; Education; Environment; Nonwhites

Hansen, W. Lee, 18n.

Harrington, Michael, 101

Hart, Schaffner, and Marx, 167–68

Havighurst, Robert J., 54, 56

Health, 73, 75, 79, 153; programs, 146, 154

Hiestand, Dale, 110, 113

High school, 92, 114; graduates, 54, 58, 177; performance, 227

High School Senior Achievement Tests, 58

Highway, 149, 150; construction, 137, 146, 161, 162

Hollingshead, A. B., 63

Hoover, Herbert, 120

Hostility, 75, 80, 81, 82, 83, 89. *See also* Aggression

Housing conditions, 10, 13, 25, 46, 56, 74–78, 100, 115, 117, 130, 214, 215, 219

Hughes, Charles C., 73, 75

Human resources, 148, 174, 176–179, 181, 187, 193, 210, 211

Hume, David, 168

Hunter, Robert, 14, 15

Husband, roles, 48, 50, 51, 78

Illness, 15, 28, 30, 209

Immigrants, 11, 26, 69; assimilation of, 13

Immigration, 69, 159, 168, 224, 226

Imports and resource availability, 152, 198

Incapacitation, 15, 84, 85, 88, 209

Incentives, 74, 193, 194, 222, 227

Income, 14, 19, 20, 100, 106, 156, 157, 169, 172, 173, 174, 177, 193–99; adequacy, 109, 183, 186, 187, 190, 214, 223, 226; Appalachia, 125, 126, 127, 128, 129, 131; average, 128; class, 26–27, 40; cut-off, 22, 32; distribution, 3, 14, 15, 118, 121, 170, 172, 173, 177n., 180, 197, 201, 202, 209, 211; family, 14, 19, 20, 26, 41, 58, 61, 64, 104, 118, 119, 120, 136, 137, 165, 172, 173, 174, 184, 185, 191, 203, 204; farm, 22, 65, 71, 180, 210; floor, 122 (*see also* Poverty line); fluctuations, 20, 28; functional, 201–02; guaranteed, 118, 119, 215, 217, 221; increase, 156, 162, 201, 214, 217, 218; individual, 184; labor, 179, 197; level, 127, 139, 141, 149, 165; low, 10, 45, 65, 99, 123, 128, 135, 144, 153, 210, 221; maintenance, 102, 117, 202, 203, 208, 209, 210, 211, 221, 223, 228; median, 113, 137, 141, 205; metropolitan, 127, 128, 129, 130; minimum, 16, 118, 119, 215, 217, 221; money, 18, 20, 22, 26, 204; national, 118, 127, 128, 177n., 202, 209, 221; Negro, 100, 114, 123, 194, 208; per capita, 87, 126, 127, 128, 129, 149, 179; personal, 19, 20, 172, 177, 201; property, 177n., 178, 179, 180, 201; relative, 122, 201–02; rural, 130; source, 175, 176; South, 107, 108; stability, 48; streams, 170, 174, 176, 177, 178; wealth paradox, 171

Indians, 84, 90, 156

Individual initiative, 215

Individualism, 7, 223. *See also* Individual initiative; Self-reliance

Industrial: change, 6; development, 11, 154; labor force, 8, 10; mix, 142; nations, 198; revolution, 174; society, 14; structure, 206

Industrialization, 7, 49, 158

Industry, 7, 17, 110, 137, 172n.; Appalachia, 137, 141; employment, 141, 142; declining, 142, 153, 154, 170, 178, 187; dominant, 155; growth, 137, 139, 155, 187; high income, 32, 206; new, 112, 114, 157, 158; resource, 153, 154, 160, 161–62

Inequities, 4, 9, 15, 17, 47, 172

Infant mortality, 40

Inferiority feelings, 66, 81

Infirmity, 5. *See also* Illness

Inflation, 109, 183, 186, 187, 188, 196, 197, 198

Informal associations, 66–69

Informal groups, 45, 77

Integration, 91, 114, 115, 224. *See also* Segregation

Intelligence, 54, 56

Intellectual adjustment, 6

Intemperance, 10. *See also* Alcoholism; Drinking

Interest: range, 66; rates, 196, 197

International monetary system, 198, 199

International transactions, 198

Interpersonal comparisons, 203

Investment, 147, 150, 155, 162, 175, 177; education, 114, 178, 219; human resources, 148, 174, 176, 177, 178–79, 181, 187, 193, 202, 208, 209, 210, 211; inducements, 145; private, 145, 149;

program, 148; public, 114, 145, 146, 170, 178; resource, 160; training, 177, 193, 219

Isolation, 84, 86, 88, 125, 226; cultural, 220, 225; geographical, 49, 215

Jim Crow, 116

Job Corps, 161, 203

Job: creation, 203, 210, 211, 220, 223; loyalty, 74; qualifications, 99; vacancies, 103

Jobs, 186; low-paying, 74; unskilled, 74

Johnson, Harry G., 169, 173, 178

Jones, James A., 57, 71

Kahn, Tom, 100

Keesing, M. Felix, 84, 85

Kentucky, 49, 58, 59, 66, 125, 128, 129, 134, 135, 143; University of, 60

Kinship: groups, 84; system, 49, 66; ties, 46, 49

Komarovsky, Mirra, 50, 64, 65

Kristol, Irving, 219

Labor: costs, 7, 158; demand for (*see* Demand: for Labor); efficient, 15, 17; farm, 100, 180; income, 179, 197; market, 21, 22, 42, 52, 62, 114, 189, 203, 223; tight supply, 193–95; manual, 112; menial, 103, 116; mobility, 178, 193, 220 (*see also* Mobility); Negro, 99, 114; organization, 172n. (*see also* Unions); services, 183–86; skilled (*see* Skilled labor); supply (*see* Supply, labor); unskilled (*see* Unskilled labor); white, 99, 110, 112, 114

Labor force, 17, 22, 28, 49, 110, 119, 136, 151, 155, 162, 180, 181, 186, 187, 191, 197, 203, 218; Appalachia, 136, 142; education, 177, 210; entrants, 136, 192; experienced (*see* Experience, job); female, 141, 178, 185; industrial, 8, 10; Negro, 100, 110, 112, 181; participation, 21, 120, 134, 136,

137, 141, 142, 187, 188, 190, 218; South, 181; unemployed, 135, 182

Land: farm, 150, 155, 168, 171; improvement, 146, 160; timber, 155, 157, 161

Landsberg, Hans H., 152

Language skills, 56, 60, 62, 63

Law, John, 168

Laziness, 13

Leaders, 49, 66, 68, 91, 92, 225; Negro, 103, 115

Legislation, 103, 124, 148; social, 200

Leighton: Alexander H., 73, 79, 85, 90; Dorothea C., 73

Leisure, activities, 64, 76

Levasseur, E., 3, 8

Levitan, Sar, 109

Lewis, Oscar, 72, 80, 81

Libraries, 62, 146

Life: expectancy, 100; lower-class, 66; middle-class, 169; of poor, 70, 72, 122, 169; style, 45–54

Lincoln: Abraham, 4, 5; University, 101

Literacy, 58

Living: cost, 196, 197; level, 64, 106, 125, 130, 152, 165; metropolitan, 130; Negro, 100, 122; rural, 130; standard, 4, 14, 15, 45, 74–75, 85, 95, 110, 120, 121, 169, 183, 201, 204; subsistence, 7, 74, 165

Locational advantage, 153, 162

London, 11, 13, 81

Louisville, 60

Low-rent areas, 66, 67

Lower-class, 48, 49n., 53, 57, 69

Lower East Side, 57

Lumbering, 86, 89, 155

Luxury expenditures, 204

Lynchburg, Va., 125

McClosky, Herbert, 82, 83

Mack, Ruth, 174

Macmillan, Allister M., 72, 73, 79, 85, 90

Maine, 155

Management of resources, 158, 160; practices, 156

Manhattan, 57

Manpower Development and Training Act, 63

Manpower training, 146, 148, 210

Manual labor, 112

Manufacturing, 7, 50, 125, 142, 155; productivity, 151; textile, 158; wage, 202

March on Washington, 100, 115

Market: capital, 176, 180; labor (*see* Labor market)

Marriage, 48, 49, 52, 53, 67, 79, 86; common-law, 76, 81

Marx, 201

Maryland, 125, 128, 134, 144

Mason-Dixon Line, 125

Massachusetts, 14

Matricentric families. *See* Female-based household

M'Culloch, Oscar C., 11, 75

Meade, J. E., 170, 173

Medical care, 106, 117, 133, 204

Medicare, 200

Membership in associations, 45, 63–70, 76–77

Menial labor, 103, 116

Metropolitan, 25, 58, 64, 127; areas, 126, 158, 159; living level, 130; population, 127, 128

Mexico, 47, 81

Michael, Stanley T., 82

Middle-class, 53, 69, 96; aspirations, 57, 59; life style, 169; living standards, 202, 203; values, 59

Midwest, 159

Migrants, 47, 94, 153

Migration, 32, 33, 40, 85, 113, 115, 125, 143–44, 155, 157, 160, 193, 220, 224 (*see also* Mobility); assistance, 187; from agriculture, 210 (*see also* Farm, movement off); Negro, 107; programs, 154, 162

Milbank Memorial Fund, 72

Military service, 188

Miller, Walter B., 53, 67

Minerals, 126, 151, 152

Minimum standards: housing, 15; living, 15, 118, 184, 186 (*see also* Living standard; Life style); wage, 15, 109, 170, 172n., 220, 223, 226; working conditions, 15

Mining, 134, 150, 153, 160 (*see also* Coal mining); employment, 141, 142; towns, 51, 156

Minnesota, 82, 84

Minority group, 87. *See also* Negroes; Puerto Ricans

Mississippi, 33, 40, 87, 205

Mobility: geographic, 40, 193; labor, 178, 193, 220; Negro, 112; occupational, 110, 112, 178, 187; upward, 57, 69, 70

Money income, 18, 20, 22, 26, 204; supply, 196

Morgantown, W.Va., 51

Motivation, 57, 74, 93, 150, 153, 154, 182, 187, 216, 224, 225; educational, 56, 59, 60

Muckrakers, 101

Mun, Thomas, 168

Municipalities, 9

Mutual aid, 51. *See also* Extended family

Narcotics, 68

National Institutes of Mental Health, 72

National Opinion Research Center, 64

National Resources Planning Board, 157

National Teachers Corps, 60

Nationalism, 167

Nationality, 46, 47

Natural resources, 74, 158, 162. *See also* Resources

Navahos, 84, 87–88

Negative income tax, 118, 172, 185, 222

Negroes, 11, 47, 51, 52, 54, 64, 68, 99, 102, 180, 208 (*see also* Nonwhites); communities, 104; discrimination against, 99, 178, 180–81, 188, 194,

205; economic position, 100, 101, 194; education, 181; employment, 110, 112, 114, 115, 116; families, 122, 176; farmer, 107, 110, 112; fertility, 107; geographical distribution, 107; high school, 114; housing, 25, 100; leaders, 103, 115; life expectancy, 100; living level, 100, 122; migration, 107, 159; Southern, 108; unemployed, 47, 103, 107, 194; youth, 103

Neighborhood, 66, 67, 69

Neighborhood Youth Corps, 203, 223, 227

Nelson, Gaylord, Senator, 60

New England, 40, 157

New Deal, 16, 217

New Haven, Conn., 65

New York, 26, 60, 65, 107, 126, 127

New York City, 8, 52

Niles, Hezekiah, 14

Nonearners, 28, 32, 76

Nonfarm: labor, 110; residents, 25, 30

Nonwhites, 28, 32, 33, 42, 107, 206, 208 (*see also* Negroes); discrimination against, 25, 189, 220; education, 41; families, 25, 106, 108, 153

North, 14, 107, 109, 114, 181

North Carolina, 125

North Central region, 40

North East, 40, 73, 158

Nutrition, 8, 78, 153

Occupational: aspirations, 57, 71; change, 110, 112, 114, 187, 194; earnings, 139, 140; equality, 112, 114; expansion, 112, 187; gap, 110, 112, 113, 114, 115 (*see also* Economic gap); groups, 113, 172n.; mix, 137, 139; mobility, 112; position, 113–14; status, 83, 94, 214

Ohio, 130, 134, 144

Old age, 25, 214. *See also* Aged

Old age insurance, 210. *See also* Benefits, old age

Old Age Assistance, 133

Ontario, 93

Operation Head Start, 61

Opportunity, 11, 12, 16, 125; Appalachia, 141, 144; creation of, 15, 70, 122; economic, 46, 94, 186, 202, 208, 212, 225; educational, 41, 188; employment, 22, 115, 136, 137, 142, 149, 154, 178, 188, 195, 202, 207, 211, 225; Europe, 193; female, 46, 194; Negro, 107, 110, 112, 113, 116, 159, 194, 208; equality (*see* Equality)

Orshansky, Mollie, 22, 105, 106, 184, 190, 191

Outdoor recreation, 150, 155, 160, 161, 162

Output per man hour, 151

Ozarks, 26, 104

Parent Teacher Association, 57

Participation: labor force (*see* Labor force); social, 84, 89, 117

Part-time employment, 62

Passamaquoddy Bay, 155

Patriarchal family, 48, 53, 69

Patten, Simon, 17

Paupers, 14, 121

Peace Corps, 96

Peer groups, 67–68, 69, 70

Pennsylvania, 124, 128, 129, 134, 139

Personality: anomic, 95 (*see also* Anomy); scales, 82, 83

Petty, William, 168

Philadelphia, 107

Philanthropy, 5, 6, 8, 9, 11

Picketing, 115

Plans: economic, 146; development, 148, 149

Planning, 154, 155

Police, 77, 79

Political: aspirations, 108; influence, 187; life, 54, 77; process, 226; structure, 108

Population: Appalachia, 143; poor, 8, 10, 26, 30, 42, 47, 192; composition, 42, 192, 200; growth, 6–7, 33, 41, 160, 169; metropolitan, 127; Negro, 154, 159; nonwhite, 206, 208

Poverty, 10–69 passim, 154; characteristics, 11, 18, 24, 25, 72; chronic, 102, 118, 154, 160; composition of, 33, 41; cultural, 13, 107n.; definition of, 3, 4, 16, 17, 18, 19, 45, 165–66, 183, 184, 191, 201, 203, 212n.; economic, 107n., 118, 121; incidence, 32, 33, 40n., 41, 42, 128–219 passim; income, 128, 139, 195, 200, 201, 203, 212, 222; income gap, 42, 117, 141, 209, 213, 220, 222, 225–26, 227; line, 14, 20, 22, 30, 42n., 104–227 passim; Negro, 110, 117; perpetuation, 14, 53, 71, 75, 77, 82, 85, 89, 187, 224; pockets, 10, 26, 220; problem, 9, 14, 15; rate, 32, 40; ratios, 139; reduction, 15, 19, 26, 32, 40, 42, 156–229 passim; reduction rate, 26, 33, 42; regional, 124; rural, 57, 80, 104, 110, 159; solution, 154, 193, 195, 198, 222; spiritual, 107n., 154; temporary, 102; types, 186–88

Power: electric, 162; water, 158

Predictions, 41, 42n., 212n., 225. *See also* Forecasts; Projections

Preferences, 166, 167, 169, 174, 176, 185

Pre-school preparation, 55–57, 60, 61, 70, 79, 225, 227

President Lyndon B. Johnson, 18, 103, 108, 200, 212, 215, 229n.

Price: influences, 188, 197, 198; parity, 223 (*see also* Farm subsidy; Government support); supports, 170, 171, 172, 220

Prices, 152, 168, 176, 214, 226, 227; agricultural, 170; consumer, 109; food, 8, 104, 220

Productive system, 7, 183, 217

Productivity, 17, 109, 120, 151, 157, 225

Progressivism, 16

Projections, 152, 210, 218

Property income, 177n., 178–80

Prostitution, 10

Protest, 103, 116. *See also* Demonstrations

Providence–Pawtucket area, 158

Psychological characteristics, 73, 84.
    See also Anomy
Psychology of poverty, 154
Public: assistance, 5, 133, 145, 188;
    benefits (*see* Benefits); costs, 131; ex-
    penditures, 131, 132–34; payments,
    197, 226 (*see also* Transfer pay-
    ments); participation by, 131–32;
    programs, 132, 133, 146, 209. *See also*
    Antipoverty programs
Public policy, 14, 20, 145, 153, 157,
    160, 173, 187, 189, 195, 199, 211, 214,
    220, 229 (*see also* Antipoverty poli-
    cies); full employment, 177, 190,
    198, 213; growth, 144, 219; mone-
    tary-fiscal, 186, 196, 203, 217, 226;
    toward demand, 189, 197
Public revenue, 157
Public utilities, 145
Public works, 50, 118, 119, 219, 220,
    223, 226
Puerto Ricans, 47, 54

Race, 45, 46, 83, 116
Racial: diversity, 223; economic in-
    equalities, 47, 99, 100, 101, 107, 115
Raw materials, 152, 153, 158, 160, 198
Reading ability, 62
Recreation, outdoor, 155, 161
Redevelopment. *See* Development
    programs
Reforestation, 160
Reform: cultural, 167; economic, 225;
    movement, 9, 15, 103; social, 102;
    tax, 173
Region, 77, 83, 92, 108, 115, 122, 124,
    125, 134
Regions, 40, 41, 103; declining, 220;
    static, 125
Regression analysis, 136, 206, 207, 208
Rehabilitation, 92–95, 102, 225, 226
Relief, 5, 8, 9, 14, 16, 50, 79, 220
Religion, 10, 47, 66, 77
Relocation, 195, 203, 219, 223
Rent, 19, 66, 67
Report of the Council of Economic
    Advisers for *1962*, 145

Research, 178
Resource: balance, 156; base, 126, 145,
    154, 157, 158, 159, 160; development,
    156, 160–61; industries, 151, 153, 154,
    160, 161–62; prices, 152; programs,
    151, 161; utilization, 150–62
Resources, 19, 95, 149, 150, 151–53,
    154, 156, 159, 162; family, 183, 209
    (*see also* Asset holdings; Wealth);
    human, 146, 148, 174, 177, 178–79,
    181, 187, 193, 202, 208, 209, 210, 211
Resources for the Future, Inc., 152
Responsibility: family, 20, 76, 80; so-
    cial, 3, 7, 8, 11, 83
Retirement, 188, 189, 200; benefits,
    221; income, 197
Retraining. *See* Training
Rezneck, Samuel, 7
Rhode Island, 157–58
Ricardo, 174, 201
Rights, 103. *See also* Civil rights
Riis, Jacob, 12, 13
River City, 56
Road, The, 72–80, 85–87, 90–95
Role: of family, 68, 69; of government,
    145, 215–16; of husband, 48, 51, 78;
    of wife, 48; reversal, 50, 51, 52
Roosevelt, Franklin, 16
Russel Sage Foundation, 125
Rustin, Bayard, 100, 103, 115

Salmon fishery, 156
Savings, 19, 93, 116, 129, 188
Scarcity, 12, 15, 16, 17, 168
Schaar, John H., 82
Schneider, David M., 5, 6, 16
School: aid proposals, 60; authorities,
    63, 90, 92; curriculum deficiencies,
    58–59; discipline problems, 55; en-
    rollment, 137, 159; failure, 62, 72;
    performance, 56, 69, 227; prepara-
    tion, 56; quality, 54, 55, 58, 79, 154;
    segregation, 57; system, 210. *See also*
    High school
Schools, 45, 54, 62, 79, 220, 225; ele-
    mentary, 56; junior high, 56; high
    school, 92, 114; lower-class, 54, 55,

56, 57; middle-class, 56, 57; pupil types, 54; rural, 57
Security: economic, 121–22; social (*see* Social insurance)
Segregation, 70, 71; school, 57. *See also* Integration
Self-confidence, 83, 84, 94, 95
Self-employed, 22
Self-esteem, 85, 87, 90
Self-help, 194, 224, 226
Self-image, 80, 87
Self-improvement, 88, 89
Self-reliance, 215, 226
Self-respect, 121
Self-supporting, 8, 14, 16
Selma, Alabama, 108, 115
Semiskilled labor, 100, 109, 110
Service industry, 112, 139, 142, 159
Service workers, 109, 110, 155
Settlement house, 66
Sharecroppers, 47, 102; Negro, 107, 110
Sharecropping, 100
Shaw, George Bernard, 224
Shipyards, 86
Sit-ins, 115
Skidmore, Thomas, 9
Skilled labor, 100, 113, 138, 150, 153, 177–78, 179–80, 181, 187, 193, 195; Appalachia, 139; Negro, 115, 116, 159, 180, 181
Skills: improvement, 90; job, 61, 75, 95, 155
Slater, Samuel, 158
Slavery, 52, 116
Slum residents, 8, 66–67, 81
Slums, 13, 46, 47, 51, 52, 53, 55, 56, 59, 60, 69, 81; city, 59, 66
Social: attitudes, 8, 12, 95, 166; characteristics, 75, 82, 84, 87, 88, 126; classes, 54, 57; conditions, 4; contact, 67 (*see also* Culture of poverty); costs, 15, 147; Darwinism, 9 (*see also* Survival of the fittest); dividend, 221; effects of poverty, 72, 73; engineers, 17; homogeneous, 69; improvement, 162; ineptness, 75–76; institutions, 7; insurance, 50, 210,

217; intervention, 11; life, 54, 75, 77; mobility, 12n.; organization, 45–71, 90, 76–77, 95, 216 (*see also* Informal associations; Formal associations; School; Street-corner groups); voluntary, 64, 66, 68, patterns, 69; problems, 10, 13, 90, 153; relations, 75, 82, 84, 94; responsibility, 3, 7, 8, 11, 83
Social security: administration, 22; benefits, 197, 221; laws, 103; services, 6; system, 9, 15, 47, 84, 87, 88, 156; theory, 12; work, 116; worker, 96
Socialist, 9, 15
Socialization, 79, 83, 95, 216
Society, 4, 5, 7, 25, 54, 100, 114
Soil: conservation, 151, 160; erosion, 150; fertility, 154, 157
Somatic symptoms, 80
South, 51, 107, 113; rural, 102, 154
South Carolina, 125
Southern: agriculture, 181; disenfranchisement, 116; farming, 181; income, 14, 107, 108; labor costs, 158; labor force, 181; locational advantage, 158; Negro, 108, 114–15, 122, 159; out-migration, 159, 193; political structure, 108; population growth, 32; poverty, 26, 28, 33, 40, 107, 181, 220; sharecroppers, 110; states, 159; whites, 107, 115
Southern Appalachia Coal Plateau, 126
Spartanburg, S.C., 125
Speculative collapses, 7. *See also* Business cycles; Fluctuations, economic
Spinley, B. M., 81
Stability: economic, 166, 192, 195; family, 107, 153; social, 83, 194
Starvation, 8, 9, 10, 11
State of the Union Message, *1964*, 212
States: Appalachian, 125, 126, 128, 129, 130, 131, 133, 135, 136, 141; employment, 155; Northern, 108; poor, 26, 33, 132; relief, 9; rich, 32, 33, 40; rights, 215, 226; Southern, 159; unemployment, 135, 141, 210

Statistical analysis, 14, 190, 191
Status, 46, 47, 70, 83; economic, 88; husband, 48, 49, 50; income, 214; occupational, 214
Sterilization, 224
Stigler, George J., 228
Stirling County, 73, 77, 84, 85, 89
St. Louis, 158
Street-corner groups, 45, 66–69, 70
Structural: change, 142; poverty, 173, 175, 176, 181, 217, 218; unemployment, 219
Structure: class, 66; economic, 124, 145, 217; educational, 207, 210; family, 45, 117, 166; industrial, 206
Structured relationships, 67, 68
Student: loan programs, 146; turnover, 55
Studies: anomy, 82; Appalachia, 125, 126; depression, 49–50; income, 121, 177; poverty, 72, 75, 85, 87, 90, 93, 104, 124
Subcultures, 47, 68, 169, 224
Subsidy, 149, 168, 172, 176; farm, 219, 220 (*see also* Price supports); housing, 219
Subsidization, 109, 171, 220
Subsistence, 165, 174; farming, 102, 125, 169; food, 165; living level, 7, 74, 165
Suburbs, 54, 159
Sumner, William Graham, 9, 10
Supply, labor, 136, 158, 193
Survey of Consumer Expenditures, 106
Survival of the fittest, 10. *See also* Social Darwinism
Sweden, 173
Synthetic fibers, 153

Taxation, 145, 166, 176, 227; burden, 226; corporate income, 179; cut, 103, 196, 219; estate, 173, 202; gift, 173; income, 172; negative income, 118, 172, 185, 222; progressive, 170, 172, 201, 202, 219; reform, 226; revenues, 222

Teachers: inexperienced, 55; turnover, 55; quality, 59, 60, 79, 91
Teaching, 60, 116; in slum schools, 60
Technical assistance, 146, 225
Technological change, 100, 112, 153, 154, 177
Teenagers, 135, 203
Television, 48, 62
Tennessee, 59, 125
Territorial expansion, 6
Texas, 26, 40
Textile industry, 7, 153, 157, 158, 160
Theory, 173, 174, 201; eugenic, 11; genetic, 225; government, 215–16; poverty, 216, 224, 225
Thompson, Sir Benjamin, 224
Thurow, Lester, 205
Timber, 155, 157, 161
Titmuss, Richard, 223
Tourism, 155, 156, 161
Townsend Plan, 102
Training, 62–63, 119, 145, 156, 157, 177n., 186, 187, 203, 212, 223; antipoverty program, 102; expenditures, 99; for diet improvement, 10; investment in, 114, 177, 193, 219; job, 150; Negro, 99, 107, 109, 114, 115; on-the-job, 192; program, 118, 161, 162, 195, 210; quality, 202; specialized, 61; system, 210; of teachers, 60 (*see also* Teachers; Teaching); vocational, 71
Tramp problem, 6, 12
Transfer payments, 118, 119, 169n., 176, 188, 195, 197, 202, 216, 220, 221, 222, 223, 225
Transportation, 158, 161
Tryon, Frederick, 126
Turnover: student, 55; teacher, 55

Underdeveloped countries, 54, 198
Underemployment, 22, 158, 186, 189; in Washington, D.C., 159
Uneducated, discrimination against, 189, 220
Unemployment, 15, 22, 28, 30, 42–69

passim, 101, 117, 126, 135, 139, 158, 162, 171–217 passim; Appalachia, 132, 135, 141, 143; benefits, 50, 202; cyclical, 49, 193; effects, 102, 193; family head, 182, 190; hard core, 126; increasing, 217; insurance, 50, 210; Negro, 107, 194; Northern, 47; rate, 135, 136, 137, 139, 141, 144, 149, 173, 191, 192, 195, 196, 197, 207, 210, 218; reduction, 197, 198; Rhode Island, 157; state, 210; Washington, D.C., 159; white-collar occupations, 139

Unions, 64, 89, 102, 170, 188
University of Kentucky, 60
Unskilled labor, 52, 65, 93, 100, 102, 113, 170, 177n., 217; demand for, 179; Negro, 109
Upper Great Lakes, 26
Upward mobility, 70, 122, 187
Urban: housing, 8; life, 66; problem, 214; residents, 25
Urbanism, 64
"Utility of poverty," 167, 169
Utilization, resource, 151, 153, 156, 157, 160

Values, 84, 93, 202, 203, 215, 224, 226, 229; antisocial, 70; cultural, 167; social, 166; system, 68; transmission of, 225
Violence, 77, 81
Virginia, 59, 125, 126, 144, 159
Vocational: education, 63, 146; rehabilitation, 133, program, 210; training, 71
Voluntary: association, 64, 68; groups, 66
Voting rights, 115, 153; bill, 108; legislation, 103

Wages, 22, 48, 84, 89, 112, 170, 187, 201, 202, 214, 220; fair, 226; fluctuating, 177n.; high, 206, 206n.; low, 117, 188,

217, 220, 221; manufacturing, 202; minimum, 15, 109, 170, 172n., 220, 223; 226; Negro, 100, 107, 109; real, 168
Wage-price guideposts, 201
War on poverty, 96, 101, 102, 103, 104, 119, 182, 183, 195, 196, 199, 200, 202, 211, 212, 213, 221, 229
Warner, Amos G., 11, 13
Washington, Booker T., 116
Washington, D.C. 100, 115, 158, 159
Water: conservation, 151, 160; development, 150, 151, 160; resources, 162
Wealth, 153, 165, 177 (*see also* Asset holdings); distribution, 9, 17, 173, 179; farmers, 171; households, 200; increase in, 178; inherited, 173; poor, 179; taxation, 173
Webb, Beatrice, 224
Webb, Sidney, 224
Weisbrod, Burton A., 18n.
Welfare: department, 77; individual, 185; officers, 79; practices, 5, 11; programs, 153, 209, 217; recipients, 53; remedial efforts, 10, 14, 84, 130, 145, 154, 157, 184; state, 219
West Virginia, 51, 53, 58, 60, 61, 125, 134, 143; State College at Institute, 62; University Appalachian Center, 61
Western: nations, 198; societies, 54
Wheat, 152
White: families, 156; labor, 99, 110, 112, 114; labor force, 110
White-collar: employment, 100, 110, 112, 137; Negro, 110; unemployment, 139
Whyte, William F., 67
Wife: beating, 77, 81; roles, 48; working, 48, 51
Williams, Lady Rhys, 221
Wisconsin, 60
Women. *See* Female
Work habits, 74
Working: age, 28; class (*see* Lower-class); conditions, 89, 110, 112

World War I, 157
World War II, 3, 16, 58, 144, 151, 170, 193
Works Progress Administration, 16

Young, Arthur, 168

Young: educational attainment, 41; family head, 32, 41; income, 192–93; labor, 192, 218; unemployment, 194, 198
Youth: Negro, 103; values, 203; workers, 62